Shakespeare and Music

Afterlives and Borrowings

For my brother, Neil; thank you for the music.

Shakespeare and Music

Afterlives and Borrowings

JULIE SANDERS

polity

First published in 2007 by Polity Press

Polity Press
65 Bridge Street
Cambridge CB2 1UR, UK

Polity Press
350 Main Street
Malden, MA 02148, USA

ISBN-13: 978-07456-3296-4
ISBN-13: 978-07456-3297-1 (pb)

A catalogue record for this book is available from the British Library.

Typeset in 11.25 on 13 pt Dante
by SNP Best-set Typesetter Ltd, Hong Kong
Printed and bound in Malaysia by Alden Press, Malaysia

For further information on Polity, visit our website: www.polity.co.uk

All art constantly aspires towards the condition of music.

Walter Pater

Why does the drum come hither?

Hamlet, v.ii.314

Contents

Acknowledgements

This is the kind of research project that not only expands a person's CD or download collection beyond recognition but also adds hugely to the list of intellectual and personal debts owed. I am grateful for the generosity of friends, family, and colleagues with ideas and references for this project, sometimes for chasing tracks, and invariably for offering advice and support. Special thanks in this regard must go to John Drakakis, Dave Evans, Sarah Grandage, John Jowett, Lucy Munro, Heather Violanti, and my family: my mum, Kay, for the love of opera and musicals; my dad, Mike, for endless lists (and copies) of Shakespeare-inspired or allusive classical music as well as childhood trips to the ballet; and my brother, Neil, for much of the folk and the jazz (and the mail-order service!). The plenary paper session at the Shakespeare Association of America conference in New Orleans, 2004, entitled 'The Duke's Man: Ellington, Shakespeare, and Jazz Adaptation' was a huge inspiration, and my thanks to the speakers on that occasion – Stephen M. Buhler, Douglas Lanier, and Frances Teague – as well as to the chair, Terence Hawkes.

My colleagues at the University of Nottingham have, as always, been a source of encouragement and support, both practical and intellectual; special thanks to Ron Carter, Janette Dillon, Brean Hammond, Jo Robinson, Mark Robson, and Peter Stockwell. The staff in the Hallward and Denis Arnold Music Libraries at the university have helped with many enquiries and chased items for me, often at very short notice; their work is much appreciated. My undergraduate and postgraduate students at Nottingham continue to be the finest inspiration of all. Particular thanks must go, though, to Daniel Grimley, friend, musical scholar, and colleague of the highest order, who read this book in manuscript form with wit and insight and undoubtedly sharpened its arguments. Remaining errors and infelicities are wholly mine.

Venues including the British Shakespeare Association Conference in Newcastle-upon-Tyne and the International Shakespeare Conference at Stratford-upon-Avon have enabled me to share some of the research and ideas for this book in stimulating environments. My thanks to all the participants in the 'Shakespeare and Music' seminar at the BSA in September 2005, and to Kate Chedgzoy, John Jowett, and Kate McLuskie for these opportunities.

Gratitude must also go to Polity Press for the initial commission, especially Sally-Ann Spencer for her early enthusiasm for the idea and Andrea Drugan, who saw it patiently and graciously through to its completion. The anonymous readers both for the original proposal and the finished manuscript were, quite simply, some of the most helpful and encouraging I have ever encountered in my career. Their enthusiasm for this project was a huge boost, and their ideas and suggestions have undoubtedly made it a far better book. Since I will never know who they were, I can only hope the work as published does their contribution justice.

And, as ever, last, but certainly not least, thank you to my constant gardener: John Higham. Only you, John, will understand and appreciate the endless sacrificed weekends and evenings that have contributed to this project and which you have, as ever, borne with patience and love. To quote Sir Philip Sidney, albeit from a rather different context: 'Now it is done only for you, only to you; if you keep it to yourself, or to such friends who will weigh errors in the balance of goodwill, I hope . . . it will be pardoned, perchance made much of, though in itself it have deformities.' Thank you for seeing me through this one; I love you more than words can say.

Prelude

If music be the food of love, play on
Twelfth Night, i.i.1

As an overture to detailed discussions of classical symphonies, operas, ballets, musicals, and film scores, among other musical genres or forms, in later chapters, I should stress that, although this is a study of Shakespeare and music, it is not about the prevalence of music as either metaphor or aural presence in the Shakespearean canon, although the influence of these processes on the musical adaptations examined here is registered at various points in the discussion. Nor is it a study of the musical traditions and associations of Shakespeare's own culture and time. Both of these subjects have been admirably explored in David Lindley's peerless recent study, *Shakespeare and Music* (2006), to which I hope this work stands as a happy complement or continuation. Lindley's book shares its main title with mine, but the fundamental difference between them as studies, perhaps, is indicated by what comes after the main title in my own, that ever salient material after the colon. For this book is about afterlives of Shakespeare's texts in music, in the quotations, borrowings, conscious citations, settings, and wholesale adaptations of the lyrics, dialogue, plotlines, and characters of his drama and the lines of his verse. My interests lie, then, entirely in the realm of what comes after those first early modern performances of his plays, and in subsequent, rather than initial, audiences and readerships.

This is a book about the reception and interpretation of Shakespeare's work by later ages and cultures, and about the wholesale reimagining of that work in a musical idiom and context. As ever, terminology plays a crucial part in understanding those acts of interpretation. I am exploring acts of adaptation and appropriation in this volume of a kind that I have long been interested in, in relation to both Shakespeare and other canonical artists and forms of Western culture (see Sanders 2001, 2006). Having offered in other domains my personal definitions of those slippery terms

1

'adaptation' and 'appropriation' (see Sanders 2006), they proved somehow inadequate for the kinds of musical creations and cultural productions I was exploring here. If, in my research, 'adaptation' has been taken to mean those works which retain a kind of fidelity to the source-text but consciously rework it within the conventions of another alternative medium or genre – novel or film, for example – then it is certainly true that a number of the musical works discussed in these pages function as adaptations. Giuseppe Verdi's nineteenth-century operatic reworkings of *Macbeth*, *Othello*, and *The Merry Wives of Windsor* are recognizably versions of their source plays. Similarly, film adaptations of Shakespeare plays by directors including Kenneth Branagh and Baz Luhrmann fit easily into this category, as do their accompanying soundtracks. Films that deploy Shakespearean texts as springboards for more contemporary themes as well as settings, often discarding his dialogue wholesale in the process, might well fall under the alternative heading of 'appropriation'. I am thinking in this field of works such as Gil Junger's 1999 *10 Things I Hate About You* or the recent *Twelfth Night*-inspired *She's the Man* (dir. Andy Fickman, 2006). Later chapters will focus on the scores to films that fall into both of these categories; others look at ballet and the musical as forms which might be located in terms of a similar epistemology, though all are active interpretations of their source material.

In truth, adaptation and appropriation seem somehow insufficient in an attempt to encompass the full range of musical responses to Shakespeare. How, for example, would we identify the 'fantasy overture' of Pyotr Tchaikovsky, based on *Romeo and Juliet* but offering nothing like a full version of the play or its *dramatis personae*? Or, indeed, Franz Liszt's *Hamlet*, a 'symphonic poem' which is really a rumination on a single character rather than the entire work from which that character derives (and based, as we will see in chapter 2, on one particular actor's interpretation of that role)? Into what column should we place the innovative jazz collaborations of Duke Ellington and Billy Strayhorn in the 1950s, the suite *Such Sweet Thunder*, which played with particular characters and speeches, sometimes combining plays together in a fascinating act of creative juxtaposition, and even invoking the overarching concept of Shakespeare's generic range? And how do we place the 'presence', sometimes acknowledged, sometimes implicit, frequently partial, of Shakespeare or lines or characters from his work in contemporary popular culture? As the study moved into these realms, it seemed more productive to me as a literary critic to look to the discipline of musicology for advice and influence. If, as the introductory chapter to this book will argue, the models of 'riff', quotation, or 'signifying' in jazz music are redeployed to think about Shakespearean musical afterlives, we begin to release more of the potential for innovative and experimental creativity that I want to argue is frequently the inherent cultural agency of these supposedly 'referential' or secondary works (see, for example, Metzer 2003; Born and Hesmondhalgh 2000).[1] Other terms from musicology such as 'borrowing' or 'sampling', which have recently held much sway and influence in the realms of rap and hip-hop (see, e.g., Schloss 2004), prove equally helpful when applied to the musical afterlives analysed here. These works might come *after* Shakespeare in one regard, in that they find their creative impulse or impetus in his works – and there is undoubtedly much to be said about the choice of plays, or specific characters, in the process of understanding, historicizing, or contextualizing that impulse – but in many other regards they are works of art that stand alone as producers of meaning, often complex and plural meanings.

Admittedly, I am hyper-conscious of avoiding what I would describe as the various pitfalls of reductionism when looking at the relationship between Shakespeare and music. While identifying source-texts, passages, or characters will inevitably prove relevant and often revealing *en route*, this is not a source study *per se*. I am interested in the new meanings or (potentially) radical alternatives offered by the musical afterlives, rather than merely identifying acts of adherence or interpolation with regard to the source. Such processes are sometimes referred to by more loaded phrases as acts of fidelity and betrayal, but I would prefer to adapt Stephen Connor's helpful phrase about fictional works that use Shakespeare as a creative springboard for their own ideas and aesthetic experiments, 'fidelity-in-betrayal' (1996: 167). Similarly, in thinking about how music has thought about, responded to, and offered its own unique interpretations of Shakespearean texts, I am keen not to seek always for simple equivalences or substitutions by one mode for another. While at times in the argument it will prove fruitful to think about the ways in which the aria of nineteenth-century opera or the set-piece 'show-stopping tune' of the Broadway musical provide variations on the particular conventions and effects of dramatic soliloquy, such easy equations between the literary and the musical form will not always be possible or even desirable. Music is a genre with its own distinct practices and traditions; it is also a genre with very particular ideas about 'text', not all of which necessarily mean the same as they do in literary criticism. Nevertheless, while acknowledging the slipperiness of terms, I hope to be able to respect the differences in the discussions which follow, despite my own literary standpoint and bias.

Equally, it is probably necessary to stress from the outset that this is a study written from the vantage point of a literary critic, one with an amateur's love of music and the forms invoked throughout, but one who is certainly not a trained musician or musicologist. To that end, this book may look rather different from one produced by a musicologist on the same theme. There will be no notational examples, and little discussion of particular musical issues such as the choice of specific notes or chordal sequences. That said, broader topics such as choice of instrumentation will prove insightful in the context of attempts to 'read' the musical works discussed and their approaches to, and negotiations with, their Shakespearean precursors.

Having declared at length what I think this book is not, I should perhaps take the time in this preface, or 'prelude', as I have opted to call it in a conscious gesture towards the encounter between the disciplines of music and literature that it seeks to effect, to say what I aim to do. One of my real concerns has been (and it is part of that attempt to avoid the reductionism already alluded to) to think about musical compositions with a 'Shakespearean' connection not in the abstract, as 'timeless' evidence of the supposed universality of Shakespeare, transcending all cultures, times, and disciplines, but in quite antithetical terms as works with their own specific cultural, historical, disciplinary, and socio-political contexts. Many of the works and composers discussed here will be studied in the context of their particular moment of cultural production. For example, the operatic 'adaptations' of Giuseppe Verdi and his librettist Arrigo Boito, or the symphonic compositions of Hector Berlioz, would not have come into existence without the Romantic movement in the arts and the particular versions, and indeed translations, of Shakespeare and his work that this produced. Similarly, the 'English pastoralism' traditionally associated with the compositions of Ralph Vaughan Williams and Gustav Holst in the 1920s is seen to affect their response to Shakespeare and their specific choices of song, plays, or characters to adapt, and the musical strategies, techniques, and traditions they bring to bear upon these choices. In turn, these musical creations impact upon the literary-critical response to Shakespeare. On several occasions in this study I will have recourse both to the agency of literary criticism in the sphere of musical composition and the undeniable impact of musical interpretations of Shakespeare, from Henry Purcell to Garbage, on academic understandings of the same. Music, sometimes described by non-specialists as an abstract form that appeals directly to the emotions, is, I would argue, born out of cultural and intellectual contexts as identifiable as they would be for any work of literature.[2] If New Historicism and Cultural Materialism have had a significant effect on the ways in which we now think about, study, and even stage Shakespeare, so a similar process of deep contextualization may help us to unlock many of the meanings and effects of musical works which have themselves become canonical in discussions of Shakespeare's cultural impact.

Finally though, to return to my statement of what this study determinedly does not seek to do. As well as avoiding a reductionist consideration of musical afterlives in terms of how loyal or disloyal they are to their source, I was determined to resist any foolhardy attempt to offer a comprehensive survey of the huge number of adaptations and interpretations of Shakespeare in music that there has been. In practice, such an attempt would always have proved too much for any single study, and would run the risk of reducing a book to the status of a mere list or catalogue. Phyllis Hartnoll and others did provide a helpful catalogue of this kind in 1966, although even that was exclusionary in some respects (jazz, my first subject here, for example, was virtually ignored in their accumulation of data). The world-wide-web now offers a rich and accessible means for bringing that material up to date, and there are various catalogues to Shakespearean music available (see, e.g., Gooch and Thatcher, 1991). I have therefore opted instead for a case study-based approach here, selecting within each generic category what I consider to be particularly salient examples of the diverse and informing practice of musical interpretation and creativity in the wake of Shakespeare. Having raised the issue of genre, it remains to add that while the chapters here are ostensibly organized by generic category – jazz, classical songs and symphonies, ballet, musical, opera, film scores, and contemporary and popular music – the historicist approach favoured by this study also serves to highlight numerous occasions when those generic boundaries are blurred, consciously transgressed, or willingly confused. Adaptation and appropriation studies, let alone the study of afterlives and borrowings, always need to be alert to complex processes of mediation, cross-fertilization, and filtration, and on many occasions the compositions and musical events described here have as deep an intertextual relationship to each other as to the originating drama and poetry of Shakespeare.

Many overtures to longer symphonic compositions and film scores offer an overview of what is to come, and this 'Prelude' aims to do something similar in terms of the focus and approach of this study, by offering a walk through the chapters that follow with the aim of highlighting the approaches, examples, and claims that are found there, as well as indicating ways in which the separate chapters might interlink. This Prelude also provides an opportunity to clarify the terminology that I am using, though this is further supported for those less familiar with the kinds of theoretical languages being deployed by the provision of a glossary at the back. This glossary, which is necessarily selective, has been aimed at the non-specialist in both musical and cinematic terminology; I hope that it will provide a helpful key to some of the more specialized material in the book. With similar intentions in mind, a detailed index is also provided, with the aim of assisting individual readers in making connections between chapters and navigating their own paths of interest through the material.

The book begins with a study of the relationship between Shakespeare and jazz music, which, as well as looking at specific examples of twentieth-century jazz adaptations of Shakespeare, such as the collaborations of Duke Ellington and Billy Strayhorn in the USA and Cleo Laine and Johnny Dankworth in the UK, argues that we might think of jazz's citational and allusive processes as a useful model for thinking about adaptation as a practice. Jazz's complex relationship with the source material that it readily quotes but also improvises and innovates upon provides a rich template for the multiple ways in which Shakespeare and the Shakespearean canon have signified – often in contradictory ways – across periods and cultures, as well as across different disciplines, including music. Jazz's assimilatory and incorporative strategies offer an example that can tell us much about Shakespearean adaptation and appropriation, although, as the introductory chapter indicates, jazz has its own precedents for this practice in early modern baroque music and its investment in patterns of developmental variation.

The second chapter, entitled 'Classical Shakespeares', deals with orchestral, choral, and symphonic responses to Shakespeare's work, as well as taking significant detours into the realms of *Lieder* and song settings, as well as the particular intimacies and conventions of chamber opera. Labels, as ever, raise their own difficulties. The term 'classical' is much contested in a musical context. Nevertheless, anyone seeking to purchase music in this category in a shop or online will invariably find themselves in a section labelled 'classical music', and in that section they will undoubtedly find the work of many of the composers discussed here: Hector Berlioz, Edward Elgar, Gustav Holst, Felix Mendelssohn, Antonín Dvořák, and many others. But the title of the chapter is also in some respects playful, echoing as it does the establishment, at least in the UK, of so-called classical radio stations, chief among them one called 'Classic FM', which play music that falls into this notional category.

As the subsequent chapter on ballet indicates, however, labels can only ever be facilitating categories, and there will always be overlap, interaction, and blurrings at the boundaries of any discipline or genre. As readers of this book will soon come to realize, it is my intention to celebrate rather than criticize those blurrings, regarding them as perhaps the most productive of cultural interstices. In this vein, in the discussion of ballet in chapter 3 – a dance form that, incidentally, has its own understanding of the designation 'classical' – Mendelssohn's incidental music for *A Midsummer Night's Dream* resurfaces in a new context, as indeed it will recur, further revised, in later discussions of film scores. The example of Mendelssohn is useful, since it captures one of the effects of musical adaptation across a wide range of time periods, genres, and contexts, which is that seminal works persistently resurface, albeit in altered form, and become in themselves exemplary of the cultural processes of adaptation, appropriation, and signification under discussion. Exploring how and why Mendelssohn's music for *A Midsummer Night's Dream* has been reworked, revised, echoed, and even parodied is a means to explore the diverse ways in which Shakespeare's text has also been made to signify differently across ages and cultures.

As already noted, I have chosen to be highly selective in this study, offering examples of musical adaptation both familiar and unfamiliar within the different fields and genres discussed. That selection has a clear rationale, which is to select those works which best exemplify the process of interpreting Shakespeare in different contexts that this study aims to make visible. They are facilitating examples, ones which it is hoped readers will use as springboards for their own considerations. With that in mind, at the end of each chapter there is a section headed 'Further examples and reading' with suggestions of where to go next.

After the discussion of ballet we move into another realm of musical drama that incorporates the language of dance into its performative frame. The American musical is often regarded as a distinctly twentieth-century phenomenon, although, as this chapter stresses, important precedents and links can be found in the semi-opera that was popular at the end of the seventeenth century in the English Restoration theatre. Nevertheless, the examples concentrated on here, Shakespearean musicals, which include such iconic shows as *Kiss Me Kate* and *West Side Story* in both their stage and screen identities, do locate us firmly in the modern era. Musicals are seen to shade into the world of the cinema, not just in terms of filmed musicals such as those mentioned above, but also in the use of allusion and pastiche in references to the form in Shakespearean films as varied as Richard Loncraine's *Richard III* (1995), Kenneth Branagh's *Love's Labour's Lost* (1999), Julie Taymor's *Titus* (2000), and Tommy O'Haver's *Get Over It* (2001).

Chapters 5 and 6 are also about musical drama, but this time the focus is opera. As well as making larger arguments about the context for nineteenth-century opera that can be found in Romantic theory and the translations of Shakespeare's work that were produced in Europe at this time, the method of analysing instructive case studies is once again deployed. In chapter 5 Shakespeare's female characters provide a focus for discussion, enabling analyses of operatic interpretations of texts as varied as *Othello* and *The Merry Wives of Windsor*; then in chapter 6 we zoom in in even more detail to offer specific examinations of Giuseppe Verdi's nineteenth-century Shakespearean operas, *Macbeth, Otello,* and *Falstaff,* as well as Benjamin Britten's and Peter Pears's ground-breaking 1960 production of *A Midsummer Night's Dream*, which is seen to have deep roots in the English theatrical tradition, consciously reaching back as it does to the work of Henry Purcell at the end of the seventeenth century.

Following the discussion of opera, we move to a wholly different medium for the next two chapters: that of motion pictures, and the very specific acts of adaptation and interpretation that are involved in the composition of film scores. The first of these chapters (7) looks at more traditional symphonic and orchestral film scores, concentrating on the work of William Walton and Dmitri Shostakovich, as well as the rather more controversial attempt to re-create their epic and lush scores in the work of Patrick Doyle for Shakespearean actor-director Kenneth Branagh. Chapter 8 then moves into the realm of 'compilation' scores, which deploy songs, often from the genres of rock and pop, to provide atmosphere, as well as additional layers of meaning for the films they accompany. As ever, the category proves permeable, since in the work of

Baz Luhrmann and Tim Blake Nelson a productive blend of the symphonic or 'classical' alongside these more contemporary musical references is seen to be a driving force of their films' narrative and aesthetic. The chapter ends with an extended analysis of the role and function of music both in the overlaid soundtrack and within the film world of *10 Things I Hate About You*, a US High School remake of *The Taming of the Shrew* (1999).

Chapter 9 brings us in some respects up to the present day with its overview of contemporary songs that allude to Shakespeare and Shakespearean texts, and contemporary performers who have offered their own arrangements of songs from his plays. But, fittingly in a study so concerned with connection and interaction, this chapter brings us full circle in terms of its discussion of settings of Shakespearean songs and the intrinsic 'musicality' of his work – not least his sonnets – since this is where the introductory chapter on jazz begins.

I have stressed elsewhere, and it is worth reasserting in this context, that 'Shakespeare' and the Shakespearean canon do not come to us – as spectators, performers, readers, critics, or listeners – free of the subsequent cultural heritage they have fostered and enjoyed. Many people today will have seen a production of *West Side Story* before experiencing a 'straight' production of *Romeo and Juliet* on the stage; certainly many may well view both through the prism of Baz Luhrmann's explosive cinematic rendering of that play. As Barbara Hodgdon (1983) has remarked, Shakespeare's plays and poems are 'expectational texts'; audiences at different times bring different or alternative sets of expectations both to Shakespeare and to musical (and other) responses to his work (cf. Rothwell 1999; Kidnie 2005). It is these complex processes of reading, reception, interpretation, understanding, and response that I have set myself the considerable task of acknowledging, and, indeed, celebrating, in the chapters which follow. Play on.

Notes

1 I am grateful to my colleague Ron Carter for discussion of, and inspiration on, the topic of creativity. See, e.g., R. Carter 2004.
2 Daniel Barenboim's 2006 Reith Lectures for the British Broadcasting Corporation (first broadcast on Radio 4, April–May 2006), entitled 'In the Beginning was Sound', were a fascinating and thought-provoking discussion of this and related ideas.

Further examples and reading

There is a considerable body of work now emerging on the general theme of Shakespearean adaptation and appropriation. For helpful introductions to the field, see Jean I. Marsden (ed.), *The Appropriation of Shakespeare: Post-Renaissance Reconstructions of the Works and Myth* (London: Prentice-Hall, 1991); and Christy Desmet and Robert Sawyer (eds), *Shakespeare and Appropriation* (London: Routledge, 1999). For a general discussion of the field of adaptation studies, which includes a chapter on Shakespeare, see my own *Adaptation and Appropriation* (London: Routledge, 2006).

1

'All That Jazz': Shakespeare and Musical Adaptation

> And as you trip, still pinch him to your time
> *The Merry Wives of Windsor*, v.v.91

Writing about the identity of jazz music, David Horn observes that it is defined by its very contradictions:

> Diversity and connectedness; distinctiveness and conformity. In the complex cultural history of the twentieth century, jazz emerged to live as one music among many, one moreover that bore the imprint of its connections with other musics – musics as diverse as the blues and Broadway show tunes. (2002: 9)

This description could just as easily serve as a summary of the contents of this book. This study of the music influenced by and responsive to the work of Shakespeare is divided generically into chapters on opera, ballet, musical, and film soundtrack, all seemingly distinct and discrete categories with their own attendant sets of conventions and practices, but, as the 'Prelude' to this volume has already made clear, these distinctions are difficult, even impossible, to sustain for long. Certain composers and compositions resurface in and across several of the chapters – Felix Mendelssohn and his Overture and Incidental Music for *A Midsummer Night's Dream*, for example, gain mention under 'classical music', 'ballet', 'film soundtrack', and even here in a chapter ostensibly on jazz adaptations; similarly, Duke Ellington emerges and re-emerges in a range of contexts. What is at stake here, beyond the mere observation of the pervasive influence of specific composers or compositions, is a sense that we can 'read' musical adaptations of Shakespeare and their influence as indicative of, even as metaphorical for, all manner of artistic, cultural, and ideological processes. In this regard, Mendelssohn's work and the compositions of Duke Ellington matter not only as significant artworks in themselves, but also as a rich means for understanding Shakespearean adaptation as a process of cultural signification.

The somewhat fluid and dynamic aspect to this book's structure is therefore, I hope, equally suggestive of many of its aims and objectives as a study of Shakespeare and his musical afterlives. I chose to begin with jazz as an identifying category partly because of its essential pluralism, its 'competing centrifugal and centripetal tendencies' (Horn 2002: 31), which seemed to me to embody many if not all of the issues of interaction, overlap, and creativity via adaptation that I want to place at the core of my analysis and approach. In deploying jazz in this representational and pluralist way, I hasten to add that I am not suggesting that diversity is necessarily ideologically neutral. Postcolonial theory has of late been eloquent on the subject of the inherent danger for autonomous identity that exists in the processes of adaptation, assimilation, and incorporation (see, e.g., Ashcroft, Griffiths, and Tiffin 1989: 38–40), and jazz has proved a central genre in this regard with its fundamentally allusive structure, albeit one with an in-built emphasis on development and reinterpretation. As both the celebratory and negative interpretations of Henry Louis Gates Jr's influential theory, discussed in more detail later in this chapter, of jazz's ability to 'signify' (1988: 123) indicate, allusions can appear as either empowering or submissive in their relationship to authority, depending on the angle of perception (see, e.g., Metzer 2003: 2; Andreas Sr 1999: 107–8). Needless to say, exactly the same arguments virtually define the academic field of Shakespearean adaptation studies, which is why the bringing together of jazz and Shakespeare in this way seemed potentially so productive.

There has been much discussion of late in this fast-emerging field of the differences between 'local' or localized Shakespeares and global or 'big-time' Shakespeares, with much analysis of the potential for interaction between these two spheres (see, e.g., Bristol 1996; Desmet and Sawyer 1999: 2; Massai 2005). Intriguingly, similar elements have been identified in jazz as a musical practice or process: 'The jazz diaspora is . . . a case-study of the negotiation between local cultural practices and global cultural processes' (Horn 2002: 39). The analogy between Shakespearean appropriation, or 'improvisation', and jazz is potentially so rich partly because it allows for and enables a celebration of the acts of creativity that I am keen to stress are at work in the adaptive process.

I am less interested in identifying who took what from Shakespeare exactly, and what they did or did not alter or change in the process, which seems simply to affirm the questionable value of fidelity to the original, than with asking: What drove them to choose that text in particular? What drove them to make the changes or additions they did? When did they do this? Why? The flurry of question-marks here is quite deliberate. Studies of adaptation and appropriation demand a very live kind of engagement with both source-text and 'new' text, and in this way the *frisson* and excitement generated by a jazz riff or improvisation upon a recognizable or 'classic' melody – or even in the case of Shakespeare a work of literature – make it a very good model to work with. In this context the source becomes not a stick with which to beat the necessarily secondary work of art that adapts or adopts it, but rather a template, a framework, a springboard, a jumping-off point, and a stimulus to the act and art of creation. Some scholars have argued that music becomes jazz solely through the particular choices made by musicians (Jackson 2002: 91). As that previous flurry of question-marks indicates, I am deeply interested in the act of choice embedded both in the specific musical works looked at in this volume and in the process of adaptation.

Writing on Shakespeare, Terence Hawkes made his own suggestive adaptation of Roland Barthes's notion of *jouissance* to talk about the act of interpretation, the reading or interpretative process, and that 'point at which . . . the garment of predictable, expected content provocatively and disturbingly gapes, and the play-text reaches out and draws us irresistibly towards itself and the *jouissance* or *jazz* which it promises' (1986: 89; see also Barthes 1977: 164). In the light of this, Hawkes's version of Shakespeare proves unapologetically plural: 'texts are texts . . . Shakespeare's plays for instance are not transparent entities, giving immediate access to single, coherent, preordained meaning, but inherently plural structures, always open to manifold interpretations' (1986: 123). Hawkes was openly influenced in this approach by the theories of Geoffrey Hartman in his book *Criticism in the Wilderness* (1980), where he argued that jazz 'with its unsettling commitment to creative re-presentation and re-interpretation . . . offers a model for a future notion of literary criticism' (Hawkes 1986: 125). If not necessarily a paradigm for all literary criticism, this is certainly one that is richly productive as an approach to works of literary and cultural adaptation and appropriation, not least all things Shakespearean. Jazz gives us a productive working model for acts of citation, allusion, borrowing, and revision that credit the created work – the adaptation – as much as the sources of inspiration. As Hawkes stresses: 'For the jazz musician, the "text" of a melody is a means, not an end. Interpretation in that context is not parasitic but symbiotic in its relationship with its object . . . interpretation constitutes the art of the jazz musician' (1986: 117–18).[1]

All of this, then, deservedly, but not unproblematically, paints jazz as a fluid, dynamic, richly digressive, and inherently adaptive musical mode.

But it is not alone in this, not even in the musical domain. I have argued in other contexts that early modern baroque music in fact shares many of these improvisatory, creative, and essentially playful qualities (Sanders 2006: 39–41). Baroque pieces often take the form of variations on 'grounds', repeating patterns, invariably provided by keyboard instrument and gamba/viol/bass, which underscore and inform the improvisatory flights that other instruments – woodwind, for example, or the human voice – make on the top of that bass or foundation. In pieces deploying the chaconne bass, there is usually an important association between the descending ground and the affective figure of lament represented by the overlaid instrument or voice.[2] Other pieces have in-built sections which allow the virtuoso violinist to improvise freely on the established musical theme in a recital. In a more contemporary context, groups such as the Third Ear Band became interested in the relationship between modern percussive music, baroque chamber music, and the repeating rhythms of Indian *ragas*, and they allowed these interests to inform their contribution to the sphere of Shakespeare and music via the soundtrack to Roman Polanski's 1971 film of *Macbeth*. That so much contemporary choral work – not least by those composers who are devising new settings for Shakespearean lyrics – openly acknowledges its indebtedness to jazz rhythms and practices further underlines the significance of interaction and crossover between all these musical fields and domains. One significant figure in this context is Swedish jazz pianist and composer Nils Lindberg, who works in a self-proclaimed 'crossover' idiom which blends jazz, folk, and choral traditions. His setting of Sonnet 18 ('Shall I compare thee to a summer's day?') has enjoyed several recent interpretations.[3]

Mervyn Cooke has written suggestively about Duke Ellington's practice of musical quotation in his compositions, finding a context for some of his allusions to classical music in the precise cultural geographical context of New Orleans. Chopin's Piano Sonata, which finds its way into the conclusion of Ellington's 1927 *Black and Tan Fantasy*, was regularly played and elaborated upon in New Orleans funeral processions (M. Cooke 2002: 163). Here we find a fascinating glimpse in Ellington's oeuvre of the merging of local and global references. The Chopin operates in this instance in a manner analogous to a Shakespeare quotation in a contemporary television programme: it juxtaposes and tests presumptions about elite and popular cultural forms; it offers a surprising sense of geography or (dis)location; it uses a global or 'universal' shared point of reference to make what is actually a very precise localized and personalized point; and it deploys the familiar (yet in an African-American context simultaneously alien) idiom of classical music while forging something highly innovative, experimental, and new.

Ellington played with many classical pieces in his compositions, including Edvard Grieg's *Peer Gynt* (1867) and Pyotr Tchaikovsky's *The Nutcracker Suite* (Op. 71, 1891–2), as well as popular Broadway musicals.[4] The playful joy he found in these encounters is unmistakably present in some of the titles he gives to his adaptations: in *Nutcracker Suite*, for example, the *Danse de la Fée Dragée* (better known as the 'Dance of the Sugar Plum Fairy') becomes 'Sugar Rum Cherry'; and who could not be won over by the joyfulness of 'Toot toot tootie toot'? There is, of course, also an implicit sexualization at play in these adaptations, signified not least by the risqué aspect of these titles. This is what musicologist David Metzer describes as 'quotation [operating] as cultural agent', in that the Chopin or other classical quotations in Ellington's work participate in, and potentially alter, the cultural discourses that surround them (2003: 2). Metzer recognizes Ellington as a chief exponent of the practice of musical quotation, identifying the hybrid references in his work with secular and spiritual idioms, classical and popular genres, and the literary as well as the musical. This connects Ellington's approach to what Henry Louis Gates Jr has called the 'signifying practices' of African-American artists. In offering a definition of what he meant by signifying, Gates turned to the medium of jazz music as his reference point, citing the way in which the compositions of Count Basie and Oscar Peterson were 'structured around the idea of formal revision and implication' (1988: 123). Metzer's deployment of Gates's theory of signifying may be even more inclusive and celebratory than its originator initially envisaged, but it remains a productive theory in application not only to Ellington's oeuvre but to my own subject of musical borrowings from Shakespeare.

In the light of this discussion, it should perhaps come as no surprise that such a creative adaptor and interpreter as Ellington also took on Shakespearean adaptation during his musical career. In a writing collaboration with Billy Strayhorn, he undertook a commission for the Shakespeare festival at Stratford, Ontario, in 1956.[5] The music was also released in LP format. What he and Strayhorn produced was a series of jazz ruminations on some of the major characters from Shakespeare's plays, as well as a remarkable exploration of the relationship between the taut poetic form of the sonnet and the art of musical composition and jazz adaptation. The interaction between musical adaptation and character criticism is both interesting and potentially fraught in a study such as this. In discursive musical genres such as opera or musical, the relationship between character and dialogue is more straightforward, although that is not to discount the creativity involved in these genres. Nevertheless, in these discursive forms a character has a literal voice and can to an extent at least 'retain their lines', be it Katherine from *The Taming of the Shrew* declaring how she hates men in Cole Porter's *Kiss Me Kate* (1948) or the 'Willow Song' aria sung by Desdemona in Giuseppe Verdi's *Otello* (1887). In the discussion of non-discursive musical modes, in particular the classical symphony, we find a similar investment on the part of composers in particular characters from canonical Shakespeare plays, but more usually for the purpose of offering musical accounts or 'imaginings' of them, rather than the sustained response to a whole play or plot narrative that we might expect to find in conventional opera. A major example of this is Franz Liszt's 'symphonic poem' *Hamlet* (1858), inspired by seeing a particular actor perform the central role in Shakespeare's Danish tragedy. Liszt coined the term 'symphonic poem' (*symphonische Dichtung*) to describe this kind of composition, which is a piece with the qualities and dimensions of a symphony but one which is far freer from convention in some respects, and which frequently deals with a poetic theme or idea.

Shakespeare's plays appear to have been especially prominent in this particular musical form, inspiring other symphonic or tone poems, such as Bedrich Smetana's *Richard III* (1862), Richard Strauss's *Macbeth* (1890), Edward German's *Hamlet* (1897), and Edward Elgar's *Falstaff* (1913; analysed in greater detail in the chapter which follows). Both German's *Hamlet* and Elgar's *Falstaff* are directly comparable to Liszt's pioneering effort, since while they strive to offer a musical description of certain events in their focus play, there is no effort to follow the entire plotline. German's piece, for example, includes the tolling of midnight and the arrival of the ghost as well as Hamlet's Act v death, a pomp and ceremony march for the arrival of Claudius, and even some ghostly music, as well as some remarkable woodwind evocations of Ophelia; but in essence it is an evocation of Hamlet, the prince – in this case an assertive figure of considerable agency – rather than all the intricacies of a five-act play. There is nothing here, for example, to suggest Gertrude or the closet scene, no Polonius, no Rosencrantz and Guildenstern, and certainly no Fortinbras or invading armies. Jonathan Bate and Jane Moody have both connected this tendency towards character criticism as a mode of response towards the plays to the Romantic era's version of Shakespeare (Bate 1997: 192; Moody 2002). If we think of the identification of actors with specific roles, such as the Prince of Denmark, Lady Macbeth, Falstaff, or Juliet, in many of the paintings of eighteenth- and nineteenth-century theatre – the likes of David Garrick, John Philip Kemble, Ellen Terry, Harriet Smithson, Sarah Siddons, Edmund Kean and others spring to mind – this view would seem to gain credence. Hans Werner Henze seems to acknowledge this previous tradition in his 1970s compositions for solo guitar, the First and Second *Sonatas on Shakespearean Characters* (recorded as *Royal Winter Music* in 2003), which include responses to characters as diverse as Richard III, Ophelia, and the comic trio of Touchstone, Audrey, and William from *As You Like It*. Romantic understandings of Shakespeare may help to explain Liszt's composition, and in part Henze's twentieth-century responses, and we will return to this idea in the chapter on classical Shakespeares that follows this, but they prove woefully insufficient as explanations either of Duke Ellington and Billy Strayhorn's focus on character, or the specific impact that their musical 'accounts' of these characters have.

If we look at the Ellington–Strayhorn Shakespeare suite, *Such Sweet Thunder* (1999 [1957]), the title itself a quotation from *A Midsummer Night's Dream* – Hippolyta's remark, 'I never heard / So musical a discord, such sweet thunder' (iv.i.116–17) – we find not only an interest in recurring groups of characters, and specific plays, but distinctly personal approaches to the realization of those characters, not least in remaking their dialogue – their 'voice' – through music and instrumentation. Two playtexts that clearly swam in and out of Ellington and Strayhorn's ken as they composed their suite were *Othello* and *Antony and Cleopatra*. The ethnic identities and associations of the major protagonists from both those plays were clearly of interest to these jazz practitioners. The original title of the opening piece (eventually renamed 'Such Sweet Thunder') was 'Cleo', and the Egyptian queen appears again later in 'Half the Fun', a musical variation on Enobarbus's 'golden barge' speech, one of the great set-piece moments of the play, and itself much anthologized and appropriated, not least by T. S. Eliot's jazz-music-influenced *The Waste Land*:

> I will tell you.
> The barge she sat in, like a burnished throne
> Burned on the water. The poop was beaten gold;
> Purple the sails, and so perfumèd that
> The winds were love-sick with them.
> (*Antony and Cleopatra*, ii.ii.197–201)

In its renamed form, however, the opening number of the suite came to stand for Othello telling his seductive tales of travel and adventure to Desdemona:

> Wherein I spoke of most disastrous chances,
> Of moving accidents by flood and field,
> Of hair-breadth scapes i'th' imminent deadly breach
> . . .
>
>   These things to hear
> Would Desdemona seriously incline . . .
>   (*Othello*, I.iii.133–5, 144–5)

The audience is being similarly positioned as recipients of the seductive tales woven and told by Ellington and his band. It is a happy analogy.

Othello recurs on two further occasions in the sequence. 'The Telecasters' brings Iago into direct confrontation with the weird sisters of *Macbeth* in a fascinating musical discussion of malevolent intent. The instrumentation here is typically suggestive: Iago 'speaks' in baritone sax, while the witches are matched as three trombones. In 'Sonnet in Search of a Moor' Ellington and Strayhorn made their own contribution to a long history of association between this play and music (see Bate 1997: 289). Here a double-bass stands for the Moor, whereas in 'Such Sweet Thunder' brass played with plungers articulated the character. Where music does engage in the kind of 'character criticism' I am describing here, the choice of instrument to 'vocalize' the part is often very revealing, and may carry traditions and conventional significations of its own. I will argue later, for example, for a long accepted link between Shakespeare's tragic heroines and the woodwind section of the orchestra in classical and operatic composition.

Speculating as to why *Othello* is such a recurrent focus in the suite, there are clearly issues of race and ethnicity implicit in the text that were relevant to Ellington and Strayhorn, but it is also worth noting that the decades leading up to their collaboration had witnessed some remarkable, benchmark performances of Othello by African-American actors in the USA, including Paul Robeson and James Earl Jones. These performances had given a new cultural agency to the role, and in this way *Such Sweet Thunder*, like Liszt's *Hamlet*, is a rich aesthetic response to the stage performances of its day. It is certainly one of the major intentions of this book to historicize the musical afterlives of Shakespeare in this way, to think about them in their own space, place, time, and context, rather than only in terms of their relationship to the originating Shakespearean text. As well as the influence of theatre history and practice, which, as we shall see on several occasions in this study, was considerable, I would argue that the majority of musicians do not work in a world abstracted from the academic and intellectual debates that rage around Shakespeare and the

Shakespearean canon. Later chapters will argue for the influence of Romantic criticism on operatic versions of the plays in the nineteenth century, and of 1950s structuralism and theories of festive comedy and saturnalia on Benjamin Britten's and Peter Pears's *A Midsummer Night's Dream*. Edward Elgar's analytical essay on his 1913 composition *Falstaff* makes clear that he was engaging with works of criticism and critical debate about the history plays, and Thomas Adès's recent opera of *The Tempest* is acutely aware of postmodernist theory and the place of Shakespeare within that school of thought. Ellington and Strayhorn, as Stephen Buhler (2004) has noted, were working at a time when New Criticism was the dominant mode of critical practice. New Criticism can in part be categorized by close textual focus and an eschewal of earlier connections between art and biography in favour of the idea of the text as a closed system (see Lodge 1972). The influence of this text-centred approach might be registered in the 'close readings' of particular scenes, or moments, or characters offered by the twelve pieces that make up *Such Sweet Thunder*.

Ellington and Strayhorn's equation of their musical ponderings on a prescribed theme and the fourteen-line sonnet is one that deserves comment, and that will also find parallels with other musical adapters of Shakespeare, not least classical composers such as Gustav Holst and Gerald Finzi, a connection that stretches right up to the present day with musical versions of specific sonnets by Finnish composer Einojuhani Rautavaara or performers such as Ladysmith Black Mambazo and Rufus Wainwright.[6] The sonnet has its own links with music and dance in the careful patternings and metrical measures that constitute an intrinsic part of its production of meaning. Ellington and Strayhorn also seem to find a potent analogue in the contained form of the sonnet – their own musical ruminations on five-act plays last just a few minutes, after all. The connection is made at more than a purely notional level; the pieces in the suite that are called sonnets (there are four in all) are mostly written in fourteen melodic phrases of ten beats to resemble the fourteen lines in iambic pentameter of the Shakespearean sonnet form. In some there are also highly audible rhyming couplets or climaxes at their close.[7] These 'sonnets' are not consciously setting particular sonnets from the Shakespearean sequence to music, although these compositions have since been used for that purpose – Cleo Laine and Johnny Dankworth, in a project I will discuss later, sang the words of Sonnet 40 'Take all my loves' along with the arrangement for 'Sonnet to Hank Cinq'. 'Hank Cinq' is of course the jazz nomenclature for Henry V, and Ellington himself described, in the original LP's sleevenotes, how this sonnet's rises and falls and changes of tempo were meant to suggest battles and the changing map of warfare. Percussion proves crucial in the achievement of this particular effect, but there is also an amazing trombone solo. Other characters who receive their own 'sonnets' are Julius Caesar, from the eponymous Roman play, and Katherine from *The Taming of the Shrew*. Her 'voice' is achieved by a trombone played with a plunger; the aural effect is reminiscent of a 1930s street scene in a Hollywood film and is wonderfully suggestive of a possible mode of staging this play in a new historical context: a 'jazz age' *Shrew* is a nice thought.

Ellington and Strayhorn are as interested in female as in male protagonists from the plays; indeed, in their riff on *Romeo and Juliet*, entitled 'The Star-Crossed Lovers', it has been remarked by several critics that Juliet's alto saxophone dominates, marginalizing Romeo's alto sax rather than offering an image of equality, as might be expected in a genuine duet. It is intriguing that Ellington and Strayhorn did not choose to have their lovers encounter each other in a musical sonnet, since this is literally the poetic form over which they meet in the play (I.v.92–105; see, e.g., Bate 1997: 279); instead they find their musical analogue in the form of blended saxophones. The choice of instrument here may be suggestive in several regards; clearly the saxophone is an iconic jazz instrument, and therefore sounds a note of assertion on behalf of the genre, but it is also one that has sexual and sexualized connotations that Ellington and Strayhorn clearly wish to bring into the frame in their interpretation of Shakespeare's tragic lovers. As another example of powerful and sexualized female agency, Cleopatra has already been mentioned, as well as the weird sisters from *Macbeth* who are so resonantly and suggestively juxtaposed with Iago. Another exquisite female character portrait is offered in the suite in 'Lady Mac'; Ellington's own words say it all: 'we suspect there was a little ragtime in her soul.' He realizes this 'ragtime' element to Lady Macbeth's character by means of a beautiful piano solo. This is for the most part upbeat in tempo; it is only in the closing chords of the sequence that we hear a hint of darker, more tragic events to come.

The Prince of Denmark is not forgotten in the sequence, represented as he is in 'Madness in Great Ones' by a striking trumpet rendition, and Ellington and Strayhorn also ruminate on Shakespeare's diverse generic practice in the closing piece, 'Circle of Fourths', which finds musical expression for the comedies, tragedies, histories, and sonnets that are so intrinsically linked to the Shakespearean canon. But one of the most remarkable pieces of characterization in the suite has to be that of Puck from *A Midsummer Night's Dream* in 'Up and Down, Up and Down (I will lead them up and down)'. The title refers to Puck's little verse of intended mischief at III.iii. 397–400:

> Up and down, up and down,
> I will lead them up and down.
> I am feared in field and town.
> Goblin, lead them up and down.

The lines refer to Puck's planned confusion of the four lovers, who have become entangled by the magic of the Athenian forest. A careful listener can hear the lovers themselves represented in the piece by the alternate pairings of clarinet and violin and alto and tenor sax. But perhaps the most remarkable moment of 'vocalization' comes at the end of the piece – at least on the original LP recording, since although the 1999 CD re-release made reference to the effect on the liner notes, it actually used a different recording which omitted the closing bars. What listeners in 1957 heard, and what Wynton Marsalis re-created when he performed the piece in New York in 1988, was Puck literally 'speaking' the line 'Lord, what fools these mortals be!' (III.ii.115), albeit articulated through the mouthpiece of a trumpet.[8]

Ellington's work has become canonical in its own right within the category of Shakespearean music. Gregory Doran recently used his incidental music for a 'jazz age' production of *Timon of Athens* originally commissioned for Michael Langham's 1963 Stratford, Ontario production (Jowett 2004: 103–4) at the Royal Shakespeare Company in Stratford-upon-Avon (1999), and subsequent jazz musicians making their own negotiations with the bardic inheritance acknowledge the influence of Ellington and Strayhorn's pioneering work.[9] In 1974, for example, the musicians who offered a series of Shakespeare-inspired pieces to celebrate the tercentenary of his birth in a concert at Southwark Cathedral, released under the title *Will Power*, were consciously following in their footsteps.[10] Mike Gibb's 'Sonnet' not only echoes the expressed form of many of the Ellington–Strayhorn compositions, but the liner notes suggest that as an opening number in the performance it consciously sought to imitate the sensuality of the portrait of Cleopatra that was embedded in the eponymous opening of *Such Sweet Thunder*. The interest in sonnets continued in the duet for female voices offered by Neil Ardley's setting of Sonnet 18 ('Shall I compare thee to a summer's day?'[11]); and Stan Tracey's 'Alas sweet lady' is a character portrait of Ophelia in music that directly imitates the Ellington–Strayhorn accounts of Cleopatra, Lady Macbeth, and others. Ophelia's journey into mental derangement is realized through a piano solo as well as the voice of Norma Winstone.

The Ophelia portrait sounds a tragic note in a performance that is elsewhere characterized by a more light-hearted sense of free play and improvisation: 'Charade for the Bard', for example, makes musical puns on Shakespeare's name. The final piece, divided into several distinct sections, also copies the Ellington–Strayhorn precedent in its willingness to juxtapose in close proximity tragic and playful possibilities. Ian Carr's 'Will's Birthday Suite' starts with free jazz improvisation and then moves into 'Heyday', which has rock elements within its rhythms. The second section, however, interprets Guiderius's and Arviragus's funeral dirge for Imogen from *Cymbeline*, 'Fear no more the heat of the sun' (iv.ii.259–70). Then 'Fool Talk' picks up on the association between Shakespeare's jesters and clowns with music and song by extemporizing on the words of the Fool in *King Lear* (an embodiment we might say of the presence of the comic at the heart of the tragic).

The interest in playfulness, creative juxtaposition, and the Shakespearean sonnet sequence evinced by this birthday tribute concert is shared by the work of Cleo Laine and Johnny Dankworth, a jazz pair who have consistently returned to the Shakespearean canon for lyrics and inspiration.[12] Songs such as 'The Compleat Works' joyfully play with an attempt to set all the titles of Shakespeare's plays and poems to music ('32 more to do', rasps Laine at one point), but they also performed settings of several Shakespeare sonnets on Laine's 1964 benchmark album *Shakespeare and All That Jazz*, and on later recordings, including Dankworth's own setting for Sonnet 18, and several of the Ellington–Strayhorn collaborations, adapting these pieces to offer precise settings for Sonnets 40 ('Take all my loves') and 147 ('My love is as a fever'). This they did in addition to offering on the 1964 album a witty exploration of the role of juxtaposition in the sonnet sequence in 'Duet of Sonnets'. Here Dankworth's setting and Laine's flexible voice bring together sonnets 23 and 24, which body forth an actor and a painter respectively, with additional reference to the creative role of writer or poet. There is a sense of shared artistry here between performers and source-text, which offers a rich reading of the poems themselves in the process of musical adaptation.

In later recordings, Laine and Dankworth returned to Shakespeare, not least to his dramatic verse and settings for actual songs from the plays, many of which, as we shall see in the next chapter, had a long history of adaptation within the classical canon. Their versions of the funeral dirge from *Cymbeline* (also embedded in the 'Will's Birthday Suite' piece from the 1974 tribute concert), Winter's song from the closing moments of *Love's Labour's Lost* ('When icicles hang by the wall', v.ii.897–912), or *As You Like It*'s 'It was a lover and his lass' (v.iii.15–38), are well aware of the considerable history of interpretation, from the seventeenth century onwards to the work of Ralph Vaughan Williams and Gerald Finzi in the twentieth century, and of the fact that they are making their own 'riff' on the subject.

The pair go further, in that they take Shakespearean dialogue from the stage and subject it to similar forms of musical description and underscoring as used for the sonnet adaptations. For example, they set the music-drenched opening speech of Duke Orsino from *Twelfth Night* ('If music be the food of love'), and, in a further intriguing hybridization that in effect offers a reading of their source-texts (again following the model of Ellington and Strayhorn and their suggestive combination of characters from *Othello* and *Macbeth* in 'The Telecasters'), they juxtapose the lines of Titania from *A Midsummer Night's Dream* instructing her fairies to attend to her new-found love Bottom's every need (III.i.144–54) with the weird sisters' cauldron chant from IV.i of *Macbeth*. As well as making the genres of comedy and tragedy play off against each other in the contrapuntal aesthetic of this number, 'Witches Foul and Fair' picks up on the fascination with the binary oppositions of light and dark, real and fantastic, and foul and fair that both playtexts indulge in and explore: 'Fair is foul, and foul is fair, / Hover through the fog and filthy air' (*Macbeth*, I.i.10–11).

Dankworth already had an established track history with jazz adaptations of Shakespeare, since he had starred in *All Night Long* (1962), a version of *Othello* with a 1950s London jazz club scenario, directed by Michael Relph and Basil Dearden. Aurelius Rex, played by Paul Harris, is the Othello-character or analogue, an American trumpet-player who is driven to near-strangle his partner, club-singer Delia, due to the covert plotting of Iago-esque drummer Johnny Cousin (played by Patrick McGoohan). Both Dankworth and Dave Brubeck played themselves in the film, as well as providing the score, in a neat trick 'authenticating' Shakespeare in the process, according to Tony Howard (2000: 304). In this modern 'take' on the play, the handkerchief transmutes into a cigarette case, and Cousin uses a tape recorder to entrap his victims in the course of a claustrophobic all-night party (see Rothwell 1999: 223; T. Howard 2000: 304). Technology, and especially recorded technology, provide in combination with the resonant jazz context an interesting response to the new possibilities of Shakespeare on film.[13]

The big band, swing, or jazz club musical context has proved surprisingly fertile ground for adaptations of Shakespeare, cinematic or otherwise. Douglas Lanier has recently offered suggestive studies of two 1930s works, *Paradise in Harlem* and *Playmates*. *Paradise in Harlem* (1939; dir. Joseph Seiden) tells the story of a black actor in the USA who dreams of playing Shakespearean roles, but is instead attacked by racist thugs. His dream of Shakespeare remains just that for most of the film. In a painful twist towards the end, he finally finds himself performing the role of Othello only to be booed from the stage by black members of the audience: 'Yeah, put *out* the light!' Lanier indicates that the film nevertheless resists this pessimistic ending by swerving away from the tragic outcome of Shakespeare's play towards a vision of a world transformed by cultural agency and black empowerment (Lanier 2004). What is crucial in the context of this study is that this transformation is partly effected through music, through the blues, and eventually through a gospel-infused choral and semi-spiritual scene with Desdemona which cedes to the ultimate performance of optimism in the deployment of the jitterbug at the very end, in what Lanier perceives as a complex attempt to assimilate Shakespeare into the 'protocols of popular culture' (Lanier 2004).

Playmates (dir. David Butler, 1941) is a rather different movie in content and tenor, but one which also flirts with the idea of a 'swing' Shakespeare via its casting of the popular bandleader Kay Kyser alongside acknowledged Shakespearean actor John Barrymore, both playing themselves in a further example of the world of the contemporary arts 'authenticating' (and presumably promoting) Shakespeare's presence on the big screen. In the film, Kyser adapts *Romeo and Juliet* into the story of 'swing musician Romeo Smith and opera singer Juliet Jones, with Juliet's father, a devotee of classical music, as obstacle to their romance' (Lanier 2002: 65). Mr Jones soon changes his tune when he realizes how well Romeo is paid for his job as a bandleader, and the happy ending is once again realized in the form of communal song and dance. As Lanier's discussion makes clear, the film offers an interesting (re)location of Shakespeare in the debates about elite and popular culture in the early part of the twentieth century. It is, he says, all 'filtered through swing, Tin Pan Alley rhymes, and the convention of musical comedy' (2002: 66), and there is certainly a question to be asked as to whether jazz and swing gain authority and status from the bard, or vice versa, in instances of adaptation and appropriation such as these.

Questions about legitimation and authorization were certainly in the air in 1939 when a jazz- and swing-inflected musical version of *A Midsum-*

mer Night's Dream, entitled *Swingin' the Dream*, was staged in New York. The musical relocated the events of the play to Louisiana in 1900, with Theseus as state governor. It had a remarkable cast – Louis Armstrong played Bottom, and Butterfly McQueen (known to many from her role as Scarlett O'Hara's maidservant, Patsy, in the film version of *Gone With the Wind*) was Puck. The lovers and the Athenian aristocrats were, revealingly, played by white actors, while African-American performers were cast either as the artisanal class, the mechanicals, or as the fairies. This was not colour-blind casting, then, although its suggestion of alternative Shakespeare was both provocative and brave in a 1930s context (cf. Teague 2002: 228).[14] The more integrated racial politics at least suggested by this casting of Shakespeare extended to the choice of musicians for the performance; the orchestra was provided by the Benny Goodman sextet, one of the few racially integrated bands of this kind in America at this time.

Just as Ellington and Strayhorn would seek to do in the 1950s, the aim was to consciously merge and hybridize classical and jazz idioms. The production even deployed the classic aural signifier of Felix Mendelssohn's Overture and Incidental Music for *A Midsummer Night's Dream* as a base, or 'ground', for the swing score, to highlight this act of appropriation or amalgam (for a fuller discussion of the significance of Mendelssohn's music for the theatre history of *Dream*, see chapter 2). But the effects proved too radical for the USA in the 1930s; reviewers complained that black performers could not recite Shakespeare 'properly', and the show closed with massive losses in less than a fortnight.[15] The climate was shifting by the 1950s when Ellington and Strayhorn made their own persuasive case for the productive relationship between Shakespeare and African-American culture, a fact evidenced by the star performances of Robeson and Earl Jones in the productions mentioned above. The mainstreaming of jazz Shakespeare by this time can perhaps be registered in the audible presence of jazz elements in the Leonard Bernstein score for another Shakespeare musical, *West Side Story*, also first performed in 1957.[16]

Certainly since the 1950s, the mutually informing relationship between popular music and Shakespeare has resurfaced in the many knowing references to swing and jazz engagements with the Shakespearean repertoire in films such as Richard Loncraine's 1995 *Richard III* (discussed in greater detail in chapter 4), and the US musical has itself revisited the subject of Shakespeare and Ellington in the 1997 *Play On!*, a less than resounding success on Broadway at its first performance, but a subsequent touring success and the focus of a PBS broadcast version in 1999. The play, as its knowing title suggests, is an appropriation of *Twelfth Night* (which opens with the declaration, 'If music be the food of love, play on', 1.i.1.) set in the period of the Harlem Renaissance, in a locale that closely resembles the Cotton Club, and with an Ellington-inspired musical soundtrack. To cement that relationship further, Ellington's granddaughter choreographed the show. The plotline is ostensibly about a woman called 'Vi' (Viola) who wants to be a songwriter and who, fearful that her case will not be taken seriously, dresses as a man to gain access to the 'Duke' who owns the club, Orsino reimagined as Ellington himself. Meanwhile the Duke is supposedly in love with a club singer, Lady Liv (Olivia). There has been some academic comment on the changes made to the events of *Twelfth Night* to recast the play in an acceptable African-American idiom at the close of the twentieth century. In a reflection of the taboo status of homosexuality in many faith-led black communities, the potential for homoerotic encounter between Antonio and Sebastian is entirely removed from the scene, and Malvolio is reimagined as 'The Rev', a Man of Islam and the club manager who this time gets to win the heart of 'Lady Liv', albeit dressed in a fittingly yellow zoot suit.

Play On! confirms a rich collaboration between Shakespeare and jazz, and Shakespeare and Duke Ellington in particular, in the latter half of the twentieth century. It is a relationship that seems set to continue. As I was completing this book, a production of *Othello*, directed by Luk Perceval and performed by German theatre company Münchner Kammerspiele, was opening at the Royal Shakespeare Company site in Stratford-upon-Avon as part of their Complete Works Festival. The show sees the play condensed to two hours, transposed into modern discourse, and performed to the continuous accompaniment of live jazz piano.[17] The beat goes on, it seems . . .

Notes

1 Though it would be a gross oversimplification to read jazz's relationship to the melody it cites as always joyful or symbiotic. Duke Ellington himself had a notoriously charged relationship with George and Ira Gershwin's music for *Porgy and Bess*, e.g., which he felt was an invidious example of white musicians appropriating and exploiting African-American music and history for personal and commercial gain (A. Knight 2001: 320).

2 My thanks to Daniel Grimley for discussion of this and much else in this chapter.

3 See, e.g., versions included on *'Shall I compare thee?': Choral Songs on Shakespeare Texts* by the Chicago *a capella* group (Cedille Records, 2005, CDR 90000 085) and on *Shakespeare in Song* performed by the Phoenix Bach Choir (Chandos Records, 2004, CHSA 5031). The work of other composers on *'Shall I compare thee?'* also exhibits the influence of jazz and its mainstream appropriations, not least Robert Applebaum, who as well as contributing another setting of Sonnet 18, alludes to the music of George

Gershwin in his 'Witches' Blues', a setting of the cauldron song and dance of the weird sisters from *Macbeth*.

4 Like many of the Shakespearean musical adaptations discussed in this book, Edvard Grieg's *Peer Gynt* suites began their compositional life as incidental music for the first stage production of Henrik Ibsen's play of the same name.

5 It is instructive how frequently a model of artistic collaboration will be invoked in this study of adaptation. It is, of course, a model that has clear precedents in the playwriting practices of Shakespeare and his contemporaries; see Jowett 2003.

6 The musical renditions of sonnets by Ladysmith Black Mambazo and Rufus Wainwright appear on film composer Michael Kamen et al.'s *When Love Speaks*, a mix of musical adaptations and readings of Shakespeare made on behalf of RADA and released on CD in 2002. The CD and its musical settings of Shakespearean verse, including the sonnets, are discussed in more detail in ch. 9.

7 I am indebted to the work of Stephen Buhler in this regard. In a remarkable performance at the Shakespeare Association of America conference in New Orleans in 2004, in a seminar on 'Ellington, Shakespeare, and Jazz Adaptation', he spoke Sonnet 40 ('Take all my loves') along to the 'Sonnet to Hank Cinq' from the *Such Sweet Thunder* suite to prove his point. This was the sonnet set by Cleo Laine and Johnny Dankworth to this composition for their own *Shakespeare and All that Jazz* album in 1964 and included on the 2002 compilation, *The Collection*.

8 Again, I am indebted to Stephen Buhler for this clarification (2004).

9 Presumably a memory of this collaborative relationship spurred the Globe Theatre to commission contemporary UK jazz musician Django Bates to write incidental music for its production of *Titus Andronicus* (dir. Lucy Bailey) in 2006. Bates is a composer and musician who works very much within the blended idiom I have been discussing in this chapter, citing influences from the classical canon and Indian *ragas* as well as contemporary pop songs. Other Globe productions have used a jazz idiom for their incidental music, notably a 2001 *Macbeth* for which Clare van Kampen composed tracks including 'Come seeling night' and 'Rat without a tail'. Michael Langham reused Ellington's *Timon* suite in a 1991 revival. For an adaptation of that music, see Silverman 1994 in the Discography.

10 The recording was re-released on the Vocalian label in 2005: see Ardley et al. (2005) in the Discography.

11 The recurring interest in providing musical settings for this sonnet (this chapter has already mentioned versions by Nils Lindberg and Robert Applebaum; Kevin Olson, a Chicago jazz musician, also contributes a setting of the 'Summer Sonnet' as he calls it to the album on which Lindberg and Applebaum's choral work appears – the aptly titled *'Shall I compare thee?'* performed by the Chicago a capella (see n. 3 above) – which blends jazz influences with the rhythms of Brazilian *bossa nova* and Bryan Ferry offers another rendition on Kamen et al. (2002)) begs the question as to why this sonnet is selected from all the others so often. The summer comparison and its memorability as an opening line in the public consciousness may be contributing factors, but the answer for musical adaptation must surely also exist in the underlying rhythm of this sonnet, its gently regular metrics perhaps lending themselves to musical scoring. The entirely monosyllabic beats of the closing couplet have a musical rhythm of their own. For a brief but lucid discussion of the history of musical settings of the sonnets, see Edmondson and Wells (2004: 172–6).

12 Laine even played Hippolyta in a 1960s 'jazz' interpretation of *A Midsummer Night's Dream* in Edinburgh (Williams 1997: 222).

13 Rothwell (1999: 223) makes an intriguing comparison with a Portuguese-language Brazilian appropriation of *Othello*, *Otelo de Oliveira* (1984) which tells the story of Otelo

and Denis, residents of a *favela*, or Rio shanty town. Otelo is the leader of a *samba* band rife with internal rivalry like the jazz band of *All Night Long*.

14 The obvious parallel was the interracial casting of Oscar Hammerstein and Jerome Kern's *Show Boat* in 1938; see Graziano 2002.

15 I am indebted for some of these details to Teague 2004.

16 Of course, Bernstein's assimilation of Latin and jazz syncopation in his music has been read as a questionable act of appropriation by a white classically trained musician. The racial significations of the score to *West Side Story* continue to be a subject of discussion and debate.

17 The adaptation was a collaboration between Turkish German writer Feridun Zaimoglu and scriptwriter Gunter Sekel.

Further examples and reading

The Oxford Companion to Music, ed. Alison Latham (Oxford: Oxford University Press, 2002) and *The Oxford Companion to Jazz*, ed. Bill Kirchner (Oxford: Oxford University Press, 2000) are invaluable reference works. Mervyn Cooke is an acknowledged authority on the complex history of jazz; see his *Jazz* (London: Thames and Hudson, 1998b), and the volume of essays he co-edited with David Horn, *The Cambridge Companion to Jazz* (Cambridge: Cambridge University Press, 2002). On the history and cultural context of big band and swing music, see Lewis A. Erenberg, *Swingin' the Dream: Big Band Jazz and the Rebirth of American Culture* (Chicago: University of Chicago Press, 1998), plus the Shakespeare-specific discussions of Douglas Lanier in his *Shakespeare and Modern Popular Culture* (Oxford: Oxford University Press, 2002) and Frances Teague in her article 'Shakespeare, Beard of Avon' in *Shakespeare After Mass Media*, ed. Richard Burt (New York: Palgrave, 2002). On Shakespeare and jazz, Terence Hawkes's work as discussed in this chapter was ground-breaking; see his *That Shakespeherian Rag: Essays on a Critical Process* (London and New York: Methuen, 1986). For additional discussion of jazz and baroque music as metaphors or templates for the adaptation process, see my own *Adaptation and Appropriation* (London: Routledge, 2006). One additional example of a jazz rumination on Shakespeare which it was not possible to discuss in detail here is Mike and Kate Westbrook's *Measure for Measure* (1992), which is a collage of verse from Shakespeare's play of the same name. This composition for voice and jazz orchestra was commissioned by the Vienna Art Orchestra and is included on Mike Westbrook's CD *The Orchestra of Smith's Academy* (1992).

On Shakespeare's language and the intricate relationship between metre, musicality, and sound, an excellent starting point is *Reading Shakespeare's Dramatic Language: A Guide*, ed. Sylvia Adamson, Lynnette Hunter, Lynne Magnusson, Ann Thompson, and Katie Wales (London: Arden/Thomson Publishing, 2001). This includes several further recommendations for reading, but one that deserves re-mention here is Delbert Spain's *Shakespeare Sounded Soundly: The Verse Structure and the Language* (Santa Barbara: Capra Press, Garland–Clarke Editions, 1988). For a rich and intriguing study of the idea of sounds and acoustics in Shakespeare's work, see Wes Folkerth, *The Sound of Shakespeare* (London: Routledge, 2002).

2

Classical Shakespeares

> I never heard
> So musical a discord, such sweet thunder
> *A Midsummer Night's Dream*, IV.i.116–17

In many respects, Shakespeare established his own precedent in the theatre for the rich tradition of providing musical settings of his lyrics and verse, since many of his plays include set-piece songs that either invite or require the provision of settings by any theatre company that performs them. The songs that punctuate the forest scenes of *As You Like It*, including the much anthologized 'Under the greenwood tree' and 'It was a lover and his lass', or that provide the darker, more morbid undertow to the romantic comedy of *Twelfth Night* (for example, Feste's delivery of 'Come away death'), or the exquisite seasonally resonant lyrics that close *Love's Labour's Lost* ('When daisies pied' and 'When icicles hang by the wall', the songs of Spring and Winter respectively), Moth's song in that same play, or that sung by the boy who entertains the melancholic Mariana at her isolated moated grange in *Measure for Measure*, have all led to memorable and frequently re-performed song settings, dating from the seventeenth century onwards. Add into this already rich picture those plays in which music is not just present for the purposes of dramatic punctuation or emotional underscoring, but functions as an integral theme and even agent – *The Tempest* springs immediately to mind, with Ariel's eerily magical songs and the affecting 'noises' of the island (III.ii.138), as does the use of trumpets and drums to signify threats both martial and otherworldly in *Hamlet* – and the significance of music to understanding the history of Shakespeare on the stage proves not only inescapable but vital.

Many Shakespeare songs found a particular prominence in the German *Lieder* tradition, with examples including Josef Haydn's late eighteenth-century setting of 'She never told her love' from *Twelfth Night* and Franz Schubert's *'An Sylvia'* ('To Sylvia') from *The Two Gentleman of Verona* (*c*.1820s). Richard Wigmore, in CD liner notes that accompany tenor Ian Bostridge's haunting performance of this and other Schubert *Lieder*, comments on the looseness of the translation by Eduard von Bauernfeld that Schubert used.[1] In another striking example of the process of cultural translation and transformation frequently involved in musical adaptation into languages other than English, in 1873 Johannes Brahms set five songs from *Hamlet*, crediting the lyrics not solely to William Shakespeare but also to the bard's German translators August Wilhelm von Schlegel and Ludwig Tieck. In subsequent chapters on opera I will argue that the Schlegel–Tieck translation is crucial not only to the dissemination of Shakespeare's work during the Romantic period in Europe, but also to understanding specific modes of interpretation and dominant understandings of the plays. Brahms's folk-song-influenced settings of Ophelia's songs from IV.v of the play, the scene of her mental distraction following Hamlet's rejection and his callous murder of her father, were written specifically for the actress Olga Priecheisen, who was making a considerable name for herself in this role on the German stage at this time, another indicator of the close relationship between Shakespeare's musical afterlife and practical theatre.[2] One of the songs 'Und kommt er nicht mehr zurück' ('And will he not come again?', IV.v.188–98), with its telling use of refrain to emphasize the inescapable plight of the singer, is heavily influenced by Brahms's own experimentations within the folk tradition, but it therefore finds kinship with later experimentation with Shakespeare songs by composers associated with the English folk tradition at the start of the twentieth century, including Gustav Holst, Ralph Vaughan Williams, Percy Grainger – who wrote a setting for the 'Willow Song' from *Othello*, which was even in Shakespeare's play readily recognizable to audiences as a traditional ballad rather than a new song by the playwright – and Roger Quilter.[3]

Shakespeare's own deployment and use of music in his plays has been much analysed and well served of late, as the 'Prelude' to this volume noted, by an astute and suggestive study by David Lindley. That work looks not only at the material contexts for the production and provision of music in Shakespeare's playtexts, as well as their performance in specific playhouses and performative environments, but also at the wider social significations and semiotics of song, dance, and instrumentation in the early modern period (Lindley 2006). But subsequent ages and cultures had their own context-specific reasons for writing the settings they did for Shakespearean lyrics, and in this respect a study of the afterlife of these songs can prove equally illuminating as a record of the plays' impact in the world of the theatre and beyond. Chapter 5, which looks at Shakespeare in the opera house, will identify an important precedent for that particular generic manifestation of Shakespeare and music in the conditions and contexts of Restoration theatre. A more detailed account of the history of textual and performative adaptation of Shakespeare in the hands of writers such as Nahum Tate and Nathaniel Lee, and its concomitant impact upon the compositional careers and profiles of Matthew Locke, Henry Purcell, and others will be offered there; but in any discussion of classical music's response to Shakespeare the setting of his lyrics, initially in a theatrical context but eventually moving out into concert halls, must take centre-stage. Ariel's songs in *The Tempest*, 'Come unto these yellow sands' (i.ii.377–89), 'Full fathom five' (i.ii.399–407), and 'Where the bee sucks' (v.i.88–96), were regularly set for late seventeenth-century theatre performances. In the twentieth century, composers such as Sir Michael Tippett continued this tradition, and it is one that persists to the present day with the more recent contributions of Harrison Birtwistle and Thomas Adès (cf. Adlington 2000).

Restoration theatre was anything but precious in its approach to Shakespearean song, and the theatres of William Davenant and Thomas Killigrew were more than willing to add songs by contemporary musicians (see Dobson 1992). *The Tempest*, *Macbeth*, and *A Midsummer Night's Dream* were all plays that saw their content regularly supplemented not only with new dialogue, scenes, and characters, but also with new opportunities for musical performance, in the form of both song and dance. Other plays which included inset dramas, such as *Timon of Athens* with its 'Masque of Amazons' (i.ii), provided further occasion for additional music. Purcell himself wrote music for the latter, as well as for Nahum Tate's productions of several history plays. These musical additions were themselves frequently recycled in a Restoration and later eighteenth-century theatre context; David Garrick, for example, was much influenced by Davenant's adaptations and alterations to *Macbeth* and *A Midsummer Night's Dream* when creating his own influential performance scripts. Such recyclings were not always produced in conjunction with the play to which the additions had initially been attached. Purcell's masque for *Dido and Aeneas* would feature, for example, as part of Charles Gildon's adaptation of *Measure for Measure* in 1700.[4] What becomes apparent from any study of the classical genre's association with Shakespeare's oeuvre is just how many of the musical responses to, or interpretations of, either specific plays or specific song lyrics from those plays have tangible roots in theatrical productions. Tippett's above-mentioned setting of the 'Songs for Ariel', although later performed and recorded for the Aldeburgh Festival by Benjamin Britten on the piano with Sir Peter Pears singing (their own remarkable and influential operatic collaboration on Shakespeare's *Dream* is explored in detail in chapter 6), was initially composed for a theatre production at the Old Vic in 1961, and was therefore intended to be sung by an actor in the role of Ariel, rather than a trained classical performer such as Pears. Tippett was far from alone in establishing this direct relationship with Shakespeare in performance. With the precedent of Purcell firmly in mind, many of what are now regarded as major classical 'suites' based on Shakespeare plays in practice derive from, or are adaptations and reworkings of, incidental music for specific theatre productions.

In eighteenth-century England, both Thomas Arne and William Boyce wrote music for the commercial playhouses, including several commissions for the leading actor-manager of the day, David Garrick. Boyce wrote incidental music for productions of *The Tempest*, *The Winter's Tale*, *Cymbeline*, *Romeo and Juliet*, and *Macbeth*. Many of Arne's settings of the Shakespeare songs mentioned at the start of this chapter are still well known today, and were published as settings as early as 1741. But their origin was undoubtedly in play performances at the Drury Lane Theatre. Arne was directly following the precedent of Purcell in this respect. Such was the impact and memorability of these musical enhancements of eighteenth-century theatre productions that songs added for the purposes of performance that were not 'by' Shakespeare or, at least, did not derive from the original playtexts (since, as Lindley rightly indicates, Shakespeare was consciously using recognizable popular songs of his own day, 2006: 70–6, 142–68), became inextricably associated with Shakespeare in the popular memory; so much so that several were published in Shakespeare song collections without proper attribution to their actual lyricists and composers. Examples include a dirge with lyrics by William Collins that Arne inserted in a production of *Cymbeline*, entitled 'To fair Fidele's grassy tomb', obviously intended to accompany the existent and much-adapted 'Fear no more the heat of the sun', and popular lyrics such as 'My bliss too long my bride denies' and 'To keep my gentle Jessie' (Cudworth, 1966: 61). Much of the additional music of this kind appears to have been used for the scenes of spectacle so beloved of eighteenth-century theatre; dirges for funeral processions and musical accompaniment for masques, as well as inset dances and ballets, are regular occurrences. We are already, then, starting to witness the blurring of the dividing line between the operatic and the theatrical Shakespeare which chapter 5 will argue is crucial to a full understanding of the operations of music in relation to

Shakespearean performance in the eighteenth and nineteenth centuries, especially in the English tradition. The 'operatization' of Shakespeare was even the topic of several nineteenth-century pastiches, including Henry Rowley Bishop's *Antony and Cleopatra*. 'Operatization' would also make its mark on European compositions now regarded as veritable benchmark works in the history of the rich creative relationship between Shakespeare and classical composers, not least the creations of Hector Berlioz, which will be discussed in more detail later.

Incidental music for the theatre is, by its nature, a very particular beast. It is context-specific, often aiding the practical and pragmatic needs of particular productions, be it to facilitate lengthy exits and entrances or complicated costume changes, or to entertain the audience during act breaks and scene changes; it frequently reflects the aesthetic and creative impulses of a particular director or company, and the particular mood or ambience they seek to create for their production, as well as the specific speeches or moments in the action they wish to emphasize. A pervasive link to the genre of melodrama can be identified here, with certain kinds of music or instrumentation used to provide rapid information for the audience about character type or scene. Such choices may even signify the geographical, cultural, or temporal settings for particular productions; one thinks of 'orientalized' productions of *A Midsummer Night's Dream* that pick up on references to spices and the East within the dialogue and infuse their productions with *raga*-influenced soundtracks.

Having made this declaration, however, that incidental music for theatre is context-specific, tied to a particular production and moment, it is intriguing to register the considerable afterlife that many such compositions have enjoyed, albeit in altered form, in the concert hall and in classical recordings. Works by Henry Purcell, Felix Mendelssohn, Claude Debussy, Jean Sibelius, and Gerald Finzi all fall into this category. In a related context, Ralph Vaughan Williams's work for Stratford-upon-Avon productions of *The Merry Wives of Windsor*, the *Henriad*, and other plays by Frank Benson's company in 1913 fed directly into his creation of the folk-song-inspired opera based on *The Merry Wives*, *Sir John in Love*, composed between 1924 and 1928.

Vaughan Williams adapted several folk-songs and tunes for use in these productions, deploying 'Greensleeves' (which he would use again both in a classical suite and in *Sir John in Love*) in the productions of *The Merry Wives* and *Richard II*. He set music for many of the set-piece songs in Shakespearean plays, including, as a young man, 'O mistress mine' from *Twelfth Night* and the 'Willow Song' from *Othello*, and settings of some of these, such as 'When daisies pied', were later incorporated into his Falstaffian opera. In *Serenade to Music*, he set Lorenzo's speech on music from *The Merchant of Venice* for multiple voices:

> Therefore the poet
> Did feign that Orpheus drew trees, stones, and floods,
> Since naught so stockish, hard, and full of rage
> But music for the time doth change his nature.
> The man that hath no music in himself,
> Nor is not moved with concord of sweet sounds,
> Is fit for treasons, stratagems, and spoils.
>
> (v.i.79–85)[5]

In an act of creative amalgam, these direct inheritances from the Shakespeare plays become bound up with the specific musical experimentation and interests of Vaughan Williams's own time, in particular English folk-song and tradition. Both Vaughan Williams and his sometime collaborator Gustav Holst were directly influenced by the new folk-song school of English music led by Cecil Sharp, and the version of an English pastoral it promulgated, when they came to adapt plays featuring Shakespeare's Lord of Misrule, Sir John Falstaff. Like Vaughan Williams's *Sir John in Love*, Holst's exquisite one-act chamber opera *At the Boar's Head* (1924), based on the tavern scenes of the two *Henry IV* plays, embeds traditional English folk-songs and dance tunes alongside a complex grouping of Shakespearean verse, more conventional operatic arias, and lyric settings of some of the sonnets. The influence of Sharp's folk-song movement was felt in many areas of cultural life in the decades surrounding the Great War, and it is telling that Sharp himself was involved in writing incidental music for theatrical productions of Shakespeare: in 1914, for example, he contributed music to a production of *A Midsummer Night's Dream* (Cudworth, 1966: 85).

Though not an English pastoralist *per se*, Roger Quilter, along with Percy Grainger a member of the so-called Frankfurt school, had just a few years earlier produced his settings for many of the same Shakespearean lyrics as would attract Vaughan Williams's attention, notably a duet version of 'It was a lover and his lass' from *As You Like It*, for productions of the plays in the commercial theatre – in this instance for a 1921 production by Lilian Bayliss at the Old Vic. Roger Fiske describes the example of musical settings for specific theatrical performances that find a future life in reworked or reimagined compositions, either operatic or symphonic, as 'incidental music that has outlived the production for which it was written' (Fiske 1966: 177). He lists examples such as Mily Balkirev's *King Lear* (1860–1); Gabriel Fauré's *Shylock* (Op. 57), written for a production of Edmond Haraucourt's adaptation of Shakespeare's *The Merchant of Venice* (1889); and Pyotr Tchaikovsky's *Hamlet* (1891). Interesting additions to this list are Claude Debussy's *Le roi Lear* (1904), which was incidental music for a production of that play directed by André Antoine, and which includes a striking fanfare for the opening scene in which Lear tests the love of his three daughters (Weller 2005: 81), and Erich Wolfgang von Korngold's suite for violin and piano 'Much Ado About Nothing' (1918), which derived from incidental music he composed for a 1920 performance of the play in Schönbrunn Castle. Originally a composition for a full orchestra, it was subsequently adapted by Korngold for a smaller group of players partway through the run when the full orchestra was required at another venue.[6] The piece has the episodic quality of much incidental music, offering four snapshots of Shakespeare's play. It opens with an engaging pizzicato violin in Hero's bedchamber as she prepares for her wedding to Claudio ('Mädchen im Brautgemach' ('Maiden in the Bridal Chamber')), and goes on to offer the humorous interlude of Dogberry and Verges's drunken escapade in 'Holzapfel und Schlehwein', a beautiful musical account of the emerging love between Beatrice and Benedict in the 'Gartenscene' (Garden Scene), and finally the set-piece ending of the 'Masquerade' in 'Mummenschanz'.

Fiske also mentions in his catalogue of incidental music for Shakespeare Arthur Sullivan's *The Tempest* (1862). Sullivan would go on to greater fame as part of the Gilbert and Sullivan partnership, but his early career is in part defined by music for Shakespearean productions; he composed incidental music for stagings of *Macbeth*, *The Merchant of Venice*, *Henry VIII*, and *The Merry Wives of Windsor*. Others involved in writing incidental music for theatrical performances of Shakespeare, such as the Russian composers Sergei Prokofiev, who wrote incidental music for a *Hamlet* in Leningrad in 1937, like Vaughan Williams utilizing Elizabethan folk airs for his score (Fiske 1966: 233), and Dmitri Shostakovich, went on to further involvement and engagement with Shakespeare in other, related media, such as ballet, opera, and film music (Prokofiev's ballet *Romeo and Juliet* will be discussed in detail in the following chapter, and Shostakovich's scores for the Shakespeare films of Russian director Grigori Kosintsev are examined in detail in chapter 7).[7]

The process of adaptation that theatre music undergoes when being reworked into a classical concert piece is often revealing. Of necessity the dramaturgic chronology that drives the music for a performance of a play can be sacrificed for an alternative narrative of central themes and characters. Sibelius's suite for *The Tempest*, for example, originally written for an extravagant production of the play at the Royal Theatre in Copenhagen in 1926, becomes less determined by the plotline or unfolding dramaturgy of the storm-drenched late play than by central themes selected for attention. We start in the classical suite, for example, with a section representative of Caliban's drunken behaviour in III.ii; elsewhere, alongside the set-piece moments of the wedding masque, we hear sections suggestive of the magus Prospero and his daughter Miranda, who are represented by contrasting instrumentation. Prospero's piece is an unsettling combination of harps and percussion, which brilliantly captures the resonant ambiguity of the character and his movement between malign and benign possibilities in the play. There is even a brief 'Humoresque', a light-hearted interlude which brings the voice of the jester Trinculo into the suite, comparable to Korngold's deployment of the comic relief of Dogberry and Verges in his *Much Ado About Nothing* suite for violin and piano.

Fascinatingly, Sibelius makes no attempt to provide musical settings for the actual songs of *The Tempest*; Ariel's 'Full fathom five' is notable simply by its absence. In his drawing out of the essences of particular characters, rather than a concentrated attempt to follow the narrative of the play in musical terms, we can, however, identify an intriguing kinship between Sibelius's project and that of the poet W. H. Auden, who wrote his own rumination on *The Tempest* in 1942–4. 'The Sea and the Mirror', a remarkable extended poem, gives literal voice to many of the play's *dramatis personae*, including all the central protagonists, such as Prospero and Miranda, but also paying attention to the so-called minor characters such as the boatswain and the mariners in the opening storm scene, and Trinculo himself, who is given a song. Auden's long poem ends in a lengthy section of prose in which his dark, ambivalent rendering of the character of Caliban directly addresses his audience of readers. Sibelius's decision to give Caliban the opening frame in his musical suite shares with Auden's poem, then, a decision to offer a personal interpretation of the play through the conscious ordering and focus of the piece. It also finds kinship with what has been a dominant note in the literary-critical history of the play in the twentieth century, not least in postcolonial readings in which the oppression and subjugation of Caliban and Ariel at the hands of the colonialist invader Prospero has been at the forefront of concerns. This angle on the play has in turn fed a rich history of adaptations, appropriations, and 'writings back' to Shakespeare that makes

Sibelius's use of Caliban as a framing device look both prescient and insightful as a reading of the playtext in operation (see, e.g., Bate 1997: 240–50; Hulme and Sherman, 2000).

Edward German was yet another English composer whose work was strongly inflected by his association with the practical theatre. He was Musical Director of the Globe Theatre from 1888 onwards, composing incidental music for productions of *Richard III*, *Romeo and Juliet*, and *Henry VIII, or All is True*, among others. His dances for the latter sealed his reputation. He continued to write music with a Shakespearean connection long after a working link with the theatre had been severed due to a collapse in personal confidence, composing music for Desdemona's 'Willow Song' as late as 1922. Of particular note is his 'Symphonic Poem' on *Hamlet*, which dates from 1897. This twenty-minute piece offers an engaging narrative of some of the play's main events, not least through a descriptive use of instrumentation. The opening has an ambience of tragic portent; a gong quietly strikes midnight, presaging the ghost's appearance. The use of percussion throughout this piece is striking. Hamlet's death is exquisitely realized in the closing bars through the use of timpani which seem to represent his fading heartbeat.[8] Fittingly, thereafter 'The rest is silence' (v.ii.310).

A descriptive or suggestive use of instrumentation is common in musical adaptations or interpretations of literary narratives. We saw in the first chapter on jazz how Duke Ellington selected specific instruments to suggest characters such as Puck in *A Midsummer Night's Dream*. German strives for an equivalent effect in his use of woodwind to indicate Ophelia's presence in his symphonic poem. She is first signified by the light touch of the clarinet, which, with its nineteenth-century associations with femininity and the 'feminized', sounds in marked contrast to the assertive, masculinized, and often militarized brass and percussion that has typified Hamlet in this composition. German's prince is very much a man of action; his sections invariably rising to a loud *crescendo*. In the more mournful passages that signify Ophelia's death and precede the funeral lament for her, the oboe performs an equivalent role. The association between Shakespeare's tragic heroines and the woodwind section of the orchestra is long established. German deployed woodwind to signify his Juliet, as did Berlioz, and as would Prokofiev in his balletic version of the play. Woodwind more generally appear to function as tragic signifiers, often bringing a tone of mourning, melancholy, lament, and loss into a piece: Elgar's *Falstaff* is a case in point, where the plaintive clarinet signifies the offstage death of the marginalized Sir John. That the clarinet in this example might also carry traces of the 'feminized' associations and connotations mentioned above in relation to Edward German's interpretation of Ophelia, thereby polarizing Falstaff in his relationship to the masculine and martial Hal, again seems to offer significant correspondences between Elgar's musical interpretation and influential veins of critical interpretations of the play.[9]

Shakespearean comedy as well as tragedy has proved a rich seam to mine for composers. Gerald Finzi's *Love's Labour's Lost* had its origins in performance, this time on radio rather than the stage. In 1946 Finzi was asked to compose incidental music for a BBC broadcast of the play produced by Noel Iliff. This small-scale radio context meant that it was originally scored for a small chamber orchestra; but in 1952 Finzi reworked it as a concert suite for performance by a full-scale orchestra at the Cheltenham Festival. Like several of the musical works discussed in this volume, Finzi's suite had not one but several afterlives. In 1953 it was further adapted and added to for the purposes of an open-air performance of *Love's Labour's Lost* by the Southend Shakespeare Society directed by Michael Greenwood. Sections such as the 'Nocturne' were composed to enable the actors to change scenes on a stage which, because of its open air nature, could not be darkened, and to allow for lengthier exits and entrances. Instruments were added, and parts for singing voices removed. As with many recordings of pieces that started life as incidental music for the theatre, what we hear now in concert halls or on audio equipment is rarely representative of the music as it operated in a play performance. As in the case of Sibelius's *Tempest* suite, the chronology often differs from that of the play proper that it purports to represent, and Finzi's *Love's Labour's Lost* is no exception. Nevertheless, such recordings still provide an intriguing insight into a composer's understanding of a play and its dramaturgic operations. Like many playgoers, Finzi identified the onstage delivery of the love sonnets by the male members of the Navarre academe in iv.iii as a key moment, and regarded the speeches as akin to soliloquies in the way they stood out onstage. To this end, he thought that they could be further highlighted by being delivered over a musical background. In this respect we might see his work as absorbing influence from mainstream cinematic practice of the time, in particular its use of music on soundtracks to heighten or underscore key scenes. Finzi also subtly differentiates the instrumentation and tempo of each sonnet.[10]

Most intriguing, however, is the subtle and suggestive musical analogue Finzi finds for the play-within-a-play when the work transfers from its stage context to its audio afterlife. In *Love's Labour's Lost* the 'Pageant of the

Nine Worthies' in v.ii is, unfittingly and hilariously, performed by the comic characters, including Costard the clown who plays Pompey, Nathaniel the curate who is Alexander, and the tiny page Moth who inappropriately performs the role of Hercules. Instead of simply offering musical accompaniment to this event, Finzi finds an alternative from the domain of music, the *quodlibet*, to substitute in suggestive ways for the play-within-a-play device. While the dictionary definition of 'quodlibet' is simply a 'light-hearted medley of well-known tunes' (*Oxford English Dictionary*), in the eighteenth century, the term was often used to describe a traditional family musical performance, usually involving the *extempore* singing of popular songs before an audience of friends and relatives. The contents of such performances were invariably secular, and both partly comic and partly bawdy in nature, and, according to contemporary records, much enjoyed by members of the audience. Johann Sebastian Bach is known to have participated in these family singing entertainments during his childhood, and Richard Egarr has suggested that the influence of this can be traced in the *Goldberg Variations*, where the final variation is given this title (2006: 7). This notion of an intimate, comic performance fits perfectly with the impact and content of the 'Pageant of the Nine Worthies' in Shakespeare's play, and is a further indication of Finzi's sensitivity to the particular demands of his medium when adapting *Love's Labour's Lost* into music. What we are witnessing in this instance is an example of music finding its own idiom in which to respond to or remake Shakespeare. The ways in which arias stand in for but also supplement soliloquies from specific plays in opera, especially in the aria-centred work of Verdi, or in which the inset song and dance routines function in Broadway or Hollywood musicals, are other cases in point. In Holst's *At the Boar's Head*, for example, the character of Prince Hal, the future Henry V, is given a major aria early on in the piece, singling him on the stage, separating him from the Eastcheap tavern community, just as he is singled out in the play for audience attention by his delivery of his machinatory soliloquy at I.ii.192–3: 'I know you all, and will a while uphold / The unyoked humour of your idleness.'[11] Shakespeare further emphasizes the separateness and cool control of his feelings by Hal at this point by having the soliloquy move effortlessly into a perfect fourteen-line sonnet at its close:

> If all the year were playing holidays,
> To sport would be as tedious as to work;
> But when they seldom come, they wished-for come,
> And nothing pleaseth but rare accidents.

So when this loose behaviour I throw off
And pay the debt I never promisèd,
By how much better than my word I am,
By so much shall I falsify men's hopes;
And like the bright metal on a sullen ground,
My reformation, glitt'ring o'er my fault,
Shall show more goodly and attract more eyes
Than that which hath no foil to set it off.
I'll so offend to make offence a skill,
Redeeming time when men think least I will.
(I.ii.201–14)

In his 'Music for *Love's Labour's Lost*' Gerald Finzi finds a similar striking meeting point between the modes of soliloquy and sonnet as used in Shakespeare's play and the musical set-pieces of his suite. As the above example from 1 *Henry IV* makes manifest, Shakespeare himself consistently played with the idea of dramatizing the sonnet – there are other vibrant examples of this kind of poetic and linguistic experimentation in *Romeo and Juliet* and *Love's Labour's Lost* – and in the genre of opera, of sung drama, the process of transformation is taken one stage further with the rendering of sonnets or soliloquies as arias. Sonnets have proved fertile ground for musical adaptation. As well as the contemporary example of Michael Kamen's *When Love Speaks* (2002), which sets several sonnets to music, we have the earlier precedent of Holst, who, taking his cue from the sonnet embedded in Hal's I.ii soliloquy, gives the prince two further arias which are settings of Shakespearean sonnets (cf. Edmondson and Wells 2004: 175). The connecting theme is undoubtedly time: in disguise as a tapster, Hal sings Sonnet 19, 'Devouring time, blunt thou the lion's paw', and later still at the end of the sequence, Sonnet 12, 'When I do count the clock that tells the time'. The theme of temporality and ephemerality may in part provide a key to comprehending Holst's particular interest and aesthetic approach in reworking the Falstaff scenes of Shakespeare's histories in a one-act chamber opera, and why he was less drawn than many of his contemporaries to the comedy of *The Merry Wives of Windsor*, in which the same character appears.[12]

In 1924 Holst was composing his evocative rumination on time and conflict in the aftermath of the supposed 'war to end all wars', the 1914–18 Great War. As the sun sets literally on his characters and Falstaff contemplates joining the others as potential cannon fodder on the battle-field, audiences in 1924 must have seen in part a reflection of their own experiences.[13] This adds immeasurably to understanding the remarkable act of resistance at the end of the piece. Falstaff's energy has departed the stage, seemingly to join his compatriots in the slow march to London and conscription, yet there is a final onstage glimmer of hope, as Bardolph lifts a curtain and shows a candle to indicate to Doll that Falstaff has stayed for one last night of lovemaking. Mistress Quickly's urgent final line – 'Run, Doll, run' – has the effect of cancelling out, or at least temporarily resisting, the realities outside the tavern window and the facts of legal time and destiny that were stressed in Hal's arias.[14] As with many of the works studied here, what might seem on the surface an act of nostalgia for 'a merry old England' that never existed, and a mythical ideal of Shakespeare, is instead a remarkable and individual piece of music that responds to and is born out of Holst's own socio-political and cultural moment.[15]

Like Holst and Vaughan Williams, Finzi, when he came to write his 'Music for *Love's Labour's Lost*', was already familiar with the process of composing musical settings for Shakespearean verse, due to his creation of a song cycle *Let Us Garlands Bring* (Op. 18) in 1942, which had been dedicated to Ralph Vaughan Williams on the occasion of his seventieth birthday. The cycle, set for baritone voice, included 'Come away death' and 'O mistress mine' from *Twelfth Night*, 'Who is Sylvia?' from *The Two Gentleman of Verona*, 'It was a lover and his lass' from *As You Like It*, and 'Fear no more the heat o' the sun' from *Cymbeline*, indicating the influence of the German *Lieder* tradition on Finzi. The pervasive cultural presence of these songs and their lyrics in English culture throughout the early part of the twentieth century is striking, and perhaps in part explains their deep resonance in the allusive and adaptational writing of the Modernists, in particular Virginia Woolf. Her meta-theatrical late novel *Between the Acts* (1941) features a village pageant with a sub-Shakespearean element and a woman director, Miss La Trobe. She is haunted by the 'scraps, orts, and fragments' of English literature in her head; the quotation is itself a telling allusion to Shakespeare's *Troilus and Cressida*, a play about war and the attendant fracturing and fragmentation of society, which must have seemed richly suggestive to Woolf, writing as she was at the outbreak of the Second World War. In other novels such as *Mrs Dalloway* (1925), lines like that from the funeral threnody of *Cymbeline* – 'Fear no more the heat of the sun' – ebb and flow within her prose narrative like half-remembered songs. It is tempting to think that an understanding of the prevalence of song settings of Shakespeare lyrics at this time provides us with an aural and aesthetic register for Woolf's literary allusiveness, and the particular musicality of Shakespeare in her work.[16]

There are, inevitably, particular plays to which the classical genre has returned again and again. Part of the reason for this may rest in the perceived 'musicality' or lyricism of those plays – *The Tempest*, for example, with its self-proclaimed interest in music as agent and force, would seem to offer rich potential for a musical response. Those plays which feature songs and lyrics as part of their action, many of the romantic comedies being a case in point, would seem to offer parallel interests.[17] In a very practical sense the act of adaptation encourages further adaptation; musicians and composers perform acts of intertextual reference with each other as much as with their early modern precursor. Benjamin Britten and Michael Tippett in the twentieth century, both composers responsible for a revival of interest in the use of the counter-tenor voice, are acutely aware of the precedent and influence of Purcell, as well as each other, in their own Shakespearean ventures.[18] Leonard Bernstein recorded a New York Philharmonic performance of Berlioz's Opus 17 on *Romeo and Juliet* at the same time as he was seeing *West Side Story*, the musical version of *Romeo and Juliet* for which he provided the music, take the stages of Broadway by storm. That musical is discussed in detail in chapter 4, but the mention of *Romeo and Juliet* ushers in another crucial factor in determining why certain Shakespeare plays become the focus of classical musical adaptation and interpretation. Jonathan Bate has described *Romeo and Juliet* as 'Western culture's archetypal myth of youthful passion' (1997: 278), and it would seem inevitable that musicians and composers would strive to respond to that mythical resonance in some way.

Such is the iconicity of *Romeo and Juliet* that we can also identify musical and literary compositions that are themselves adaptations of adaptations: Frederick Delius's 'music drama in six scenes' *A Village Romeo and Juliet* (1899–1901), based on Gottfried Keller's work of prose fiction *Die Leute von Seldwyla* ('The People of Seldwyla'), set in mid-nineteenth-century Switzerland and depicting the experiences of feuding farmers and their children, is one such example. Others inspired more directly by Shakespeare include the Norwegian Johan Svendsen's *Romeo og Julie* (Op. 18, 1876) and the Swedish Wilhelm Stenhammar's *Romeo och Julia* (1922).[19] One of the best-known symphonic renditions of the story of the star-crossed lovers has to be Pyotr Tchaikovsky's 'fantasy overture', which dates from 1869–70. It does not follow the strict progression of the play, but uses instrumentation and modes of repetition and refrain to suggest specific characters and key moments in Shakespeare's drama. Most recognizable, perhaps, is the 'love theme' that attaches to Romeo and Juliet, first bringing them together at the ball, but also representing their later encounters on the balcony, in Juliet's bedroom, and, ultimately, in the tomb. It is a technique for identifying the lovers that has been much repeated, influencing Nino Rota's development of a love theme for the young protagonists in Franco Zeffirelli's 1968 film version of the play and Baz Luhrmann's designation of a similar role to Des'ree's 'Kissing you' in his screen interpretation. Chapter 8 on film scores will further suggest that Luhrmann looks to other archetypal classical compositions on tragic love, in particular the *Liebestod* from Richard Wagner's opera *Tristan und Isolde* to perform a complementary function in the closing sequences of his film. In the 1930s Sergei Prokofiev, another composer influenced by the Wagnerian technique of *leitmotif,* responded to *Romeo and Juliet* in the alternative medium of ballet.

A century earlier, Hector Berlioz had opted to eschew the dramatic voice almost entirely in his rendering of the tale of the star-crossed lovers; his lovers are famously silent, rendered only at the level of musical harmony. His work is entitled a 'Symphonie dramatique', but it is one directly inspired by and responsive to the theatrical context, indeed to one specific performance of the play which he saw at the Odéon theatre in Paris in 1827. Berlioz's emotive response to that production, staged by a visiting group of actors from Britain, is recorded in his personal writings and has been much discussed, not least because he went on to marry the actress who played Juliet on that occasion, Harriet Smithson (see, e.g., Bate 1997: 278; Kemp 1992: 38). He did not respond immediately in his music, although his interest in the play interlinks with his other musical excursions into the theme of romantic desire, not least in the *Symphonie Fantastique* (1845 and 1855), and his 1829 cantata *La mort de Cléopatra* ('The Death of Cleopatra'), includes a quotation from *Romeo and Juliet* at the start of the 'Méditation' section: 'How if, when I am laid into the tomb . . .' (iv.iii.29). The quotation is apposite in that the entire piece, written for a mezzo-soprano voice, focuses on Cleopatra's ruminations on her death prior to her encounter with the 'vil reptil', but it also indicates that the play of doomed youthful love is equally on Berlioz's mind as he responds to Shakespeare's counterpart tragedy of mature love in this composition.[20] It would be a further decade before Berlioz would actually take on the task of writing a dramatic symphony based on the story of Romeo and Juliet, and in doing so he was, as Ian Kemp has rightly stressed, not paying an empty act of homage but 're-creating Shakespeare in his own terms' (1992: 46). This is not descriptive music that can be mapped on to the dialogue or actions of specific scenes. The characters suggested by the music are drastically pared down from the original *dramatis personae,* but this kind of direct comparison, more revealing perhaps in relation to the staged musical drama of opera, seems unhelpful here anyway. There are few moments when we can halt the music and point to the suggestion of specific characters, except in the case of the two lovers themselves; there is no 'killing of Mercutio', and the Queen Mab speech becomes a much altered *scherzo* in the final movement of the symphony. Nevertheless, Berlioz offers an insightful reading of and response to the play.

We start with 'Romeo seul', the wandering melodies of these sections an indicator of his unsettled state of mind prior to the self-altering encounter with Juliet at the Capulets' ball. The ball is brilliantly evoked in a section entitled 'Grand fête chez Capulet'. We are given sudden surges in orchestration, volume, and register that help us to distinguish this brasher, more vulgar public event from the intimate encounters that will take place between the lovers. It is a brilliant aural precursor to the distinctions between public and private space suggested in Luhrmann's 1996 film version.

In Berlioz, once together with Juliet, Romeo's melody becomes more fixed and certain; he has found the place and space in life where he wants to be and the symphony represents their coming together in the 'Scène d'amour' though the use of harmony. Music which elsewhere plays with counterpoint and dissonance to suggest the feuding Veronese families here suggests the perfect match between the two lovers. That harmony is, however, only ever temporary and fitful; Ian Kemp has expertly discussed the comings and goings of *crescendo* and *diminuendo* in this scene, which while offering moments of exquisite union and complementarity, also, ultimately, suggests the unsustainable nature – at least in a secular context – of this 'perfect' love. Similar ideas will be rendered visually rather than aurally by film versions of the play in the twentieth century, not least in Luhrmann's 1996 interpretation. Ian Kemp also comments on Berlioz's choice of the musical metaphor of the *rondo* to express the couple's union, as the viola or cello that invariably suggests Romeo's melody and the oboe or clarinet that represents Juliet interweave (1992: 64, 67). The music offers variations on a theme; it returns again and again to the same point, the star-crossed lovers themselves, the centre of Shakespeare's play, with a kind of thematic discursiveness – circling away and back in musical terms from that central focus – that is dramatically apposite. This is also another version of the kind of innovation and experimentation on a ground which we identified in the introduction as a useful musical template for thinking about the process of literary adaptation in general and of the adaptation of Shakespeare into music in particular: 'Berlioz's musical metaphor here is a *rondo*, the *rondo* theme always coming back to the same thing . . . yet always different, and, in the episodes, allowing for fresh discoveries' (Kemp 1992: 67).

What is noticeably different in Berlioz's account of the play in this dramatic symphony and in his writings about that composition is the ending, at least as compared to Shakespeare's playtext. In this aspect of his work he was deeply influenced by the 1827 production of the play. For what was performed at the Odéon that year was in fact a truncated version of David Garrick's eighteenth-century adaptation of *Romeo and Juliet*. There was no Rosaline, for example, since Garrick felt that this encouraged audiences to question Romeo's status as a romantic hero; and in a moment of heightened pathos, Juliet awoke before Romeo died from swallowing the poison, allowing one last tragic onstage reunion between the lovers. As Jonathan Bate notes: 'From a structural point of view, it is clear that Berlioz is following Garrick. He read Shakespeare in the French prose translation of Pierre Le Tourneur, whose version of *Romeo and Juliet* was based on Garrick's' (1997: 281).

In his own writings, Berlioz went so far as to suggest that Garrick had actively improved on Shakespeare in respect of the ending, 'incomparable in its pathos' (cited in Kemp 1992: 37). In truth, Garrick himself was adapting the dramatic innovations of Restoration interpreters of the play, in particular the work of Thomas Otway and Theophilus Cibber (see Marsden 2002: 27). Baz Luhrmann appears to have been equally persuaded by Garrick, Otway, Cibber, and Berlioz when he restaged the tomb scene in similar terms towards the end of the twentieth century, on this occasion through the medium of cinema. By opting for a classical musical soundtrack at this point in his score, not Berlioz but Wagner's *Tristan und Isolde*, Luhrmann appears to make his sense of that adaptational inheritance explicit. Already, then, we are beginning to register a rich tapestry of influence and cross-fertilization between different moments of Shakespearean adaptation and between specific works of interpretation, but we need also to register the reverse impact that musical adaptations of the tenor and influence of Berlioz's symphony have had on readings and stagings of their Shakespearean precursors. Ian Kemp is persuasive on this subject:

> Berlioz's love scene does not have the light-fingered enchantment of Shakespeare's balcony scene. It is more inward, its discoveries more knowing, its courses less volatile. Yet a thousand books would fail to explain its secrets, subtleties, compositional mastery and the peculiar

alchemy by which the balcony scene is never quite the same once you've heard the *Scène d'amour*. (1992: 64)

One play that has certainly never looked (or, indeed, sounded) quite the same again since the creation of one particular musical composition is *A Midsummer Night's Dream*. It seems scarcely possible nowadays to see a stage production or film version or even a television adaptation of that romantic comedy that does not in some way feature the Overture and Incidental Music for the play composed by Felix Mendelssohn. In truth, Mendelssohn's Overture to *A Midsummer Night's Dream*, an attempt to capture several main aspects of the play in one short composition, was intended originally not for a dramatic entertainment but for a piano recital. He was, however, later invited to compose additional incidental music for the theatre, for an 1843 production of the play staged at the King of Prussia's playhouse in Potsdam (Fiske 1966: 223). Thereafter both his Overture and Incidental Music became inextricably bound up with theatrical productions of *Dream*, not only throughout Europe in the nineteenth century, but well into the twentieth. His Shakespearean composition made a similar mark in the medium of cinema, when it was used by German directors in exile, Max Reinhardt and William Dieterle, as the soundtrack to their spectacular Hollywood sound-motion film of the play in 1935 in arrangements provided by Erich Wolfgang von Korngold (Gooch and Thatcher 1991: 11.1020–1).

The use of Mendelssohn's music in a theatrical context had coincided with a huge increase in 'pictorial' or spectacular Shakespeare in the proscenium arch theatre of the nineteenth century. Seemingly it provided the perfect orchestral accompaniment to the balletic set-pieces which had become an almost inevitable aspect of staging the *Dream* (see Schoch 2002). There was already a strong trend towards the musical in productions of the *Dream* when Mendelssohn composed his Overture and Incidental Music, which stretched back as far as the seventeenth century and adaptations such as *The Fairy Queen* in which Purcell's additional music and songs played a major role.

In 1826, an operatic version had been staged with Elizabeth Lucia Vestris singing the part of Oberon. But Mendelssohn's music undoubtedly marks a watershed in the history of *Dream* in performance. Jay L. Halio (1994: 27) sees Charles Kean's 1856 production as a defining moment; Kean cut more than 800 lines from the play and instead used huge swathes of Mendelssohn's composition as well as other music. In an 1859 production in New York, directed by Laura Keene, Kean's text was used alongside ballet and Mendelssohn once again. Intriguingly, this production also cast an opera singer Fanny Stockton as Oberon, establishing a trend for feminized or androgynous Oberons that both looks back to Purcell's counter-tenors but also influenced Benjamin Britten's work on the play for his 1960 opera. Reinhardt and Dieterle's film displayed similar interests in, and commitments to, the staging practices of the nineteenth century.

Mendelssohn's composition is, then, one that has a deep and complex afterlife of its own, and one to which I can only gesture in this context. In 1843 it established a benchmark for theatrical production, and it became the norm for major composers to be commissioned to write new music for new productions of the plays, in Britain, Russia, and elsewhere. It is in this receptive climate that composers like Arthur Sullivan and Edward German found a veritable occupation in writing for the theatre. In the twentieth century, changing theatre practices would begin to alter that relationship between playhouse and classical composer. Fewer theatres after the two World Wars could afford to maintain full orchestras, and some composers who in an earlier era might have found a niche in composing incidental music in the commercial playhouses turned to the new arena of film, William Walton and Dmitri Shostakovich among them (see chapter 7).

As is perhaps inevitable with any work that becomes canonical and even conventional in this regard, there was a conscious backlash against the identification of Mendelssohn's music and Shakespeare's play. If in 1935 it was still (just) possible to use Mendelssohn's music for *Dream* in a non-ironic fashion, even on the cinema screen, it was clear that theatre productions in the UK were at least starting to offer genuine alternatives to the expected Mendelssohnian opening bars to the 'Wedding March' in Act v. In a 1914 Harley Granville-Barker production, the stage and setting represented a fantasy world inspired by the Paris ballets of Diaghilev, but in the musical accompaniment there was a notable shift from Mendelssohn to Cecil Sharp and the English folk-music tradition that I have already identified as an influence on the Shakespearean compositions of Vaughan Williams and Holst. Interestingly, Granville-Barker used the familiar Elizabethan tune of 'Greensleeves' for the bergomask section in this production of *Dream*, which Vaughan Williams incorporated into his opera *Sir John in Love*, as well as the ballad 'Lord Willoughby's Wedding' for the wedding sequence (in a pointed alternative to Mendelssohn: it was, says Halio, a production 'Rooted in Warwickshire soil' (1994: 35)), which Holst would use in *At the Boar's Head*. Again, the case for the direct influence of theatrical productions and staging conventions on musical composition seems compelling.

One Angela Carter short story in her *Black Venus* collection responds to Mendelssohn's associations with *A Midsummer Night's Dream* as well as 'Victorianized' versions of Shakespeare:

> The wood we have just described is that of nineteenth-century nostalgia, which disinfected the wood, cleansing it of the grave, hideous and elemental beings with which the superstition of an earlier age had filled it . . . It is Mendelssohn's wood. (1985: 69)

A benchmark modern, subversive staging of *A Midsummer Night's Dream* in the British theatre with similar objections to the Victorian 'version' of the Athenian forest was undoubtedly Peter Brook's 1970 'white cube' production for the Royal Shakespeare Company, which drew influences from Chinese acrobatics, the circus, and the theories of Carl Jung. Halio records that the first section of Brook's production ended with 'a grand triumphal procession' as the fairies bore Bottom the Ass aloft 'to the music of Mendelssohn's 'Wedding March' . . . It is a great celebration of eroticism, the satirical intrusion of Mendelssohn's music along with everything else flouting the grandiose traditions of nineteenth-century productions, which it is Brook's clear intention to demolish' (1994: 64). Mendelssohn became an easy signifier of the production's deviation from the norm in Ron Daniels's 1981 staging, also at the RSC. Here was a Victorian pastiche writ large, set not in a forest but in a deserted music hall with Mendelssohn reduced to the faint tinklings of an offstage piano (Halio 1994: 74). These parodic references and productions were clearly an influence on Carter's short story, as was Peter Hall's 1959 stage version (filmed in 1962), with its muddy fairies and its overt emphasis on the English landscape and weather, which opted to eschew Mendelssohn entirely, having almost no non-diegetic music (cf. Halio 1994: 93).

The trend continues both in the theatre and on the big screen. The most recent film adaptation of *A Midsummer Night's Dream* directed by Michael Hoffman (1998) opted for a nineteenth-century Italian *mise-en-scène*, and at various points in its soundtrack deployed snatches of recognizable operas including the 'Brindisi' or drinking song from Verdi's *La Traviata* and 'Una furtiva lagrima' from Gaetano Donizetti's *L'elisir d'amore*. There are interesting moments in the film when the use of opera extends beyond serving as a cultural geographical or historical signifier and contributes to our understanding of character as it is being interpreted. This is especially true of sequences involving Bottom, with whom opera in its bombast, hubris, but also sheer performativity and entertainment value, is regularly associated. 'Una furtiva lagrima' plays not only as he leaves the first play rehearsal in a state of comic humiliation, but also when we see him at home. This domestic version of Bottom is a significant interpolation in the film, albeit one without dialogue. We see a shrunken version of the public persona, as Bottom tries to find respite in the aesthetic beauty of the opera song playing on his gramophone, but instead finds himself subjected to the scornful gaze of his, by implication, dominant wife.

Opera is not the only musical signifier in the film's sign system: the opening sequence, as well as several others that take place in the fairy domain, is hedged round with the familiar chordal sequences of Mendelssohn's Overture and Incidental Music. The 'Wedding March' does indeed play over scenes of the celebrations of the multiple marriages at the Athenian court in Act v, and elsewhere Mendelssohn's music provides a familiar point of access to the fairy world of the forest. It is telling that during the panning shots of the opening sequence, which depict the preparations for the nuptial festivities, we catch a glimpse of a young boy carrying out a gramophone horn. Both boy and horn (he is, presumably, the changeling boy made visible onscreen) reappear in the fairy world as records float away on rivers and snatches of classical music float in and out of audience consciousness, not least during Bottom and Titania's lovemaking.[21] Some critics have suggested a parodic deployment of Mendelssohn in this film, but the sustained attention it pays within the diegetic world of both mortals and fairies to the significance of music, as inspiration, memory, respite, shared experience, and more, casts doubt on these claims. Parodic or not, the point is, however, that all these productions, in their performance of enchantment or rejection, reassert the centrality of Mendelssohn to productions of *Dream* in all media. His music is notable either for its presence or for its absence, or even for its conscious marginalization, but in this way it continues to be a major force in the afterlife of this particular text, not least in understandings or representations of the fairies of the play.

A Midsummer Night's Dream continues to influence composers; one Shakespearean offshoot of the trend for 'contemporary classical' in the later decades of the twentieth century, which had expressed itself in the popular music charts in the form of progressive rock, with its self-conscious interest in the adaptation of literary source material, is former Genesis guitarist Steve Hackett's 1997 suite for classical guitar and supporting orchestra based on *A Midsummer Night's Dream*. Hackett's composition is much enthralled by the language of Shakespeare's play; the titles of each piece derive from specific lines and quotations from the text. As a whole, it provides a fascinating link to Henze's Shakespearean guitar compositions of the 1970s and a throwback to the English pastoralists' versions of Shakespeare at the start of the twentieth century. There is little space for Bottom and the mechanicals in Hackett's self-confessed romantic account of the play. The only reference he makes to their comic play-within-a-play performance of the tragic love story of Pyramus and Thisbe is through the absolute romanticism of Hippolyta's question to Theseus as to how Thisbe will find her lover in the darkness; his reply – 'She will find him by starlight' (v.i.309) – provides the title for the piece based on this moment in the play, 'Starlight'. Instead of many of the mechanicals' comic exchanges, the suite conjures up various of the play's pastoral locales and settings, both actual and evoked, such as the 'pavèd fountain' at which Titania recounts former meetings with Oberon taking place (ii.i.82–5), and the site where Oberon saw Cupid's arrow strike the flower of 'love-in-idleness' with its potent powers in 'Between the Cold Moon and the Earth' (see ii.i.155–7).

To return to the specific example of Hector Berlioz, however, and the inspiration he drew from witnessing an actual performance of *Romeo and Juliet*, as well as the specific decisions made by that production in terms of staging and performative emphases, it is clear that another important history of classical music's engagement with Shakespeare can be written through an account of its engagement with the body of the literal performer onstage. If Berlioz's Juliet is in part written through Harriet Smithson's 1827 interpretation of the role, so Franz Liszt's *Hamlet*, part of his *Symphonic Poems* (1858), and described by the composer himself as 'a musical outline of the Danish prince' is not a response to the play *per se* but rather a response to a particular interpretation of the central role of the troubled Prince of Denmark.

Liszt witnessed and was heavily influenced by a Weimar production of the play in which the role of Hamlet was performed by Bogumil Dawison. Reviews and responses at the time saw this as an unusual, even startling, interpretation, since it portrayed Hamlet as an intelligent and active prince, and not the passive dreamer who had figured in most productions staged in the post-Goethe Romantic tradition. Jonathan Bate has written evocatively of the deep influence of Romantic readings of Shakespeare on the subsequent theatre history of the plays, and in particular of interpretations of the major roles such as Hamlet. Goethe's romanticized reading of Hamlet the thinker was expounded in his influential *Bildungsroman* entitled *Wilhelm Meisters Lehrjahre* ('Wilhelm Meister's Apprenticeship'), which not only shaped the thoughts of Samuel Taylor Coleridge on this play but the influence of which can be traced as far as the literary criticism of A. C. Bradley and the film interpretation of the prince in Olivier's 1948 cinematic adaptation. What Liszt saw, however, ran counter to this Romantic tradition, restoring the political and practical elements to the prince that the Romantic emphasis on the abstracted aesthetic had suppressed, and this in part explains the assertive tones and registers of his intimate symphonic portrait of the prince (it lasts no longer than ten minutes in performance).

A similarly personalized account of a particular moment in a Shakespearean tragedy is offered by Antonín Dvořák's overture on *Othello* (1892). The Czech composer's piece is striking, since it expresses no visible (or audible) interest in the character of Iago who so often dominates literary-critical accounts of the play. Instead, he concentrates on the closing act of the play and on two specific characters, exploring Othello's murder of the innocent Desdemona. This specific emphasis indicates that, like the Giuseppe Verdi–Arrigo Boito operatic adaptation, *Otello*, which is discussed in detail in chapters 5 and 6, Dvořák was working in the context of a nineteenth-century tradition that focused on the tragic plight of these characters. The overture is an early experiment in his canon in the form of the symphonic poem, and features telling deployments of woodwind instruments to vocalize Desdemona's character. The overture begins with her in quiet prayer, but this is soon interrupted by the ominous bass notes that signify Othello's intrusion into the bedchamber. Initially she pleads her innocence with him, with some degree of assertion, a fact realized through the sounds of the oboe, but later in the sequence this switches to the submissive dying notes of the flute. To the knowing auditor – the listener who hears the piece alongside a reading of the play as it were – the composition offers an intriguing narrative on the scene and on the relationship of the two characters. The central movement, for example, offers more intertwined waltz-like rhythms to suggest the previous harmony and attraction of their coupling – standing in, as it were, for earlier acts and scenes of Shakespeare's play – but the return of Othello's repeating jealous notes soon wrenches us back to the present and his murderous intent. Dvořák's *Othello* overture is a perfect example of how symphonic poems, which are ostensibly free interpretations of their poetic or dramatic source-text, benefit from a drama- and Shakespeare-literate listener, one who reads the narrative into the developing musical themes and orchestration. It is a particular kind of audibility that insists on something far more integral and ongoing in the relationship between source-text and musical outcome than straightforward readings of 'influence' are always able to demonstrate or allow for.

Both Liszt's and Dvořák's compositions are indicative of another nineteenth-century trend in musical engagement with the Shakespearean canon: what Bate has called the Romantic trend for 'character criticism' (1997: 252): 'Characters such as Hamlet, Macbeth, Romeo, and Juliet took on a mythic force. They no longer needed their plays, they were recreated in other media – first painting, then forms as diverse as the novel and music' (1997: 252). One of the examples or templates for this kind of criticism and its impact proffered by Bate is an essay by Maurice Morgann, published in 1777 under the title *Essay on the Dramatic Character of Sir John Falstaff*:

> Morgann set out with the apparently quixotic ambition of proving that Falstaff was not a coward. Before long, he found himself giving Sir John a complete life-history. The character becomes at the very least more like someone in a novel than a play. (Bate 1997: 252)

This is a working example of what Bate refers to as character criticism shading off into 'mythmaking' (1997: 253). Falstaff is rendered iconic by this kind of literary-critical and scholarly attention, and this focus on specific characters and their psychologies proved a huge influence on the Romantic movement and subsequent Shakespeare scholars.

According to Bate, A. C. Bradley was 'Steeped in the poetry and philosophy of Romantic idealism' (1997: 258) when he came to write his epochal work, the 1904 *Shakespearean Tragedy*, which Bate describes as one of the 'most influential books on Shakespeare written in the early years of the twentieth century' (1997: 191–2; see also Hawkes 1986). John Bayley has suggested that Bradley may not have known the work of his amateur eighteenth-century predecessor Morgann (Bradley 1991 [1904]: 6). However, Morgann's essay on Falstaff was published in 1902 as part of an edition of *Eighteenth-Century Essays on Shakespeare*, which at least opens up the possibility that Bradley had direct contact with these arguments.[22] The Romantic and, specifically, Hegelian inflection of Bradley's scholarship is, however, important to my consideration of classical composers' engagement with and understanding of Shakespeare at this particular historical juncture, and it goes a considerable way to shedding light on a work that has become central to a history of Shakespeare and music, Edward Elgar's 1913 symphonic study *Falstaff* (Op. 68; its full subtitle is 'Symphonic Study in C minor'). Elgar's analytic essay on this piece, first published in the *Musical Times* prior to the *première* of his composition, gives us tremendous insight into the thinking behind the work, and indicates that he was offering a tragic interpretation of Falstaff's character, something not readily offered by a reading or viewing of the *Henry IV* plays, but one heavily shaped by the dominant critical trends of his day. Elgar quotes directly from Morgann's 1777 essay, and to back up the point, he marked up a gift presentation of a miniature score of the work that he gave to Alice Stuart-Wortley on the occasion of the *première* as '*Falstaff* (Tragedy)' (Fiske 1966: 218; Grimley, 2002).

As already observed, the contemporary critic who shared this tragic reading of Falstaff's character was A. C. Bradley, and while Elgar does not openly acknowledge his influence, it seems likely that he was readily exposed to Bradley's theories in contemporary lectures on Shakespeare which we know he attended regularly.[23] The tragic emphasis of Elgar's symphonic study can be registered not only in the decision to set it in the key of C minor, which had pre-existent tragic connotations in the musical lexicon, but also in the climax to the work.[24] Daniel Grimley indicates that the ending caused Elgar much concern, and he was unsure what to do with it until very late in the compositional process. His ultimate decision underscores the tragic reading he offers of Falstaff's character: although on the surface the final section depicts the progress of the newly crowned King Henry V, the melodic refrain of the clarinet returns us to his rejected friend and colleague ('I know thee not, old man', v.v.47):

> This is a classic Elgarian device: the music offers a snatch of a faintly-remembered tune (never heard in its full actuality), that inspires thoughts of melancholy, loss, and nostalgia, as well as the sense of a singing presence . . . Set off from the main body of the work, and isolated within its own other-worldly context, the melody is a graphic representation of the moment of Falstaff's death. (Grimley 2002: 5)

The coda to the piece is, however, harsher in the tragic experience it offers. The ending of the final eight bars returns us briefly, suddenly, but also seemingly incontrovertibly, to the *realpolitik* of the new king's reign – Elgar's own commentary clarifies this point: 'the man of harsh reality has triumphed' (cited in Grimley 2002: 8). The ambiguity of this ending which musicologists continue to debate – is it positive or negative? – is indicative of Elgar's participation in the literary-critical debates of his day about these plays and about the character of Falstaff through the very act and art of his musical composition. Elgar's careful labelling of the different sections of his symphonic poem, with subtitles such as 'The return through Gloucestershire' and 'The repudiation of Falstaff, and his death', also indicates his search for the kind of active audibility that I was identifying in the earlier account of the listening experience of Dvořák's *Othello* overture as central to the form of the symphonic poem. Each section relates to a particular moment or scene in the plays, and offers Elgar's reading or interpretation of the same. Furthermore, the symphonic poem's engagement with issues of Englishness and heroic masculinity, and a sense of both in crisis, is highly indicative of its time of composition, just as Holst's chamber opera remakes the *Henry IV* plays for his specific post-war context.

Extrapolating more widely from the Elgar–Bradley–Morgann interaction, as well as registering the influence of theatrical tradition and innovative practice on specific composers, and the impact of particular performances of certain plays, we must now add into our interpretative frame for musical adaptations the critical scholarship in which composers may have been trained or at least exposed to during their educational or compositional careers. All of these factors aid us in carrying out the kind of contextualization and historicization of Shakespearean musical adaptations that I argue for in this study. I want to close this chapter, however, with a specific example of the way in which Shakespeare, music, and significant historical events are also inextricably bound together in cultural experience and memory. In 1997 the funeral of Diana, Princess of Wales, took place amid great state-authorized pomp and ceremony at Westminster Abbey. Pop singer Elton John's delivery of his own Marilyn Monroe-inspired song 'Candle in the Wind' for the occasion provided one musical set-piece; but so did the performance of classical composer John Tavener's remarkable 'Song for Athene'. Originally written in 1993 as a commission for the BBC, this choral work is a memorial to Tavener's friend Athene Harriadis. Its text is an amalgam of lines from the Bible and from Horatio's tribute to his dying friend in the closing act of Shakespeare's *Hamlet*: 'Good night, sweet prince, / And flights of angels sing thee to thy rest. –' (v.ii.312–13). It must have seemed remarkably apposite in its combination of Shakespeare, theology, and monarchy to those organizing the state funeral of the Princess of Wales, an 'almost' English queen (see Sanders 2000: 149). Tavener's composition, along with Elton John's emotional performance of the specially adapted version 'Candle in the Wind', has now become inseparable from the vivid cultural memory of that event.[25] In time, however, I suspect that as those memories fade and settle, 'Song for Athene', with its resonant reflections on death and friendship, will find its rightful place in the wider and immensely rich canon of Shakespeare-inspired classical music, and that its presence there will prove the finest tribute of all.

Notes

1 See Schubert 1998 in the Discography.

2 The five songs set by Brahms are 'Wir erkenn ich dein Treulieb?' ('How should I your true love know?', 23–6), 'Sein Leichenhemd weiss' ('His white shroud', 29–39), 'Auf morgen ist Sankt Valentins Tag' ('Tomorrow is St Valentine's Day', 47–65), 'Sie trugen ihn auf der Behre bloss' ('They bore him barefaced on the bier', 165–7), and 'Und kommt er nicht mehr zurück?' ('And will a not come again?, 188–97). Versions of these can be found on the *Shakespeare's Kingdom* CD, performed by Sarah Walker (mezzo-soprano) and Graham Johnson (piano) (Various Artists 1988 in the Discography), which also includes Shakespearean song settings by Franz Schubert, Camille Saint-Saëns ('La mort d'Ophélie'), Percy Grainger and others. This was far from constituting Brahms's sole venture into the Shakespearean canon; he had also composed a choral setting for 'Come away death' and a comic opera based on *The Taming of the Shrew* in 1828.

3 Quilter also set 'Come away death' among other songs; a moving rendition of this version, also performed by Ian Bostridge, is to be found on Quilter 2003 in the Discography.

4 For a fuller survey of these theatrical settings, see Cudworth 1966: 53–7. An interesting modern variation on this theme was the 1999 RSC production of *Timon of Athens*, dir. Gregory Doran, which used Duke Ellington's compositions for that play as its own incidental music and soundtrack.

5 In 1930 Ralph Vaughan Williams also wrote a *Henry V Overture* for brass band.

6 A version of the Debussy fanfare is included on *Shakespeare in Music* (Various Artists 2001 in the Discography). I am indebted for details of the Korngold, *Much Ado About Nothing*, to the CD liner notes to Korngold 2002.

7 Korngold also worked on films, having been introduced into Hollywood by the German Shakespearean theatre and film director Max Reinhardt, whose work is discussed in this and later chapters. As noted later, Korngold provided the arrangements of Mendelssohn's music for *A Midsummer Night's Dream* for Reinhardt's 1935 screen version of the play.

8 The CD liner notes to a recent BBC Concert Orchestra recording of German's Shakespearean music by Ray Siese (German 2005 in the Discography) are particularly helpful in identifying these narrative tropes in the composition.

9 On gender and the history plays, see Howard and Rackin 1997.

10 The recording of the 'Music for *Love's Labour's Lost*' used for the purposes of research was that on Finzi 2001. The sleevenotes are by Andrew Burn and Diana McVeagh.

11 In the playtext, this scene actually takes place in Hal's apartment; Falstaff exits just prior to the 'I know you all' soliloquy, having arranged a future rendezvous with Hal at Eastcheap. Holst's decision to bring this speech into the tavern adds to the deliberate intensity and intimacy of his single setting for the chamber opera.

12 For a quite brilliant reading of the sonnets in the context of a shift towards 'mechanical time' in the period, see John Kerrigan's introduction to his Penguin edition of *The Sonnets and Love's Pilgrimage*, 1986: 33–45. Kerrigan makes a specific distinction between cyclical or seasonal time, the mechanical time of the clock, and musical time, all of which Holst incorporates in his rumination on Shakespeare in this opera.

13 Verdi's opera also deploys the motif of the setting sun, presumably evoking Falstaff's own ageing and ailing physical state, a matter of some concern to the composer as a writer at a very advanced stage of his own career.

14 Holst may well have had in mind a similar line and sentiment in Andrew Marvell's renowned seventeenth-century *carpe diem* lyric 'To His Coy Mistress', which ends with the following assertion:

> Let us roll all our strength, and all
> Our sweetness, up into one ball:
> And tear our pleasures with rough strife,
> Thorough the iron grates of life.
> *Thus, though we cannot make our sun*
> *Stand still, yet we will make him run.*
> (Marvell 2005: ll. 41–6; italics mine)

15 The solar imagery and the ideas of resisting time may also reflect Holst's interest at this period in Eastern philosophy and mysticism (in 1908–9 he had created another one-act chamber opera of thirty minutes' duration based on the Sanskrit epic *The Mahabharata*, which he translated and adapted; see Mark 2005: 211). Death in this context would figure as a cyclic renewal. I am very grateful to Daniel Grimley for this point.

16 On Woolf and Shakespeare, see Sanders 2001: 4; and on her literary echoes, see Gillian Beer's introduction to Woolf 1992 [1941]. There is a larger discussion to be had of Modernism's engagement with music in its literary and artistic productions. Wassily Kandinsky collaborated with composer Arnold Schoenberg, and the theatre practitioner Vsevolod Meyerhold experimented with a vibrant combination of Wagner, opera, theatre, and colour theory in a 1909 production of *Tristan und Isolde* (McBurney 2006). James Joyce also famously engaged in a sustained manner with Wagner's music and musical theory in his prose (see Martin 1991).

17 On Shakespeare and the 'musicality' of his language, see, e.g., Bradshaw 1983.

18 Presumably a similar frame of reference and tradition was being invoked by the use of the counter-tenor Andreas Scholl on the soundtrack to the recent film version of *The Merchant of Venice* (dir. Michael Radford, 2004). Interestingly, as well as singing musical settings of Shakespearean lyrics from the playtext of *The Merchant of Venice* itself (music by Jocelyn Pook), Scholl sings a song with lyrics taken from John Milton's provincial masque, *A Mask at Ludlow Castle, 1634*, better known as *Comus*, thereby underlining the connections between seventeenth-century masque and musical adaptations of Shakespeare that I have been arguing for in this chapter and which will be extended in later chapters on opera.

19 Stenhammar's *Romeo and Juliet* suite is yet another composition that started life as incidental music, in this case for a theatrical production in Gothenberg. He also wrote incidental music for a production of *As You Like It* in 1920, as well as for productions of Strindberg at this time. An interesting collection of this music is available on a CD Stenhammar 2002.

20 Berlioz would also compose music in response to *Hamlet* (*La mort d'Ophélie*), *The Tempest*, and *King Lear*.

21 A punning reference is also possible to *Das Knaben Wunderhorn* ('The Boy's Magic Horn'), a collection of German romantic folk-tales, edited by Clemens Brentano and Achim von Arnim, and set to music by Gustav Mahler and others (1805–8), which was a major influence on the folk-song (*Volkslied*) tradition in Germany in the nineteenth century. The gramophone/horn is, of course, also a phallic symbol, suggestive of the sexualized nature of the fairy world, which has long fascinated musical adapters, including Benjamin Britten in his 1960 operatic version, co-created with his own partner, Peter Pears, which is examined in more detail in chapter 6. My thanks to Daniel Grimley for discussion of this point. For additional discussion of the use of opera and other forms of music on the soundtrack to Hoffman's film and within its diegesis, see Jones 2004.

22 The collection was edited by D. Nichol Smith and published in Glasgow by James Maclehose in 1902. On the additional influence of Edward Dowden's criticism on Elgar, see Wells 2002: 364.

23 On the influence of Bradley's work in the field of Shakespearean criticism, see K. Cooke 1972. I am hugely influenced in my own work here by Daniel Grimley's excellent study of Elgar's *Falstaff* and the influence of A. C. Bradley on the account of the *Henry IV* plays given by his compositional emphases: see Grimley 2002. My thanks to Dan for allowing me to use this piece prior to publication and for ongoing conversations about Shakespeare and music.

24 Alexandra Maria Dielitz's CD liner notes to the Münchner Rundfunkorchester's recording of *Falstaff* (Elgar 2006) observes that Hamlet, Prince of Denmark, would have been a more obvious subject for a 'Symphonic Study in C Minor'.

25 In an intriguing account of the event's musical connotations, Simon Frith has observed that Elton John's 'pop music' song was perceived very much as a 'performance' by gathered crowds who watched the event on big screens outside Westminster Abbey, their applause for his performance spilling over into applause for Earl Spencer's angry funeral elegy which was regarded by many as a trenchant attack on the House of Windsor, whereas Tavener's music, more obviously in a classical (and spiritual) musical register was not (Frith 2001: 93–4). In the specific case of spectator applause and response in the moment, Frith's argument is correct, but it seems to me that Tavener's music has, nevertheless, become as linked in the cultural memory to that high-profile historical event as Elton John's song. Frith does note in the same article that, following the funeral, listeners to the UK radio station Classic FM duly voted it one of their favourite works from the classical canon (Frith 2001: 94).

Further examples and reading

Once again this chapter has focused on detailed case studies of selected symphonic, orchestral, and choral compositions. Readers wishing to pursue issues raised here through listening to and exploring other Shakespeare-related music could look, for example, at Pyotr Tchaikovsky's fantasy overture on *The Tempest* (1873), Robert Schumann's *Julius Caesar* concert overture (1852), or Paul Dukas's *King Lear Overture* (1883), as well as the various interpretations of *Romeo and Juliet* listed within the body of the chapter, including those by Johan Svendson and Wilhelm Stenhammar. Dvořák's son-in-law Joseph Suk made his own venture into Shakespearean adaptation with a concert overture on *The Winter's Tale* in 1894.

For additional examples of the specific compositional style of the symphonic or tone poem such as Elgar's *Falstaff*, Franz Liszt's 1858 *Hamlet* is a useful starting point, as is Bedrich Smetana's *Richard III* (1862) or Richard Strauss's *Macbeth* (1890). For recordings, see Liszt 2003, Smetana 1995, and Strauss 2005 in the Discography. A less well-known example is *Hamlet and Ophelia: A Symphonic Poem* by the American composer Edward McDowell (1885). Readers might also wish to look at additional Shakespearean compositions by composers discussed here such as Hector Berlioz, or at some of the many *Lieder* or settings of Shakespeare songs that are available dating from the seventeenth century to the present day. Numerous recordings of these are listed in the Discography at the back of this volume, several under the heading of 'Various Artists'. For recorded examples of many of the settings of Shakespeare's songs for the eighteenth-century theatre by Arne and others discussed in this chapter, see The Parley of Instruments 2004.

Useful sources of information relating to the composers, as well as dates and titles for all these, can be found in the superlative resource, *A Shakespeare Music Catalogue*, 5 vols, ed. Bryan N. S. Gooch and David Thatcher, with Odean Long and Charles Haywood (Oxford: Clarendon Press, 1991). An additional resource which includes discursive essays as well as a catalogue of works that is extensive, if now slightly overtaken by the time passed since publication, is Phyllis Hartnoll (ed.), *Shakespeare in Music: Essays* (London: Macmillan,

1966). The world-wide-web is an excellent resource for tracing recordings and performances of these Shakespeare-related works.

On the interaction between different cultures and times and particular texts by Shakespeare, as well as the notion or concept of 'Shakespeare' as, by turns, English national poet and German Romantic icon, Jonathan Bate's *The Genius of Shakespeare* (London: Picador, 1997) is an enlightening read. On the particular context of late seventeenth- and eighteenth-century adaptations and adoptions of Shakespeare, Michael Dobson's *The Making of the English National Poet: Shakespeare, Adaptation, and Authorship, 1660–1769* (Oxford: Clarendon Press, 1992) is a rich source of argument and information. For those interested in pursuing the postcolonial critical history of *The Tempest*, as well as the discussion in Bate's *The Genius of Shakespeare*, a fascinating collection of essays on the play's adaptation in a range of mediums and contexts is available in *'The Tempest' and its Travels*, ed. Peter Hulme and William H. Sherman (London: Reaktion Books, 2000).

For more general contextual material on some of the composers concentrated on here, several excellent studies are available. On Jean Sibelius see *The Cambridge Companion to Sibelius*, ed. Daniel M. Grimley (Cambridge: Cambridge University Press, 2004); on Edward Elgar, see *The Cambridge Companion to Elgar*, ed. Daniel M. Grimley and Julian Rushton (Cambridge: Cambridge University Press, 2004); and on Hector Berlioz, see the collection of essays in *Berlioz Studies*, ed. Peter Bloom (Cambridge: Cambridge University Press, 1992) and Julian Rushton, *Berlioz: 'Roméo et Juliette'* (Cambridge: Cambridge University Press, 1994).

3

'Shall we dance?': Shakespeare at the Ballet

> Come now, what masques, what dances shall we have?
> *A Midsummer Night's Dream*, v.i.32

The place of dance in the history of stage productions of Shakespeare's plays was well established from the late seventeenth century onwards, when Restoration tastes for ballet, songs, and music deeply affected and shaped the adaptations of Shakespeare, and other early Stuart playwrights, which were frequently performed in the London commercial playhouses. The work of William Davenant, John Dryden, Nahum Tate, and Nathaniel Lee bears witness to the interest in dance as a means of conveying dramatic meaning. In a later chapter it will be argued that this same hybrid aspect to the performance languages of Restoration drama played a crucial role in the emergence of opera as a distinct genre in England in the eighteenth and nineteenth centuries, one which had particular effects on realizations of Shakespearean drama in an operatic context. But the other obvious strand of the performing arts to which it was a major contributor in terms of influence and practice was undoubtedly ballet. In the 1920s, composers such as Gustav Holst and Ralph Vaughan Williams, in an attempt to try and re-create a specifically English theatrical tradition, experimented with hybrid combinations of dance, opera, and theatre in their stagings of Shakespeare in direct imitation of their Restoration predecessors.[1]

There is not world enough and time to give sufficient pages over to the full complexity of the adaptation of Shakespeare into dance forms across the centuries, though it is a tremendous means of studying how one medium encounters and makes sense of another. Choreographer John Neumeier, for example, describing how he reworked *Hamlet* for the Royal Danish Ballet in 1986, as *Amleth* – a ballet entirely set to music from the *Triple Concerto* by English composer Sir Michael Tippett – explained why he turned not only to Shakespeare's playscript but also to the 'pre-history' of the play in Saxo Grammaticus: 'In the play, knowledge of what has happened previously is essential to an understanding of the plot. Shake-speare's text provides the necessary background. In ballet, however, the dancer cannot dance the past tense.'[2] Aspects of the transformation of spoken dialogue and staged action into the specific performance semiosis of dance and movement will resurface in the following chapter, which focuses on the very twentieth-century genre of the musical, in both its stage and its film manifestations.[3] Ballet is, perhaps, the most elite of the song and dance incarnations of the Bard, which has its own effects on the ways in which Shakespearean drama has been interpreted and reinter-preted by choreographers. As ever with the question of generic conven-tion and practice raised by this study, ballet actually has a felt presence in many productions of Shakespeare which are or were not strictly full-scale dance dramas. The Restoration fondness for balletic sequences has already been mentioned, and music- and dance-rich plays such as *The Tempest* and *A Midsummer Night's Dream* proved ripe for this kind of performative inter-polation. As a playtext, *Macbeth* comes less readily to mind in the context of a discussion of dance, but it is true to say that the weird sisters provided Restoration adapters such as Davenant with considerable material to which to give a dance inflection. Indeed, it was David Garrick's inherit-ance of Davenant's staging practices with regard to the witches which in turn influenced Giuseppe Verdi's decision in one of his earlier ventures into the realm of Shakespearean opera to include a ballet sequence around the cauldron.

In film Shakespeare also, ballet has jostled for space and attention alongside conventional dialogue and performed action on screen – featur-ing, for example, as a major part of the aesthetic of Max Reinhardt and William Dieterle's consciously spectacular version of *A Midsummer Night's Dream* in 1935. In that film, it was specifically the fairy sequences which were realized within a sub-balletic idiom, sequences which were notably choreographed by Bronislawa Nijinska, sister of the famous Russian dancer-choreographer. The 1936 Hollywood screen version of *Romeo and Juliet* (dir. George Cukor) was also inflected by contemporary perform-ances of ballets of the same play, and, in what appears to be a related move, deployed the music of Pyotr Tchaikovsky in its score. In 1948 the musical version of *The Taming of the Shrew*, *Kiss Me Kate*, which featured songs by Cole Porter, told the Bianca–Hortensio–Lucentio subplot through the medium of dance as opposed to the songs that elsewhere characterized the Petruccio–Kate relationship.[4] Ballet also contributed to the dance vocabulary of later screen versions of musicals such as *West Side Story* (1961), choreographed in both its theatrical and its cinematic incarnation by Jerome Robbins of the American Ballet Theater (that particular musical adaptation of *Romeo and Juliet* will be discussed in more detail in the following chapter).

Film influenced the staging of ballets in turn; Dmitri Shostakovich's score for the 1964 Grigori Kosintsev-directed *Hamlet* (Riley 2005: 98; the film and score are discussed in more detail in chapter 7), which featured an Ophelia much associated with the visual and aural semiotics of music and dance, was used in several Russian ballet versions of the play. More recently still, the trope of ballet and dance as part of the register and frame of reference for a Shakespeare adaptation was used in Peter Greenaway's postmodern baroque interpretation of *The Tempest, Prospero's Books* (1991), where the notion of Caliban speaking a language other than that of the incomers to the island – 'You taught me language, and my profit on't/Is I know how to curse' (i.ii.365–6) – is articulated through the strictly corporeal medium of dance. A controversial dancer of the day, Michael Clark, famed for sexually and politically inscribed performances, offered on screen a phallic, confrontational, and eroticized rendition of Caliban in a film memorable for the absolute need of its audiences to read its visual semiotics in intense detail, since many of the screen images are conscious reworkings of Renaissance and baroque paintings. Clark dances out Caliban's speeches to the accompanying score of Greenaway's long-time musical collaborator Michael Nyman, who adds to the baroque sensibility informing the whole by playing with counter-tenor voices amid the lush synthesizers and orchestral strings of his soundtrack.[5]

While this is ostensibly a study of Shakespeare's musical rather than danced afterlives, it seems important in an effort to understand the contribution of classical composers to the domain of ballet to think about the specific demands and effects of dance on Shakespearean playtexts. To this end, I have elected in this chapter to concentrate on two Shakespeare plays that have become, perhaps, most canonical in the world of ballet, at least among Western ballet troupes: *Romeo and Juliet*, most famously realized in the 1930s version with music composed by Sergei Prokofiev, and *A Midsummer Night's Dream*, a ballet with several contrasting choreographies, but always performed to Felix Mendelssohn's Overture and Incidental Music (already discussed in the context of classical music in the preceding chapter).

Mendelssohn's romantic score for *Dream* was, like many of the Continental European musical adaptations of Shakespeare considered here – not least the significant operatic collaborations between the Italian artists, composer Giuseppe Verdi and his librettist Arrigo Boito – informed by the dominant German translation of August Wilhelm von Schlegel and Ludwig Tieck. Gary Williams has described the Schlegel–Tieck version (the shorthand by which it is commonly known) as 'one of the most prominent occasions of the German appropriation of Shakespeare as cultural capital' (1997: 104).

Mendelssohn's Romantic interpretation played a major role both in the popularity of his Incidental Music in stagings of *Dream* and the use of ballet sequences in those same productions. Audiences came to productions with as much expectation of hearing Mendelssohn's Wedding March at the start of Act V as they did of seeing gauzy winged fairies, invariably played by child actors, a renowned example of the Victorian predilection for the presence of children onstage. The presence of dance in these nineteenth-century productions made it perhaps inevitable that Mendelssohn's music would eventually be used to score a full-scale ballet and that, in turn, the romanticized readings and understandings of the original play that these forms of staging encouraged, and even by default endorsed, would influence the highly pictorialized and romanticized versions of the *Dream* that held sway on the commercial stage right through the nineteenth century and the first half of the twentieth. Perhaps the biggest surprise is that ballet as a distinct genre came surprisingly late to the play. In the previous chapter we noted the fact that Mendelssohn's becoming so omnipresent in theatrical productions of *Dream* occasioned a kind of backlash in the work of Harley Granville-Barker, Peter Hall, Peter Brook, and others. Yet it was not until the very moment when these parodic allusions to Mendelssohn began to be established as a convention in their own right in the theatre of the later twentieth century that ballet opted to take the play on in the fullest sense.

The roots of this seemingly belated decision to bring 'the traditions of Mendelssohn and moonlight, roses and tulle . . . over into the classical ballet' (Williams 1997: 192) can, however, be found in the theatre itself. In 1954, a production of *A Midsummer Night's Dream* at the Old Vic Theatre in London revived the Mendelssohn score almost as a conscious countermove to the anti-Romantic backlash. The Old Vic production was also one that restored ballet to the performance languages of the play. The show was choreographed by Robert Helpmann, and Moira Shearer, best known as a lead ballet dancer and for her starring role in Michael Powell and Emeric Pressburger's seminal film about dance *The Red Shoes* (1948), took the part of Titania. Helpmann's assistant on that occasion – he choreographed the dance sequence to the Nocturne which Mendelssohn had originally written as an *entr'acte* between Acts IV and V – was Frederick

Ashton, who went on to become director of the Royal Ballet. This experience clearly encouraged Ashton to choreograph a one-act ballet to Mendelssohn's score in 1964. His version ends with Bottom's restoration to his non-donkey self and his puzzled memories of his 'dream': 'Methought I was – there is no man can tell what. Methought I was, and methought I had . . .' (iv.i.205–6). But Ashton was not the first to look to the play as source material in this way; George Balanchine had done the same just two years earlier, and it is the work of Ashton's predecessor that I want to concentrate on here as a case study of *Dream* as ballet.

Balanchine was, like Ashton, influenced by previous encounters with *A Midsummer Night's Dream* in a theatrical context. As a child performer he had danced the part of an elf in a 1912 St Petersburg performance, and in 1958 he choreographed the fairy sequences for a US production of the play in Stratford, Connecticut. It will already be clear that when ballet did feature in stagings of Shakespeare's *Dream*, the dance sequences tended to be located in the fairy realm and to attach to the non-mortal characters. Dance in this context becomes a means of communicating the otherworldliness of the forest inhabitants, including Titania and Oberon and their attendant fairies, and the hobgoblin Puck, better known in folklore as Robin Goodfellow. The play provides ready precedent in this respect: the fairies' dialogue is full of references to song and dance. Titania and Oberon resolve their quarrel with a dance: 'Come, my queen, take hands with me, / And rock the ground whereon these sleepers be. *Oberon and Titania dance* / Now thou and I are new in amity' (iv.i.84–6), and the blessing of the bridal bed of Duke Theseus and his new bride Hippolyta in Act V is realized in the form of song and music.[6]

Dance, music, and magic are in this way inextricably bound up with one another in the interpretative framework of *A Midsummer Night's Dream*. When a full-scale ballet is created, however, the language of dance must also speak for the mortals in the play, and we can register both the possibilities and the problems this poses in Balanchine's very individual interpretation. Unlike Ashton, Balanchine opted for a two-act structure with an interval. He compressed most of the play's plotline (its first four acts in fact) into the first act, or half. Instead of opening as the playtext does in Theseus's palace, Balanchine's ballet thrusts us straight into the heart of the wood and the fairy world. In this respect, his dramaturgy resembles operatic encounters with *A Midsummer Night's Dream* such as Henry Purcell's late seventeenth-century *The Fairy Queen* and the Purcell-influenced work of Benjamin Britten and Peter Pears for the 1960 Aldeburgh Festival (both explored in chapter 6). After a dance of the *corps de ballet*, we see Puck and soon after Oberon, to whom the dancing fairies pay homage in their steps, with only a glimpse of the plotline of the lovers provided by the fleeting movement of a melancholic Helena across the stage.[7]

The quarrel between Titania and Oberon over the changeling boy is then played out. In the ballet, the boy is visibly present onstage, whereas he is only referred to in the play, one of several examples of a resonant offstage presence in the Shakespearean canon (others include Sycorax and Claribel in *The Tempest*). The visible presence of the boy in the ballet follows a long-established tradition of using children, often in consciously commodified and exoticized ways, in the genre. The ballet based on Pyotr Tchaikovsky's *The Nutcracker Suite* (1892) is one well-known example, but the fairy dances in the ballet *Dreams* invariably feature the youth as well as adult wings of the *corps de ballet*.[8]

It is at this point in the ballet that we see the mechanicals, Peter Quince and his fellow would-be actors, onstage for the first time. They function as a veritable subplot to the main action in the refined atmosphere of ballet. Their entrance, cider pots and all, allows for a highly contrasted form of dance and movement to the high pointwork and exquisite lifts of the main characters; the comic dance routines of the mechanicals function in ways analogous to the parodic or raucous choreography of early Stuart court anti masques, which would be followed by the decorous movement of the main masque, equivalent to the main sequences of a modern ballet. Later, in related fashion, the *pas-de-deux* between a quite literally 'charmed' Titania and Bottom, complete with his donkey's head, which offers its own particular challenges in terms of weight, movement, and carriage to the dancer in that role, offers a grotesque, albeit oddly charming, version of one of ballet's main visual signifiers. Bottom cannot perform the kinds of powerful lifts or high jumps which would more usually characterize a lead male dancer on the stage (the movements performed throughout by Lysander and Demetrius, for example), and in this way the particular grammar of dance achieves an instructive equivalence with Shakespeare's own verse–prose distinctions between his elite characters and the 'hempen homespuns' (III.i.71).

The vocabulary of the *pas-de-deux* is particularly revealing in this ballet. As a genre, ballet frequently enacts the female dancer's dependence on male strength, and in ballet versions of *A Midsummer Night's Dream* this becomes a potent means of articulating Titania's dependence on Oberon. There is a felt absence when she dances in her bower, parted from Oberon by their quarrel over the changeling boy. In his absence she requires the assistance of a 'cavalier', another male dancer, to support her in certain moves; without his aid in the lifts, she is quite literally grounded from fairy flight. This gives additional significance to the fact that Oberon and Titania's eventual reunion is performed as dance, a coming back together both physically and emotionally. In the spaces in between all this Oberon will perform his mastery and power for the audience through the visual signification of the height and complexity of his jumps. In most performances of Balanchine's *Dream* he controls both the central stage space and the spotlight.

Dance is undoubtedly a highly kinetic discourse,[9] and part of the way in which it articulates the romantic comings and goings of the various lovers in the labyrinthine Athenian woods in *Dream* is through the construction and production of space, of nearness and distance. The *pas-de-deux* is a particularly striking expression of these spatial dynamics. In the case of the confused lovers, Helena, Hermia, Demetrius, and Lysander find themselves constantly coupled and uncoupled by the operations of Puck's magic, and the performance of *pas-de-deux* is constantly realized and then disrupted, with rejected partners being spun off into the wider spaces of the stage. This is especially true of Helena's treatment at the scornful hands of Demetrius in the earlier sections of Act I, and this is an action which Hermia will unknowingly mimic when she rejects Demetrius's attentions in turn.

In accordance with the reified romanticism and established power structures and hierarchies of ballet as a form, the scenes involving the mechanicals in *Dream* are vastly reduced and compressed in Balanchine's version. Although he is happy to place the transformation of Bottom at the heart of Act I, there will be no room in the Act II 'Divertissement', which ostensibly equates to Act V of the play, for the mechanicals' entertainment at Theseus's court. Instead of their tragic-comic performance of the play-within-a-play, the 'tedious brief scene' (v.i.56) of Pyramus and Thisbe, Balanchine extemporizes on his dance theme, substituting a series of balletic set-pieces to provide the wedding entertainments for the courtly newlyweds. There is, as a direct result of this innovation, a massive expansion in the ballet of the élite signifiers of the playtext at the expense of its more plebeian content. Shakespeare's carefully achieved contrasts are sacrificed in favour of showcasing the more familiar hierarchized and decorous vocabularies of the genre.

Gary Williams has rightly noted that both Ashton's and Balanchine's dance versions of the play are conceived in a 'neo-romantic idiom' (1997: 199). In other respects, however, Balanchine's version of *A Midsummer*

Night's Dream retains its experimental air in terms of both dramaturgy and choreography. So-called non-tutu ballets such as this, often ballets which are literary adaptations, enable freer choreography than the 'classics', and Balanchine extends these possibilities further by including song as part of his production's loyalty to the Mendelssohn score. Mendelssohn featured the voice of both soprano and mezzo-soprano as first and second fairy respectively. Reinhardt and Dieterle's 1935 film has also somewhat unfairly acquired a rather saccharine reputation. Admittedly, it now seems dated, not least in its treatment of the lovers and the courtly characters, a product of 1930s class and gender politics, but in the ballet sequences the film responds with subtlety to many of the darker and more experimental tones in Mendelssohn's score. Williams rightly highlights the sequence involving the abduction of the first fairy by Darkness (1997: 183), another radical interpretation of the convention of *pas-de-deux*:

> Their dance is elegantly fluid; their bodies briefly touch suggestively, pelvis to pelvis, just before the powerful, masked figure lifts her and slowly carries her off. The camera lingers long on her undulating hands, gradually disappearing; stars fleck the darkness, and Mendelssohn's Nocturne resolves peacefully on low tonic notes on the double bass. (1997: 185)

If *pas-de-deux* is a defining element in the grammar of dance as it is performed in balletic interpretations of *A Midsummer Night's Dream*, it is equally central to the syntax of Shakespeare's romantic tragedy *Romeo and Juliet*, whose very title performs the act of coupling that is central to the plotline and metaphorical basis of this play. *Romeo and Juliet* has proved fascinating to composers and choreographers alike in the twentieth century. In 1926, Sergei Pavlovich Diaghilev commissioned Constant Lambert to write the music for a balletic 'version' of the *Romeo and Juliet* story for the Ballet Russe. The piece's meta-theatrical framework prefigures John Madden's 1998 film *Shakespeare in Love*, which also used *Romeo and Juliet* as its defining romantic intertext. Lambert's plot told the story of an actor and actress rehearsing Shakespeare's tragedy of love, enacting in the process their own doomed relationship (see Fiske 1966: 237). The seminal interpretation of the play proper in balletic and musical terms, however, is surely that of Sergei Prokofiev, a work produced in Russia in the mid-1930s. Prokofiev had written music for several ballets during his period of exile in Paris in the 1920s, under the influence of Diaghilev and Igor Stravinsky, but by the time he turned to Shakespeare and *Romeo and Juliet* for his raw material, he was back in Russia and working to a commission from the Kirov Ballet. He fell out spectacularly with his patrons when he sought to write a 'happy ending' for the play. As a result, the ballet was premiered in Czechoslovakia but then taken up in 1940 by the Bolshoi, only to be dropped once again with the claim that Prokofiev's score was far too experimental for dancers to cope with. Notoriously, Prokofiev had taken no advice from a choreographer when scoring his ballet (Fiske 1966: 237). Ironically, at this point the Kirov renewed its interest, and it was with their star dancer Galina Ulanova as Juliet and Leonid Lavrovski's choreography that the ballet in its earlier incarnations is best remembered.

What was deemed so experimental in Prokofiev's score was the rapid shift of rhythms and registers, an aspect particularly difficult for the formal dancers of the Bolshoi to adjust to. In the later part of the twentieth century it was to gain an immense reputation as a ballet, if a surprisingly unstable history of choreographies. Unlike *Dream*, where Ashton's movements have dominated in the UK and Balanchine's in the USA, there have been various interpreters of *Romeo and Juliet*, including Ashton himself for a 1955 Copenhagen production; John Cranko in Vienna in 1958 and Stuttgart in 1963; Kenneth MacMillan in London in 1965; John Neumeier in Frankfurt in 1971; and, perhaps along with MacMillan providing one of the most respected versions, Rudolf Nureyev, who having danced the part of Romeo as early as 1966, choreographed the ballet for a 1977 London Festival Ballet performance, itself revived in Paris in 1984.[10] These multiple interpretations have all, however, relied on Prokofiev for their score.

Characterized in performance by ensemble scenes of fighting, feuding, and dancing, all three often merging into one, Prokofiev's score is typically adroit in its distribution of instrumentation among the *dramatis personae*; characters can be easily identified by their running themes, or *leitmotifs*, in what has been described as a sub-Wagnerian structure of repetition and refrain. Richard Wagner is a figure whose influence on Shakespearean musical adaptations has been considerable, even though his personal involvement in adapting Shakespearean texts to music was surprisingly limited – he composed an opera based on *Measure for Measure*, *Das Liebesverbot* in 1836. His writings of and writings on opera more generally, however, have made enduring contributions to both practice and thinking not only in the domain of opera – Verdi consciously composed his later Shakespearean operas, *Otello* (1887) and *Falstaff* (1893), as a counterthrust to Wagner and Germanic traditions in the genre – but also in film music, where understandings of his ideas of the melodic throughcomposition of music drama and the specific use of developing refrains, or *leitmotifs* (however misplaced or misrepresentative – a topic I will discuss in later chapters on film scores) have dominated the scene. Wagner is therefore a subject to which I will return at various points in this study, but his idea of the *leitmotif* deserves further explication in this context. Wagner himself described the use of *leitmotifs* as 'guides-to-Feeling through the whole labyrinthine building of the drama';[11] but a more helpful breakdown of his theory is provided by literary critic Timothy Martin in his ground-breaking study of Wagner's influence on the writings of James Joyce, which defines the *leitmotif* as 'the brief phrase that, repeated and varied, comes to represent the character, object, idea or emotion in connection with which it sounds' (1991: 150). The idea of repetition with development is crucial to any study of *leitmotif*, be it in its musical, visual, literary, or danced interpretation.[12]

In the ballet versions of *Romeo and Juliet* we can see ideas of *leitmotif* operating at both the level of the music and that of the dance, where repeated movements or positionings of the body can operate as visual *motifs* comparable in their linking effects to the identification of character with a particular melody or even instrument. If in Prokofiev's composition Friar Laurence is represented by the subtle use of cornets, Juliet is once again represented by woodwind instruments, in particular solo flute. Cellos frequently carry tragic portent into the schema; they can be heard, for example, in the sombre scenes conducted at Friar Laurence's cell. The ensemble dances are realized through familiar folkloric tunes – waltzes, minuets, tarantellas and gavottes – while more dissonant sounds and structures surround the scenes of feuding and street brawls that typify and punctuate those scenes when Romeo and Juliet's intense and intimate passion is not centre-stage.

The ensembles provide an obvious contrast to the *pas-de-deux* sequences that characterize the lovers' intimate onstage encounters. Most memorable of all the aural *leitmotifs*, perhaps, is the 'Knights' Dance', which first sounds when the male guests 'perform' at the Capulet ball in I.ii of the ballet. Rita McAllister has described this as a literal show of strength in both orchestral and dance terms: 'This is the ballet's prototype music of enmity and male feuding. Its dotted rhythms, angular melodic outlines and ponderous basses return at the most menacing moments of the drama.'[13] The music returns in the fighting between Romeo and Tybalt, and, perhaps most chillingly, when Juliet's father asserts his patriarchal control over her in violent terms when she refuses to marry Paris. In this way the violent masculinity identified by McAllister equates to or substitutes for the aggressive language in the text:

... fettle your fine joints 'gainst Thursday next
To go with Paris to Saint Peter's Church,
Or I will drag thee on a hurdle thither.
Out, you green-sickness carrion! Out, you baggage,
You tallow-face!

(III.v.153–7)

The dance equivalent to the aural *leitmotif* or refrain of the musical score rests, then, in the shapes and movements of the body of the performer. Nowhere can this be better located in a performance of the ballet of *Romeo and Juliet* than in the corporeal development and expression of the dancer in the lead female role. In the play this is in part achieved linguistically. Even at the moment of their first kiss, Juliet is teaching Romeo to be himself, to leave behind the clichés of romantic love that have until now coloured his performance as the archetypal Petrarchan lover. After their first kiss, she tellingly informs him: 'You kiss by th' book' (I.v.109). The ballet, like the play, subsequently charts her rapid growth to maturity. A dancer can represent this development not only through the more assertive notes of the woodwind associated with her character as the score progresses but by means of an ever more confident demonstration of Juliet's ability to perform what are perceived as 'adult' moves in the strictly codified world of the ballet. One recent Royal Opera House performance of MacMillan's version of *Romeo and Juliet* was defined by Tamara Rojo's interpretation of the role of Juliet in this regard: her *leitmotif* became the constant arching of her back into arabesque.[14] She grew ever more confident in this movement as love seemed to spur her on to self-assertion and discovery. This only made it all the more tragic when she arched her back one final time as her body fell over the tomb following her decision to commit suicide in the face of Romeo's death. Body and score operated here in perfect union to offer a rich alternative means to dialogue of responding to and staging Shakespeare's ultimate tragic scene.

We have already established in this chapter that dance is a kinetic discourse that partly expresses itself through the performance of space. *Romeo and Juliet* is a play whose tragedy is partly enacted spatially. The tomb is of course one striking version of the irony that Romeo and Juliet seem able to find peace and privacy only in death. The iconic balcony scene visibly enacts for audiences the impossibility of permanently bridging the social and cultural divide between the two lovers, at least in this 'mortal coil'. Later chapters on film will consider how Baz Luhrmann finds innovative visual alternatives to these spatial dynamics and how music in the soundtrack to his 1996 film reproduces the effects of *leitmotif* familiar from Tchaikovsky's fantasy overture or Prokofiev's ballet. Just as Nino Rota, composing a 'love theme' to operate as a refrain in Franco Zeffirelli's 1968 film version of the play, was conscious of his classical musical precedents, so Luhrmann located his 'love theme' in Des'ree's 'Kissing You'. As ever, in the discussion here of both *A Midsummer Night's Dream* and *Romeo and Juliet*, the carefully established generic distinctions between ballet, theatre, opera, musical, and film begin to blur and overlap in intriguing ways, ways productive in their own right of new insights into Shakespeare's plays or new means of understanding the long traditions and legacies of interpreting these plays in a diverse range of media and contexts.

If Prokofiev's ballet translated the parry and thrust of Shakespeare's play into the complicated languages of dance and the performing body in new and telling ways, so ballet would influence the more self-consciously populist medium of the stage and film musical in the twentieth century. Just as we cannot now watch Luhrmann's 1996 film without recourse to *West Side Story*, so *West Side Story* in its realization of urban gang warfare in the high kicks and pirouettes of modern dance recalls its origins on the stages of London, Paris, and Moscow, and Prokofiev's remarkable ballet. Similarly, the history of *A Midsummer Night's Dream* is forever connected to Mendelssohn and the balletic achievements of Ashton and Balanchine. A recent example of the ongoing negotiation with Mendelssohn's music in balletic adaptations of *A Midsummer Night's Dream* can be found in the work of choreographer Heinz Spoerli, who in 2000 set a new version for the Finnish National Ballet to a postmodern combination of music by Mendelssohn, Philip Glass[15] and Steve Reich. Directors and performers may choose to eschew this obvious line of influence but that very act of choice reminds audiences of these musical legacies and inheritances, even at the moment of disavowal, and in the process reaffirms their resonance.

Notes

1 The first decade of the twenty-first century has also witnessed a revival of interest in these late seventeenth-century or baroque operas, in which music and dance are equally balanced in the compositional aesthetic, witnessed not least in the oeuvre of New York choreographer Mark Morris, whose production of John Dryden and Henry Purcell's *King Arthur* at the London Coliseum in 2006 was described by critics as a very contemporary exploration of Englishness. Morris's choreographic style readily blends ballet, modern dance, and vaudeville in an eclectic aesthetic. See, e.g., Jennings 2006a. We might also recognize this interest in more hybridized art-forms in recent interaction between music theatre and instrumental composition, as demonstrated in the work of Harrison Birtwistle and others (see Adlington 2005).

2 Cited from a web article on Neumeier's *Amleth* on <http://www.michael-tippett.com/mthamlet.htm> (last accessed 25 July 2006).

3 Although, as Katherine K. Preston (2002) points out, that very twentieth-century form had obvious precedents and provenance in musical theatrical forms of the eighteenth and nineteenth centuries, including ballad operas, vaudeville and variety theatre, and melodrama.

4 Casting in the 1953 MGM film version of the musical confirmed this fact in that Bianca, Lucentio, and Hortensio were played by well-known dancers: Ann Miller, Tommy Rall, and Bob Fosse (who went on to become a significant choreographer).

5 The Nyman–Greenaway collaboration, though lengthy, has been fraught, and has occasioned considerable public disagreement between them.

6 This sense of the play as one driven by ideas of performance, music, and dance was borne out in spectacular fashion by a 2006 multilingual, intercultural performance of *A Midsummer Night's Dream*, directed by Tim Supple and staged by the Dash Theatre Company as part of the Royal Shakespeare Company's Complete Works Festival (2006–7). Titania and Oberon's reunion was marked by an extended dance on the part of the couple and the wider company of actors, and the bergomask that ends the mechanicals' performance of 'Pyramus and Thisbe' at the ducal court was just one example of dance that provided a finale to the show – a candlelit song and dance by the fairies as they blessed the bridal bed of Theseus and Hippolyta was another memorable moment in a production largely defined by its use of physical theatre and corporeal semiotics. Supple's company featured performers from the Indian sub-continent, picking up on an established association of this play with ideas of Asia and the East, an association encouraged by embedded references within the play: Titania, for example, describes the deceased mother of the changeling boy as sitting 'in the spicèd Indian air' (II.i.124). For these reasons, in ballet versions of *Dream*, including Balanchine's, the boy is often depicted in Indian costume or performed by an actor of Indian or Anglo-Indian ethnicity (the same is true of Reinhardt and Dieterle's 1935 film interpretation); for a postcolonial reading of this tradition in terms of the nineteenth-century history of the British Empire, see Williams 1997: 85–6. Another significant production that deployed Indian iconography and philosophy to read the play was Baz Luhrmann's 1994 interpretation which he took to the Edinburgh Festival that year.

7 My reflections in this chapter on Balanchine's choreography are heavily influenced by the performance of the Pacific Northwest Ballet at Sadlers Wells Theatre, London, in 1999, directed by Ross McGibbon, and screened on BBC2 that same year.

8 In an intriguing cross-reference, Adrian Noble's film version of his stage production of *A Midsummer Night's Dream* (1996) is framed by the story of a young boy which directly imitates the narrative structure of *The Nutcracker* ballet. For a discussion of this film, see Burnett 2000.

9 I am consciously adapting this phrase from S. Howard (1998).

10 Nureyev is said to have read and reread the Shakespearean playtext for the purpose (see Peter Noelke's sleevenotes to *Dancer's Dream*, a French documentary about Nureyev's ballets, TDK DVD 1999). On a personal note, as a very young girl I was fortunate enough to be taken to see Nureyev in the London Festival Ballet performance by my father. It was my first encounter with ballet in a live performance context, and I was lit up with the magic of it all. It feels doubly poignant to revisit that memory in this context.

11 Quoted in Martin 1991: 151.

12 For additional discussion of the concept of *leitmotif*, see chs 6, 7 and 8.

13 The quotation comes from her sleevenotes to the Deutsche Grammaphon recording of the ballet score (Prokofiev 1987: 423-268-2).

14 I am deeply indebted for this analysis of Rojo's deployment of the *arabesque* as a visual *leitmotif* to the various reviews by Luke Jennings in *The Observer* newspaper of this production and its revivals between 2004 and 2006.
15 The Philip Glass music on this occasion derived from his *Concerto for Violin and Orchestra*. That same composition was also used in 2000, along with extracts from other Glass compositions, including *Anima Mundi, Mishima*, and *In the Upper Room*, for a new ballet based on Shakespeare's *Hamlet* choreographed by Stephen Mills for the Ballet Austin in the USA.

Further examples and reading

An obvious starting point for those interested in exploring Shakespearean ballets more widely would be to look at productions that have utilized Frederick Ashton's choreography for *A Midsummer Night's Dream* – also set to Mendelssohn's music – to provide an obvious point of contrast and comparison with the Balanchine choreography. Both men had very distinct aesthetic styles; whereas Balanchine is associated with more experimental movements and contortions of the dancer's body influenced by work in modern dance, Ashton's choreography is often classified as typically 'English' and conservative, demonstrating as it does a late twentieth-century interest in English dance in elegant forms. Luke Jennings (2006b) has written of the 'swooping Romanticism that Ashton's choreography demands', identifying one of the 'most recognizable characteristics' of his work as the use of *épaulement*, or the 'oppositional torsion of shoulder and waist with shoulder' which became in turn a marker of English balletic style in the twentieth century. Gary J. Williams, *Our Moonlight Revels: 'Dream' in the Theatre* (Iowa City: University of Iowa Press, 1997) has some very useful history of ballet versions of the play.

Other Shakespeare plays which have been reworked in ballet form include *Hamlet* – both John Neumeier's version, *Amleth*, which uses the music of Sir Michael Tippett, 1986, and Steve Austin's version set to the music of Philip Glass in 2000 are briefly mentioned above. There is also the work of Boris Blacher who, in addition to adapting *Hamlet* both as a symphonic poem in 1940 and a ballet in 1950, wrote music for the ballet *Der Mohr von Venedig* based on *Othello* in 1955. *The Tempest* has also been made into a ballet; in one 1889 version the musical score was composed by Ambroise Thomas (*La Tempête*, 1889) who will be discussed further in the chapters concerning opera.

For a far more comprehensive listing of Shakespeare-related ballets than it is practical to provide here, see Alan Brissenden's informative entry on 'Ballet' in the *The Oxford Companion to Shakespeare*, ed. Michael Dobson and Stanley Wells (Oxford: Oxford University Press, 2001).

New versions and revivals of productions mentioned here are, of course, appearing all the time, and reviews in newspapers are often an excellent source of material and ideas. My own work on dance, it will have been noted, is especially indebted to the writing of Luke Jennings in *The Observer*, a former dancer who describes his subject with insight, elegance, and wit. For those interested in pursuing theories of dance and the performing body further, recommended books are: Helen Thomas, *The Body, Dance, and Cultural Theory* (Basingstoke: Palgrave Macmillan, 2003); and Simon Shepherd, *Theatre, Body, and Pleasure* (London: Routledge, 2005). For a general introduction to dance scholarship, see Alexander Carter (ed.), *The Routledge Dance Studies Reader* (London: Routledge, 1998), or Jane Desmond (ed.), *Meaning in Motion: New Cultural Studies of Dance* (Durham, NC, and London: Duke University Press, 1997). On the adaptational relationship between ballet and narrative, a useful work is Susan Leigh Forster, *Choreography and Narrative: Ballet's Staging of Story and Desire* (Bloomington: Indiana University Press, 1996).

4

'Shakespeare with a contemporary musical twist'

I have a reasonable good ear in music. Let's have the tongs and bones.
A Midsummer Night's Dream, IV. i. 28–9

In the recent Shakespeare allusive 'teen-flick' *Get Over It* (dir. Tommy O'Haver, 2001), Dr Forrest-Oates (played by Martin Short), the outrageously flamboyant and egotistical director of the high school musical *A Midsummer Night's Rocking Eve*, describes his new opus as 'Shakespeare with a contemporary musical twist'. While the artistic value of his production remains questionable throughout the film's comic depiction of auditions, rehearsals, and ultimately performance, Dr Forrest-Oates is in remarkably good company in his decision to update Shakespearean comedy into a contemporary musical idiom. There have been several attempts to rework Shakespearean plotlines within the parameters of the modern musical, from Gilbert Seldes and Erik Charell's 1939 *Swingin' the Dream* (discussed in chapter 1), Samuel and Bella Spewack's 1948 reworking of *The Taming of the Shrew* as a meta-theatrical backstage musical with songs by Cole Porter, *Kiss Me Kate* (made into a film in 1953, dir. George Sidney and starring Howard Keel, Kathryn Grayson, and Ann Miller), through to more recent hip-hop updatings of *Romeo and Juliet* and *The Comedy of Errors* as *Rome and Jewels* – created by Rennie Harris and the Philadelphia-based Pure Movement Dance Theater, and 'filtered through' another musical adaptation of that play to be discussed later, *West Side Story* (Lanier 2002: 79) – and *Da Boyz*, itself an updating of a previous musical adaptation of that play, the 1938 Rodgers and Hart collaboration *The Boys from Syracuse*.

Along the way there have been rock musical versions of *Twelfth Night*, *The Two Gentlemen of Verona*, and *Othello*. In 1968, *Your Own Thing* created by Danny Apolinar, Hal Hester, and Donald Driver, adapted *Twelfth Night's* themes of androgyny and sexual possibility for the psychedelic era. An off-Broadway production, it told the story of a rock band desperate for a gig and was able to achieve a contemporary version of the confusion over the twins, Viola and Sebastian, in Shakespeare's play by means of the gender-bending hairstyles and clothing of the day (Warfield 2002: 235). That same year, Jack Good's *Catch My Soul*, which was relocated for its 1973 film version (dir. Patrick McGoohan) to New Mexico (Rothwell 1999: 226), depicted a religious commune in which Othello is a charismatic cult leader, Desdemona a naive new convert, Emilia a hippy dropout, and Iago a malcontent member of the sect (see Lanier 2002: 71; T. Howard 2000: 304; and Teague 2002: 234). In 1971 Joseph Papp's production of a musical version of *The Two Gentleman of Verona*, another update designed to appeal to a youth audience, was distinguished by having a libretto by John Guare and a musical score composed by Galt McDermot, who had been responsible for the global hit musical *Hair* in 1968. One contemporary reviewer described the score as a 'mix of rock, lyricism, [and] Caribbean patter'.[1]

There have also been musicals based on works themselves derivative of Shakespearean playtexts, such as the 1950s retro-musical *Return to the Forbidden Planet* (1985), which adapted the 1956 science fiction film based on *The Tempest*, *The Forbidden Planet* (dir. Fred McLeod Wilcox). Perhaps most famously of all there was also a relocation, or displacement, of the fated love story of Romeo and Juliet to the sidewalks and concrete playgrounds of New York in order to speak about 1950s racial tension in urban America, the enduring *West Side Story* (1957; dir. Robert Wise and Jerome Robbins, book by Arthur Laurents, and with music and lyrics by Leonard Bernstein and Stephen Sondheim: it was made into a film in 1961). What each of these texts and performance events offers is an insight into the cultural updating of Shakespeare for particular moments and audiences, what the French theorist Gérard Genette describes as the 'movement of proximation' (1997 [1982]: 304), or Lawrence Grossberg calls 'context-specific appropriations' (1997: 70). They provide a means of interrogating how the parameters and conventions of the genre of musical respond to the challenges posed by the source-text in each instance, not least via the possibilities and potentials of song and dance, but also through the form's hyper-realism or conscious meta-theatricality.

Kiss Me Kate deals with a group of actors touring with a musical version of Shakespeare's *The Taming of the Shrew* as *The Shrew*. The two stars of the show, Fred Graham and Lilli Vanessi, are former partners, a fact which leads to some heated backstage, and indeed onstage, exchanges. Cole Porter's songs (there are fourteen in all in the production) are a mixture of tunes that form part of the 'onstage' show of *The Shrew*, and therefore make direct use of Shakespearean verse-lines, such as 'I come to wive it wealthily in Padua' (I.ii.74), and 'backstage numbers', including the show-stopping 'Brush Up Your Shakespeare', delivered by two comic gangsters who are pursuing one of the touring show's star performers Bill Calhoun (Lucentio in *The Shrew*) over a gambling debt. This song, with its multiple clever puns, rhymes, and *double-entendres* on the titles of various Shakespeare plays, has become iconic in its own right within the history of Shakespearean appropriation, and fittingly provides one of the shaping epigraphs to *Wise Children*, British novelist Angela Carter's remarkable 1992 novel about Shakespeare on the stage in both its legitimate and illegitimate incarnations, from elite London theatres to music hall and vaudeville.

As a response to the problematic sexual politics of *The Taming of the Shrew*, *Kiss Me Kate* is very much a product of its time, with an uncomfortable propensity to make comic capital out of domestic abuse. In one 'onstage' scene Fred is seen spanking Lilli into submission, and that image even featured in publicity for the film. Writing about the sub-genre of the backstage musical into which this production squarely falls (for useful definitions, see Cohan 2002: 131), John Mundy has noted: 'It is often argued that no other genre stereotypes women as savagely as the backstage musical does' (1999: 61). This issue aside, however, it is clear that the implicit and inevitable meta-theatricality of the backstage musical fits beautifully with the meta-theatrical frame to Shakespeare's play, where the induction involving the drunken Christopher Sly establishes the idea that the entire taming scenario between Petruccio and Katherine is a play-within-a-play staged by the Lord for Sly's benefit. In the 1953 film version, the induction is literally substituted by an audition scene at Fred Graham's apartment, complete with Hamlet portrait on the wall and Rick Randell playing the part of Porter himself.

West Side Story has a significant place in the history of the musical as a genre, not only because of its wholly integrated deployment of different modes of dance, including modern and ballet, within its action, and in its screen manifestation in 1961 for the full arrival on the scene of the choreographer-director as a phenomenon, but also because of its politicized treatment of its Shakespearean subject matter (see, e.g., Graziano 2002: 75; and Laird 2002: 201). The musical was a response to a specific moment in US cultural history. The 1950s had witnessed serious urban gang violence, particularly in New York City, in the wake of large-scale Puerto Rican immigration and settlement on the city's west side. Taking as its cue Shakespeare's tragedy of young love across feuding families, *West Side Story* brilliantly reworked the balcony scenes and masked balls of *Romeo and Juliet* into the fire escapes and dance hall environments of 1950s New York. Like the film adaptations of *Romeo and Juliet* that we will consider later, this was an updating of Shakespeare that sought to speak to a specifically young audience, the newly emergent social category of teenagers, and the film's *mise-en-scène* underscores this fact by featuring very few adults, and none of those in a strictly parental position. As well as the racist and ineffectual Officer Krupke and his New York Police Department officers (the comic butt of one of the songs performed by the Jets' gangleader Riff), we have the peace-preaching Doc, owner of the local drugs store, in a witty reworking of Friar Laurence and his questionable knowledge of herbal lore, and the somewhat comic figure of the dance hall compère who tries to keep peace between the rival gangs, but none of these mature voices in the production seems able to stem the flow of violence. Parental authority, so present in the play, for example, in terms of Capulet's violent manipulation of his daughter into a propitious dynastic marriage, is here displaced, offscreen, present only in the 'noises off' of Maria's mother and father in the 'balcony scene', in this case conducted on the external metal fire escapes typical of New York mid-twentieth century architecture.[2] Surrogate roles as parents and mentors are instead played by best friends and newly created siblings, in keeping with the youth dynamic and emphases of the musical; in Maria's case her brother Bernardo, a reworking of Tybalt, and in Tony's case, his gangleader friend Riff, a reworking of Mercutio that renders him central to the gang ethos rather than situated on the edges of it, as Mercutio so poignantly is in the play (hence his dying curse, 'A plague o' both your houses' at III.i.91).

It is Tony and Maria who, fittingly, share the central duets of the musical. One particular lyric, 'There's a place for us', like the reworked balcony scene mentioned above, directly reflects the crushing spatial semiotics of their world, especially in the film version. As with Shakespeare's star-crossed lovers, while they may sing of union and togetherness, the visual images invariably tell a different story. The metal frameworks of the fire escapes and the wire netting that surrounds the basketball courts which are dotted about the concrete jungle deployed as the 1961 film's *mise-en-scène* – and from which the opening sequence makes such rich aesthetic capital, zooming in from the skyscrapers to the caged animals in the poorer ghettos of the city, away from the green open space of Central Park to a place defined by concrete and sidewalk, sewage pipe and metal – merely encase and entrap the inhabitants of this environment. As in the play, where the iconic balcony scene enacts spatial and social separation at the very moment of the lovers' profession of togetherness, the only true space of union for Tony and Maria must be a world elsewhere of fantasy and imagining. The informing idea here is undoubtedly also one derived from the operatic canon of composer Richard Wagner (whose theories of *leitmotif* were identified as an influence on balletic interpretations of *Romeo and Juliet*, not least Sergei Prokofiev's, in the previous chapter): the notion of *liebestod* or 'love-in-death' which he deployed in Isolde's aria of the same name in his 1865 *Tristan und Isolde*. Touchingly, the couple play-act their wedding in the dress shop where Maria works, with lyrics enacting the bodily and spiritual union of marriage vows: 'Make of our hands one hand'; it is a beautiful, but ultimately hopeless, reimagining of the sonnet encounter in which the pair first meet each other on the Shakespearean stage: 'For saints have hands that pilgrims' hands do touch, / And palm to palm is holy palmers' kiss' (I.v.98–9).

The spatial semiotics that control and produce meaning in the film are nowhere better played out than in one of its central musical moments, the dance hall encounter between the Jets and the Sharks, imagined by the hapless adult organizers as an attempt at peace making but in truth an opportunity for tribal display and enmity. The gangs enact their rivalry through the medium of dance, offering very different choreographies and gendered practices as bold statements of their ethnic differences. This is just one of several remarkable sequences in the screen version of the musical when violence is displaced into the performance language of dance; the kicks and clicks and rhythms and staged throws of dance making the violence 'presentable' and bearable in some respects, but in an odd way emphasizing its troublingly ritualistic and performative aspects in the context of gang warfare.

The dance is held in a youth centre that clearly operates most of the time as a sports hall (the section of music attached to this sequence in Bernstein's score is entitled 'Dance at the Gym'); the basketball hoops and lines of play on the floor are clearly visible throughout. The dance/sport/physical violence metaphors do not need to be pointed out, although it is a fine working example of Will Straw's observations on the cultural geography of dance: 'The history of popular dancing in the Western world is partly a history of places in which that dancing has occurred' (2001: 160; see also Straw 1991 and 1993, *passim*). In the film version of the musical, the dance hall tableau reinforces the framework for understanding the operations of these urban gangs established by the aforementioned opening sequence, where at one point the dancers steal balls from other street kids playing basketball on the outdoor courts through which they stride. It is only the first encounter between our Romeo and Juliet, Tony and Maria, that, for a brief moment at least, can challenge these over-riding images. The film version deployed its medium to stunning effect by making the couple the still point in this turning world; but by blurring the dancers swirling around them into an indefinable whole, the film also made them a point of clarity amidst the madness. The dance mode shifts accordingly from the hot-headed rivalry of the salsa, tango, and rock-and-roll idioms of the Jets and the Sharks to a gentler, slower, deliberately almost balletic language – the couple dance the modern musical equivalent of the *pas-de-deux* – while the lights are transformed into a starry sky over the head of the couple as they quite literally fall in love before our eyes. This balletic register should, not perhaps, surprise us in view of the choreographer-director Jerome Robbins's own roots in ballet and his previous collaboration with Leonard Bernstein on a wartime ballet about sailors home on leave, *Fancy Free* (1944), which was in turn adapted to become the Broadway musical *On the Town* that same year (McClung and Laird 2002: 174–5).[3]

When the world of threatening whistles and clicks re-enters the sonic environment, Tony and Maria are forced back into real time. Those clicks, which first heralded in the gang members at the start of the film, have in truth never entirely gone away, underscoring as they do the ballet sequence; but it is the whistle intended to break up an emerging fight, once again the sports analogy being played up, that definitively end-stops the romantic interlude. If the duet, or *pas-de-deux*, is one of the musical's primary means of identifying the relationship between its central protagonists, it must be stressed that in contradistinction to the usual tradition of the happy ending in this escapist genre, *West Side Story* resists the play's offer of the Wagnerian *Liebestod*, the tragic union in death, and instead insists that Maria survives, enduring to tell the gangs of the consequences of their bitter enmity, and ensuring that Tony's death is the promoter of a long-awaited truce. This is no less tragic an ending, but it is a tragedy of a different order and one with a different message for its contemporary audiences.

Baz Luhrmann's recent music-powered film reworking of Shakespeare's play in the context of even more modern gang and gun warfare opts, as we will see in detail in chapter 8, to heighten the *Liebestod* ending of Shakespeare's tragedy rather than adapt it in the manner of *West Side Story*, but the influence of the Wise–Robbins–Bernstein musical on the style and aesthetic of his film should not be underestimated. From the dance idioms that are evoked in the opening attention-grabbing gas station sequence – Tybalt's appearance is full of allusion to flamenco and tango

– and the divisions of his gangs and groupings along racial and ethnic faultlines to his film's highly legible spatial semiotics, Luhrmann pays direct homage to his musical source as well as to the Shakespearean one. It is, perhaps, not an unexpected allusive framework for his movie adaptation, since Luhrmann's career began with a film centred on the social and sexual semiotics of dance, *Strictly Ballroom* (1992), and he has since confirmed his interest in both musical and opera as informing influences in his postmodern pastiche of the film musical *Moulin Rouge* (2001). That film blended references to *La Bohème*, Madonna, and T-Rex with ease, but I would argue that Luhrmann does more than just gesture towards musical convention in all these works; he capitalizes on the possibilities of frame breaking, meta-diegetic interpretation, and the range of performance languages that the genre of musical enables, and in doing so responds with genuine depth to both the achievements and, with hindsight, the problems, not least in terms of ethnic representation, of *West Side Story*.

The influence of *West Side Story* can be traced in other musical updatings of *Romeo and Juliet*, including the aforementioned hip-hop version *Rome and Jewels*; but it is perhaps in a more general sense of its politicization of the musical reworking of classic texts, and not least Shakespeare, that its impact has been lasting. This politicization of the genre is most visible at the edges of its practice rather than in mainstream West End or Broadway musicals, although the potential for contemporary commentary in the conventional form should not be entirely dismissed; US military action in Vietnam and the Second World War provide the settings for *Miss Saigon* and *South Pacific* respectively, and the 1927 Oscar Hammerstein–Jerome Kern creation *Show Boat* was a brave attempt to deal with US race relations.[4] Nevertheless, it is within smaller theatre groups, often with ethnic diversity at their core and as a defining part of their performance ethos, that some of the most intriguing recent sociopolitical rewritings of Shakespeare in musical terms has taken place. The choice of texts through which to achieve these re-visions is sometimes, however, on the surface at least, rather surprising.

The Comedy of Errors, 'unique' according to Stanley Wells (2002) in that as a playtext 'it makes no explicit use of music' (131), has proved remarkably fertile ground for musical adaptation, as has *The Merry Wives of Windsor* in an operatic context, both challenging the erstwhile canon of commonly performed Shakespeare plays. *The Bombitty of Errors* (1999), memorably described by Douglas Lanier as a 'hip-hopera'(2002: 73), is an example of the practice of 'sampling' familiar from the musical genre of hip-hop as applied to Shakespeare. The show deployed rap as well as actual lines of Shakespeare. In its sampling practices, however, this off-Broadway show, originally devised by New York University students, was actually following in an established musical tradition of responses to this particular play that find their provenance in the 1938 Rodgers and Hart Broadway show *The Boys from Syracuse* (filmed in 1940; dir. A. Edward Sutherland). According to Frances Teague, none of these adaptations is deeply concerned with its Shakespearean precursor, instead deploying the source play as a 'shell' within which to explore other kinds of more contemporary points or issues (2002: 226). She observes that *The Boys from Syracuse* retained only two actual lines from Shakespeare, and that when these were delivered in the original production, a character poked his head out from behind the stage curtain to yell 'Shakespeare!' at the audience.

In 2003, *The Boys from Syracuse* was itself updated as *Da Boyz*, a hip-hop-inspired musical, staged by Philip Hedley at the Theatre Royal Stratford East in London, a theatre with a strong history of radical performance aimed at the local neighbourhood and at an alternative audience to the elite patrons of West End theatre. The musical emerged from the work-shopping practice that has long been a common tradition at Stratford East, which was formerly the home of Joan Littlewood's experimental group Theatre Workshop. While *Da Boyz* drew some critical fire because it was an update rather than an 'original' work, a fairly dubious line of attack on theatrical and artistic creation at the best of times, it was Hedley's defence of the project that proved most revealing. He stressed that the essence of hip-hop practices was 'borrowing influences from unlikely places', describing it in one interview as 'a cannibalistic medium' (Ojumu 2004: 7). In this respect he echoed the theories of musicologists such as David Metzer and Susan McClary, who have made persuasive cases for the presence and creativity of borrowing practices in musical tradition (Metzer 2003: *passim*; McClary 1998). What is refreshing about Hedley's approach to the workshop reinvention of *The Boys from Syracuse* in this way is that he regards the evolutionary and adaptational process as entirely open and ongoing, envisaging that *Da Boyz* will itself adapt and transmute for each new space, place, and time, and each new context of performance:

> I could see someone putting it on in Southside Chicago or Johannesburg and doing their own story. Or schoolchildren could put it on and update it because it's a year old now, and instead of doing something like *Guys and Dolls* or *Oliver!* because those are really the music of their parents and grandparents. (Ojumu 2004: 7)

It is this idea of people 'doing their own story' that is the direct impetus behind another Hedley and Theatre Royal Stratford East musical reworking of Shakespeare. In 2004 the theatre staged *The Big Life*, a re-envisioning of the plotline of *Love's Labour's Lost* in the context of the 1950s 'Windrush' generation, the Caribbean immigrants who came to England, and in particular to London, on the *SS Windrush* at the direct invitation of the British government to supplement an ailing post-war work-force and in search of the proverbial 'better life' in the 'mother country'. The not unproblematic centrality of Shakespeare to Anglo-Caribbean educational structures, and therefore to local discourse in the West Indies, has been explored by indigenous writers like Derek Walcott in plays such as *A Branch of the Blue Nile*, where he represents attempts by a group of actors to stage a production of *Antony and Cleopatra* (see Döring 2005). The experiences of the Windrush generation themselves in London and elsewhere were the subject of several remarkable 1950s novels by Sam Selvon and others (see Head 2002: 164–7). *The Big Life* responds to, and takes it stimulus from, this complicated set of inheritances.[5] Written by Paul Sirett (the Royal Shakespeare Company's literary manager at the time of the show's composition), with a score by local reggae musician Paul Joseph, it transforms the King of Navarre and the celibate academy he creates at the start of *Love's Labour's Lost* into a decision taken by four hopeful immigrants on the *Windrush* who decide to eschew the company of women while they concentrate on making a success of their lives in the British capital. It is a decision that, like that of the king and his men in the play, is short-lived. One scene finds the men onstage beneath the statue of Eros, which is suggestive not only of the geographical location of Piccadilly Circus but of the considerable sexual temptations the big city puts in the men's way. In this sequence as it was staged in the *première* production of the musical, the statue, in suitably Shakespearean fashion if we remember the fifth act of *The Winter's Tale*, came to life, tap-danced onstage, and led the men in a rousing rendition of the song 'Getting Hot', which was performed in the ska idiom adopted by this production to suggest the 1950s acoustic and cultural environment in which events were located.[6]

Love's Labour's Lost might seem on the surface an odd play in which to find such topical and local resonance in contemporary multicultural heteroglot London; yet, for all its courtly idiom and aesthetics, it is at its heart a play rooted in the media of music and dance (see, e.g., Brissenden 1981: 25): songs, dances, and in-built performances, which, as we have already seen in chapter 2, also inspired classical composers from Arne to Finzi to find acoustic equivalents. It is this understanding of *Love's Labour's Lost* that undoubtedly formed the impetus for Kenneth Branagh's screen version of the play which recast it in the style of a 1930s musical.

Branagh's considerable output of cinematic Shakespeares is discussed in greater detail in chapter 7, when we look at classical musical scores for Shakespearean films. But his 1999 *Love's Labour's Lost*, unlike his *Henry V*, *Much Ado About Nothing*, or *Hamlet*, opted not for a classical orchestral score in the style of William Walton's work for Laurence Olivier or Dmitri Shostakovich's for Grigori Kostinsev, but one with the register of a Broadway or Hollywood musical. Branagh further emphasized this choice by selecting a late 1930s *mise-en-scène*. His decision to work within the genre of the musical radically altered his approach to the Shakespearean script in this instance, in that, more so than in any of his other film versions of Shakespearean plays, he made substantial cuts to the language and dialogue, invariably replacing soliloquies with songs and dialogue with dance routines.[7]

Taking his cue from the playtext's own frequent allusions to song and dance, Branagh transformed *Love's Labour's Lost* into a full-scale musical spectacular, replete with show-tunes by Cole Porter, Jerome Kern, and the Gershwin brothers, alongside dance routines reminiscent of both Fred Astaire and Ginger Rogers's seminal screen partnership and the set-piece musical interludes familiar from the Hollywood cinematic tradition of Busby Berkeley and others. Initially, Branagh had toyed with the idea of commissioning new songs from his long-time musical collaborator Patrick Doyle in the style of Cole Porter, with an obvious nod to the precedent of *Kiss Me Kate* in this respect; but in the end, the pair jointly selected a medley of existing songs, ones with their own resonant film history (on the allusiveness of these songs, see Wray 2002). The resulting film, however, persistently teetered on the edge of being pastiche and, at times, in its seemingly untroubled melding of the Second World War context with the conventions of the American film musical, a potentially offensive pastiche.

Undoubtedly, *Love's Labour's Lost*'s heavily embedded deployment of the sonnet form – for example, the King of Navarre opens proceedings with a sonnet, and the set-piece scene at IV. iii is one where each erstwhile male suitor's attempt at sonneteering is read aloud on the stage – can be related to comparable musical and dance motifs, not least in the careful choreographic patternings they encourage between couple(t)s and quartets (or quatrains), and between various combinations of 2, 4, 6, and 8. Barbara Trapido made witty play on this idea in a Shakespeare-drenched novel, *Juggling*: 'I really like those matrices . . . The way they come together . . . They're sort of like dancing the galliard . . . Sort of like writing a sonnet' (1994: 168). In subsequent chapters on Shakespeare and opera (see chapters 5 and 6), the equation between aria and soliloquy recurs in the analysis of specific operatic texts at regular intervals. The role of sonnets in the context of dramatic verse in plays by Shakespeare, ranging from *Love's Labour's Lost* to *Romeo and Juliet*, where, as already noted, the lovers first encounter each other in sonnet form, to the history plays, allows for comparable moments of heightened aural awareness on the part of the audience of the carefully created, rhythmical operations of the speech they are hearing. In some instances, classical composers deliberately selected sonnets as the subject matter or 'lyrics' for their arias with these effects in mind: witness Gustav Holst's deployment of Sonnets 12 and 19 to boost Hal's time-conscious repertoire in his remarkable one-act opera – or 'musical interlude' to use Holst's own phraseology – *At the Boar's Head*, which was based on the Falstaff tavern scenes from the two parts of *Henry IV*. Elsewhere, particularly in the influential operatic oeuvre of Giuseppe Verdi in the nineteenth century, the aria offers equivalence with the operations of Shakespearean soliloquy or sonnet (or both) in terms of dramaturgic placement and the establishment of an intimate relationship with the audience; Iago's multiple soliloquies carefully located in the first half of *Othello* are reduced to the single but insightful 'Credo' in the Verdi–Boito *Otello*, and Lady Macbeth's particularly striking arias in Verdi's earlier opera actually serve to give her a dominant role in the early sections of the show which clearly reflects the stage dominance of her character in any theatrical production of *Macbeth* (see Kliman 1995: 1).

Branagh's musical director Patrick Doyle was clearly influenced by these links and equivalences when thinking about the operations of song in the film of *Love's Labour's Lost*. In an interview about the soundtrack, he noted: 'I came to see them almost as arias, there to heighten the action . . . I think my job was to make the narrative accessible through the musical numbers and to put these songs on the plinth they deserve.'[8] Doyle created around these 'plinth' numbers a typically lush and enveloping score and, as with his controversial soundtracks for the Branagh-directed *Henry V* and *Hamlet*, he consciously harked back to an earlier period of cinema. The nostalgic aspect to the soundtrack is clear from the opening credits in which, to quote Heather Violanti, 'cursive scrawls . . . unfurl against a theatrical red silk backdrop' (2005: 4). Doyle made a direct link to the films dating from the Hollywood Studio era when describing the aural environment he sought to create; the title music, he states on the notes to the published soundtrack of the film, 'needed to sound like those old MGM overtures, which I will always associate with childhood Sunday afternoons, accompanied by the smell of home cooking'.[9] That the opening credits were devised as an 'overture' also immediately conjures up a nostalgic memory of 1930s Hollywood film Shakespeares, especially the Reinhardt–Dieterle *A Midsummer Night's Dream* (1935), which so consciously used Felix Mendelssohn's Overture dating from the nineteenth century.

Branagh's *Love's Labour's Lost* initially equates its *faux* Oxbridge setting with a form of scholarly asceticism, albeit a short-lived one, when the King of Navarre makes his proclamation of three years' abstinence. As in Shakespeare's play, the oath is sustained only momentarily, due to the arrival of the Princess of France and her ladies-in-waiting, but the film underscores the futility of the oath by demonstrating the king's willing, even eager, participation in a song-and-dance ensemble which declares a wish to enjoy the fun things in life: 'I'd rather Charleston'. All of the songs selected for performance in the film encourage the audience to read, see, and hear co-textually on a number of levels. The instructive equation of verse and the strict rhythms of song and dance routines is spelt out in a scene where Branagh, as Biron, beats out the iambic pentameter for his colleagues. The codas and conventions of the musical segue suprisingly easily with the sexual tensions and battles of wit that define the playtext. The French women's independence of mind and action finds expression here in Jerome Kern's 'I won't dance'. But the co-textuality operates not only at the level of lyrical allusion and analogue, since many of the songs chosen themselves featured in high-profile films, including several starring Fred Astaire. The associations of that 1920s–1940s era of Hollywood film musicals with romance and escapism feeds into Branagh's resonant if idealized relocation of the play to an England on the edge of war. The interspersed and comic use of Pathé newsreels contributes to the over-riding sense of a world in unstoppable transition, and further emphasizes the temporary nature of the king's scholarly academe.

Branagh's use of 'show-stopping' numbers in this way has not been without its critis, however. In a particularly trenchant article, which also describes *Love's Labour's Lost* as one of Shakespeare's 'weakest plays', Kelli Marshall (2005: 83) has condemned Branagh's use of the song and dance numbers in a completely non-integrated and disruptive way in terms of the narrative and the plot drive of the film, suggesting that this constitutes desecration of, rather than adherence to, the conventions of the very film musicals he aspires to re-create (a similar condemnation of the film's understanding of musical conventions appears in Friedman 2004).

Marshall's case is particularly persuasive in its discussion of the inapposite, explicit, and sadomasochistic sexuality of the dance segment that supposedly equates to the masked dance of Shakespeare's play at v.ii; this would never have taken place in an RKO musical!

In terms of conventions, the Astaire-era musicals are perhaps most recalled now for their prominent use of the duet, Astaire being best remembered for his routines with his dance partner Ginger Rogers in a series of RKO-produced films in the 1930s. In those films – there were nine made between 1933 and 1939, including *Top Hat* and *Swing Time* – Astaire and Rogers played romantic leads to an often comic foil of an older pair (Cohan 2002: 8). Branagh repeats that trope in his feminizing of Holofernes to Holoferna to enable Geraldine McEwan to play out a comic partnership with Richard Briers as Nathaniel.[10] The Astaire–Rogers musicals worked to a very recognizable formula, and it was one that moved from solo routine to challenge dance between the two stars to a romantic duet and then a big production number to close (Cohan 2002: 8). *Love's Labour's Lost's* formal interest in the figures of pairings (couplets), and quartets and octets, and the poetic form of the sonnet has already been mentioned, but the musical's focus on the duet, the shared song, often performed by the lover-protagonists of a given work, also echoes the play's focus on particular linguistic pairings: Dumaine and Katherine, Longeuville and Maria, and of course the King of Navarre and the Princess all have their important dialogues and duologues, re-visioned in Branagh's film as song and dance pairings. But it is in the central combat of wit between Biron and Rosaline, one which follows on from Petruccio and Katherine in *The Taming of the Shrew* and prefigures the 'merry war' of Beatrice and Benedick in *Much Ado About Nothing*, that Shakespeare offers a rhythmic versified equivalent to the shared duet of song. In II.i, despite their surface quarrelling, Biron and Rosaline share rhyming couplets in their stichomythic banter:

> ROSALINE: Is the fool sick?
> BIRON: Sick at the heart.
> ROSALINE: Alack, let it blood.
> BIRON: Would that do it good?
> ROSALINE: My physic says 'Ay'.
> BIRON: Will you prick't with your eye?
> ROSALINE: *Non point*, with my knife.
> BIRON: Now God save thy life!
> ROSALINE: And yours, from long living.
> BIRON: I cannot stay thanksgiving.
>   (II.i.184–93)

The mixed register of resistance and seduction that this exchange offers finds a ready equal in the choreography and feisty partnerships of the 1930s RKO musicals.

The casting of Branagh's film musical is, as ever, an intertextual gesture – in all his films audiences are actively encouraged to read in other parts and associations with specific performers, and to be aware of the actors in the individual Shakespearean roles, as well as the history of those roles themselves. The Olivier undertow to any readings of Branagh's performance as Henry V and Hamlet is just the tip of the iceberg in this respect. The most salient example in *Love's Labour's Lost* of consciously intertextual casting is that of Nathan Lane, Broadway musical supremo, in the role of Costard. Lane's Costard in his oversize coat is described in the film script as a vaudeville comic who has played in every music hall 'from Broadway to Baden-Baden'. Lane is given the literally show-stopping Irving Berlin number 'There's no business like show business' towards the end of the film, complete with Busby Berkley-style aerial shots of spectacular geometries and shapes made by the dance ensemble. That particular sequence is 'show-stopping' in that it is dissociated from the main frame of the action in a typical Busby Berkley move. It seems to do nothing in plot terms (cf. Marshall 2005), but it does offer the big production number typical of the closing moments of many RKO and MGM musicals in the 1930s and 1940s; spectacle here appears to be an end in itself (Cohan 2002: 60).

Yet the sequence is 'stopped' in another way by the arrival of a messenger from the French court to inform the Princess that her father has died and that she must now take on the mantle of Queen. Branagh finds an equivalent within the codas and conventions of musical for the jarring juxtaposition of comedy and tragedy achieved by Shakespeare in the atypical ending to *Love's Labour's Lost*. The closing number of the film proves actually to be another song-and-dance routine performed by the octet of lovers: Irving Berlin's 'They can't take that away from me', which celebrates the joys of romance in the very jaws of death as the Oxbridge scholars prepare to enlist for service in the war. This is a song-and-dance less of coming together than of farewell, and is not unlovely in that respect. Its delivery captures something of the melancholy resonance of Shakespeare's own convention-resistant ending: as Biron notes, 'Our wooing doth not end like an old play' (v.ii.860). Sadly, though, in this film it does end like an old musical; Branagh cannot resist the Hollywood happy ending, and ensures that his 'heroes' make it back unscathed from the war, the horrors of that experience reduced to a black and white montage sequence and the closing scene transformed instead into one of glorious Technicolour reconciliation and celebration.

In Branagh's upbeat and morally rather dubious film, then, the darker side of the 1930s and the rise of fascism are held off to the very edges of the screen, glimpsed only fleetingly in the form of warning or premonitory news headlines and in that all too brief montage. Ramona Wray has written somewhat forgivingly of the film's willing exposure of a 'politics of distraction' (2002: 174); for other critics, like Kelli Marshall, it constitutes wilful negligence of the real issues at stake. It rests with another 1930s-set film Shakespeare to handle the rise of fascism in more chilling depth, Richard Loncraine's 1995 *Richard III* with Ian McKellen repeating a stage performance in the title role. Here the musical and show-tune references are more deliberately unsettling, creating discord and unnerving the viewer, rather than functioning as part of the sugar-coated nostalgic aesthetic and revisionist history of the Branagh film.[11]

Kenneth S. Rothwell has astutely noted the influence of the British television work of Dennis Potter, and in particular his piece *The Singing Detective*, on the use of music in Loncraine's *Richard III* (Rothwell 1999: 231). Potter's knowing, part-ironic segues into song and dance in his television dramas from *Pennies from Heaven* onwards are in a sense a postmodern reaction to the (glorious) suspension of disbelief demanded by the genre of film musical, where characters suddenly break into song in the most incongruous of locales and nobody bats an eyelid. Onstage this is less problematic than in the essentially realist context of film, and Potter's use of witty resonance and sometimes deliberately jarring anachronism in his choice of songs has had a deep impact not just on British television and film, but on the postmodern aesthetics of Luhrmann and others. Loncraine takes this a stage further to add to the unsettling effects of Richard's all-knowing and uncomfortably intimate relationship with the audience in any stage production of *Richard III*. In this respect he appropriates the effects of Potter's deployment of 1930s songs in his work, where, as Peter Holland has astutely observed, they 'mark the gap between the sordid and painful action . . . and the language of sentimental song' (1997: 87).

A similarly disjunctive mode allows Loncraine as director to make Richard deliver several direct addresses to camera, a sort of knowing film response to the importance of stage soliloquy in the play from its opening moments onwards, and the intimacy and confidence which that represents to any theatre audience. In the process, this unexpected frame breaking unnerves audiences, as does the dissonant juxtaposition of song and dance with the gruesome events they are witnessing unfold on the screen. A prime example of this in operation is the moment following the grim mortuary 'seduction' of Lady Anne. After her capitulation, and as he leaves the hospital full of injured people to whose woes he has presumably contributed, Richard celebrates his acting skills with a stairwell performance deliberately reminiscent of Fred Astaire routines on steps and stairs to the accompaniment of an offscreen jazz tune. McKellen's Richard appears here to adopt the incongruous role of screen matinee idol, incongruous because it is so at odds with his behaviour elsewhere as Fascist dictator and murderous thug; but this is a part which we see him performing self-consciously on several occasions, not least through his iconic deployment of his cigarette.[12]

The role of music and, in particular 1930s musical tunes, in the interpretative diegesis, or meta-diegesis, of this film is established early on when we move from the interpolated history of the York–Lancastrian battles into the dance hall scene, where the York family celebrate their victory.[13] A twenty-piece band led, as Rothwell observes, by a 'Glenn Miller lookalike' performs a 1930s setting of a Christopher Marlowe lyric, 'Come live with me and be my love', from music stands wittily emblazoned with the initials 'WS' (1999: 233).[14] There is a self-consciousness about the interpretative frame here that borrows something from musical's own persistent disruption of diegesis on film. Something similar is effected by a combination of musical and intertextual (or, more precisely, intercinematic) reference in the closing sequence of the film, which contributes further to our understanding of the performative in Richard even at the point of his death. In a chilling modern take on the Tudor propaganda of Shakespeare's playscript, this also impacts on our response to the Duke of Richmond, who at the very point of Richard's demise, a figural descent into hell as he falls backwards from the ruined building into flames below, looks to camera with a knowing smirk that we elsewhere associate with Richard's Machiavellian performances of power. There is little sense here of a conquering hero; more a chilling sense of *plus ça change*. An Al Jolson song, 'I'm sitting on top of the world', plays ironically as Richard falls to his death (is the reference to Richard or to Richmond? – the ambiguity is surely deliberate) and, as James Loehlin has brilliantly demonstrated, the aural framework is further enriched by a visual and verbal allusion to the James Cagney gangster movie *White Heat* (dir. Raoul Walsh, 1949). Cagney's character is pursued by policemen to the top of a gasworks and 'shoots into the tanks, and destroys himself in a fiery explosion after proclaiming "Made it, Ma, top of the world!" ' (Loehlin 1997: 75).

Another Shakespearean film adaptation that has deployed 1930s cabaret, musical, and big band jazz music in the context of an eclectic and at times deliberately jarring – both in terms of audible sounds and in its effects of juxtaposition – soundtrack is Julie Taymor's *Titus* (2000) (as its title suggests a cinematic interpretation of *Titus Andronicus*). The music for the film was provided by her long-term artistic collaborator Elliot Goldenthal. In keeping with the eclectic costuming and temporal settings of the film's aesthetic, where locations moved between the Roman Coliseum and the 1930s Fascistic palaces of Benito Mussolini and others, and where armour-clad centurions following Titus readily mingled with Chiron and Demetrius who were dressed in glam-rock androgynous shiny jumpsuits, Goldenthal produced a score that moved between epic orchestral scoring for those scenes involving Titus himself, heavy rock music for Chiron and Demetrius (a punning reference perhaps to their status as 'Goths'), and a 1930s musical idiom for scenes at Saturninus's palace.

As with Loncraine's *Richard III*, the use of 1930s music encourages an intertextual reading on the part of knowing film audiences. Early on, amidst the excessive and indulgent celebrations for Saturninus's wedding to Tamora, a big band plays swing within the diegesis of the scene; the analogy is of jazz age decadence with the stereotypical notion of the Roman orgy. But the intertextual readings also occur at the level of casting, since Saturninus was played in the film by Alan Cumming, a British actor then best known to US audiences for a recent award-winning performance as the master of ceremonies in the Broadway revival of *Cabaret* (dir. Sam Mendes). In this instance, then, the 1930s acoustic framework also acts as a point of dissonance and disjuncture within the diegetic frame of the film, inviting us as spectators to read above and beyond what is happening at the level of plot.[15] As in Loncraine's *Richard III*, this was deliberate pastiche on the part of Taymor and Goldenthal, rather than the coincidental, and frequently happenstance, detrimental effects of Branagh's loving re-creation of 1930s RKO musicals, and was rather more trenchant in its effects, both aesthetic and political, as a result.

Loncraine's and Taymor's films, like the work of Dennis Potter, make knowing contributions to the canon of postmodernism in their ready play with 'complex allusiveness' (Loehlin 1997: 75), and their deployment of theories of camp, with its 'heard' or registered quotation marks. Their work sits readily alongside the Shakespearean cinematic creations of Derek Jarman and his punk-pastiche version of *The Tempest* (1980). The sequence I am particularly interested in in the context of this study occurs at the end of his film: the displaced wedding masque sequence. Instead of

Iris, Ceres, and Juno, as in the playtext, we get blues singer Elizabeth Welch as 'The Goddess' singing a stunning rendition of 'Stormy Weather'. The Shakespearean resonance of the 'Stormy Weather' lyric has already been noted by Samuel Crowl; the refrain 'Keeps rainin' all the time' conjures up the Fool's song from both *King Lear* and *Twelfth Night*: 'The rain it raineth every day' (cited in Rothwell 1999: 208). The movement from masque to musical in a twentieth-century referential framework is equally suggestive, and Jarman underscores that movement via the presence of his chorus of dancing sailors, an obvious Gilbert and Sullivan pastiche, but also reminiscent of countless MGM musicals with sailors home on leave, including the previously mentioned Leonard Bernstein–Jerome Robbins collaboration, *On the Town*.[16]

As is argued elsewhere in this study, the influence between Shakespearean theatrical practice and musical adaptations, be they operatic, balletic, or cinematic, is rarely mono-directional, and the conventions and commercial successes of musicals in the twentieth century had considerable impact on the ways in which directors thought about staging Shakespeare's plays, in particular the romantic comedies. The Royal Shakespeare Company Archive at Stratford-upon-Avon readily throws up examples of productions of *A Midsummer Night's Dream* with extensive musical accompaniment and self-aware allusions to the musical genre *per se*, productions of *The Two Gentleman of Verona* delivered in 1930s style complete with Cole Porter musical settings and singers, and a version of *The Merry Wives of Windsor* reworked with 1950s costumes, settings, and songs.[17]

If the musical as a genre and form with a distinct set of conventions, practices, and effects (not least the combination of song and dance as part of its performative semiotics or discourse, but also its conscious slippage between realist, non-realist, and spectacular modes as discussed above) has influenced theatrical stagings of Shakespeare plays during the past decades, and indeed pop songs – Stephen Buhler suggests that many contemporary allusions to *Romeo and Juliet* in popular music are filtered through a memory and knowledge of *West Side Story* (2002: 251) – then its influence both on and in contemporary film culture also deserves acknowledgement. Later chapters on film soundtracks will interrogate in more detail what John Mundy has recently described as the impact of 'music video aesthetic' on contemporary cinema (Mundy 1999: 226), but an interesting alliance between the recognizable coda of musicals and the aesthetic style of the music video is worth pointing up in this context. Mundy has rightly noted that 'The alliance between popular music and the screen media – cinema, television, and video – sits at the heart of contemporary popular culture' (1999: 1), and his study of the role of popular music onscreen acknowledges the role of musical as a genre in that tradition and history. What is striking in the context of a study of Shakespeare and music, however, is how contemporary film updates or reworks classical works of literature, for which there was a particular vogue in the 1990s, many of them relocating the plotlines from Shakespeare and other canonical texts including Jane Austen and George Bernard Shaw to a US high school environment,[18] frequently deploy, in a very knowing but nonetheless celebratory way, the coda and conventions of the traditional Broadway and Hollywood musical. The high school environment allows for the classic convention of the inset school play or musical and Shakespeare's own penchant for this meta-theatrical trope of the play-within-a-play (they feature in *The Taming of the Shrew*, *Love's Labour's Lost*, *Hamlet*, and *A Midsummer Night's Dream*) makes him ripe for adaptation under these circumstances.

A perfect example of this film cliché (and the movie is joyfully aware of its contribution to that tradition) is the preparation for the spring musical that forms the backdrop to the events and love affairs of *Get Over It*, the film alluded to in the introduction to this chapter. The school's rock-musical version of *A Midsummer Night's Dream* is the happy occasion of some predictably awful scenes – a personal favourite is the boy band-style delivery of the lines 'Oh, Hermia, I'll make you love me / Oh, Hermia, I'll make you care' – and the usual easy jokes at the expense of Shakespearean language in the modern era: 'I'm understanding about every other word of this shit'; 'Will Shakespeare's a wonderful poet, but Burt Bacharach he ain't!'. Puck even delivers a version of these views within the school performance: 'Tonight we're going to make things clear / Coz Shakespeare's dead and we're all here.'[19]

Elsewhere the film offers a wiser nod to the dominance of music, and in particular the pop song, in teenage culture and its own carefully prescribed courtship rituals. The film's hapless 'Lysander', Berke Landers, sings a woefully out-of-tune version of Elvis Costello's 'Alison' up to the bedroom window of his ex-girlfriend of the same name in a modern take on the Romeo and Juliet balcony scene. He will eventually fall in love with the film's 'Helena' through the medium of a song she wrote, but perhaps, best of all, the opening credits unfurl to the musical accompaniment of a Captain and Tenille cover version of the Neil Sedaka song 'Love will keep us together'. The sequence playfully tests the boundaries between the film world and that of an overlaid soundtrack (in strict terminology, the diegetic and non-diegetic soundscapes) by having Berke walking at the front of the frame carrying the box of personal belongings that Alison has rather callously returned to him at the moment of their breakup (perhaps a witty take itself on Ophelia's 'I have remembrances of yours / That I have longèd long to redeliver' from *Hamlet* (III.i.95–6)), while a group 'performing' (lip-synching) the Captain and Tenille tune emerge from Alison's garage behind him. As the long tracking shot follows Berke down the street, other performers and dancers join them, including postal delivery and garbage collection workers, a newly married couple, and an entire brass band, complete with cheerleader. The image is a parodic one from mid-twentieth-century film musical, which was not afraid to have spectacular interludes of this kind regularly breaking into the 'real' diegetic world of the film, and we are never entirely sure whether Berke has simply not noticed them because he is so wrapped up in the trauma of his breakdown. The film, like Shakespeare's *Dream*, plays throughout with an uncertainty between what Berke experiences and what he imagines, and the scene does jump to a shot of him waking up in bed and screaming out loud. This kind of comic juxtaposition is one the intended audience for this teen film, however, would be entirely comfortable and familiar with from the medium of the pop video, as played daily and often without interlude, on the MTV channel. Indeed, several recent pop videos had paid comic homage to the style of the old spectacular musical, such as the Spike Jonze-directed video for Björk's 'It's oh so quiet'.[20]

I would argue that in the same way that teen films can knowingly pastiche Shakespeare and retro-music such as the songs of Neil Sedaka or, indeed, Hal David and Burt Bacharach, so they have returned to 'borrow' from the genre of musical with genuine delight. Postmodern self-reflexiveness has no dis-ease with the reality-challenging modes of the musical where characters regularly break into song and dance in otherwise 'realist' frameworks and settings, and many contemporary romantic comedies actively allude to it. As we will see in later discussions of a companion film to *Get Over It*, *10 Things I Hate About You*, the ready allusion to Shakespeare, musical, and contemporary pop culture is part of these films' playful approach to the relationship between non-diegetic and diegetic soundtracks. In this way, then, both in its politicized reworking in fringe or non-mainstream theatrical venues and in the highly commercialized space of modern cinema and the pop video, the Shakespeare musical has come right up to date and is enjoying a new lease of life, indeed a new relevance, in the present age.

Notes

1 The description is from Clive Barnes's review in the *New York Times*, 2 Dec. 1971 (cited in Warfield 2002: 236). At much the same time MacDermot worked on another off-Broadway musical *Shakespeare, The Tales of Cymbeline*. *Hamlet* was also adapted for Broadway as *Rockabye Hamlet* in 1976, with music and libretto by Cliff Jones. *Hair*, incidentally, features a song that alludes to *Hamlet* in its title, 'What a piece of work is a man'.

2 Fascinatingly, an outline and synopsis for an earlier version of the musical discussed by the eventual collaborative team as early as 1949, which cast the young lovers as if from Italo-Catholic and Jewish backgrounds respectively, and which set events during the religious festivals of Easter and Passover, featured a far more overt adult presence, as well as retaining many of the names from the Shakespearean source. The outline can be found in Leonard Bernstein's papers held in the Library of Congress (see Laird 2002: 201). The working title of the piece in those papers is *Gang Bang* (Laird 2002: 274 n. 15).

3 As a further indication of the mutual influence and crossover of different genres and modes of adaptation upon each other in this way, Bernstein went on to adapt his music for the dance sequences of *On the Town* for a symphonic work, *Three Dance Episodes from 'On the Town'* (see McClung and Laird 2002: 175).

4 *Show Boat* is about a riverboat family and their troupe of actors and deck crew, a story told across the time period of three generations. One of the actresses in the troupe, Julie, is trying to pass as white, but when her true ethnicity is discovered, she is made to leave the boat, along with her white husband (for a fuller discussion and analysis of this musical, see Graziano 2002: 74–5).

5 The theatre is in the London borough of Newham, which, according to the last census, has a 61 per cent proportion of ethnic minorities contributing to its population.

6 Other productions at the Theatre Royal Stratford East have sought to continue the investment in music and the musical as a means of attracting local audiences. These productions include an adaptation of poet Benjamin Zephaniah's novel *Gangster Rap* about a hip-hop band in Newham for which rapper Rodney P was commissioned to provide the music (Ojumu 2004: 7).

7 My thanks to Heather Violanti for her paper 'Are the Songs of Berlin Harsh after the Words of Shakespeare?: A Look at *Love's Labour's Lost*', which she contributed to the seminar on 'Shakespeare and Film Music' at the 2005 British Shakespeare Association conference at the University of Newcastle-upon-Tyne, and for discussions with her about the musical content of Branagh's film.

8 Quoted in Rayner 2000. Doyle repeats the equation in his notes to the Sony soundtrack of *Love's Labour's Lost* (2000). My thanks to Heather Violanti for this reference.

9 The quotation derives from notes to the soundtrack written by Doyle (see n. 8 above).

10 In a different kind of feminizing impulse, he also gives one of Fred Astaire's songs from *Top Hat* – 'No strings (I'm fancy free)' to the Princess and her ladies to perform (Friedman 2004: 138).

11 It is worth adding that 1930s race issues are also subjected to this sugar coating. Debarrings and prohibitions do not feature in Branagh's account of 1930s dance. Thanks to Bridget Escolme for her discussion of this issue.

12 Rothwell (1999: 234) refers to this as 'cigarette semiology', citing the work of Gus Parr, 'S for Smoking', *Sight and Sound*, 7 (1997): 30–3.

13 The diegesis is the literal film world of the characters' experience. Diegetic music would include a CD or record played by a character onscreen. Diegetic music is heard within

the film world, whereas non-diegetic music is overlaid for the audience's benefit. The term 'meta-diegetic' gestures at those moments when music plays a role in the interpretation of what is being seen onscreen. Of course, most films involve a complex interplay between all three modes. For further discussion of these terms and their specific application to film music, see Gorbman 1987.

14 There are actually examples of settings of Shakespeare songs in this format, including Al Bowlly's 'It was a lover and his lass' with the fantastic female backing line 'A ding-a-dinga-a-ding-a-ding'. Bowlly's performance was included as part of a special feature on Shakespeare and music broadcast on BBC Radio 3 as part of a St George's Day exploration of ideas of 'Englishness' in which Shakespeare loomed large in the day's proceedings (23 April 2006).

15 For a fuller reading of the deliberately mixed messages of Goldenthal's score for the film than I can offer here, see Walker 2002.

16 This scene has been expertly analysed elsewhere, not least by Chedgzoy (1995: 204), Harris and Jackson (1997) and M. Taylor (2000).

17 John Caird's 1989 *A Midsummer Night's Dream* featured particularly musical fairies, including a Puck who played the accordion and led the company in a full number at the end of the show; Bill Alexander's 1985 production of *The Merry Wives of Windsor* had a 1950s *mise-en-scène*; David Thacker directed the 1991 production of *The Two Gentlemen of Verona* referred to. Peter Holland has suggested that this production also registered the influence of Dennis Potter's television dramas (1997: 87; for an excellent discussion of that production overall, see pp. 87–91). In 2006, the Royal Shakespeare Company also announced a newly commissioned musical version of *The Merry Wives of Windsor* to be performed as part of its Complete Works Festival, with music by Paul Englishby, a regular composer of incidental music for RSC performances.

18 Examples in the Shakespearean category would include Gil Junger's 1999 *10 Things I Hate About You* which is discussed in greater detail in ch. 8. This film itself continued a tradition for movies with a Shakespeare and education connection, which includes Peter Weir's *Dead Poets' Society*, with its remarkable inset *A Midsummer Night's Dream* school play sequence (1989), and *The Last Action Hero* (dir. John McTiernan, 1993), with its knowing deployment of Olivier's film *Hamlet* in a classroom context (the class is taught by the actress Joan Plowright, recognizable to many audience members as Olivier's widow). The updates of Austen and Shaw were respectively *Clueless* (dir. Amy Heckerling, 1995; loosely based on *Emma*) and *She's All That* (dir. Robert Iscove, 1999), a reworking of Shaw's *Pygmalion*, itself the subject of a renowned musical updating in *My Fair Lady* (filmed in 1964, dir. George Cukor).

19 There is, surely, a further layer of parody here with knowing nods to a popular 1980s performing arts school-located television series, *Fame*, itself a film offshoot, where the students, who were forever breaking 'musical-like' into song and dance relevant to the week's themes, staged a rock opera version of *Othello* with the memorable big number 'Oooh my Desdemona'.

20 See also Björk's song numbers in the Lars von Trier film, *Dancer in the Dark* (2000). Jonze, is, of course, one of several current directors who move easily between the genres of motion picture film and pop video. His recent work for cinema includes *Being John Malkovich* (1999) and *Adaptation* (2002); other award-winning videos include work for Fat Boy Slim (Norman Cook).

Further examples and reading

An excellent starting point for considerations of the musical as a genre is *The Cambridge Companion to the Musical*, ed. William A. Everett and Paul R. Laird (Cambridge: Cambridge

University Press, 2002). This collection includes detailed analysis of *West Side Story* as well as discussion of rock music adaptations of Shakespeare, including *The Boys from Syracuse*, *Your Own Thing*, and *The Two Gentlemen of Verona*. Especially recommended is Bruce D. McClung and Paul R. Laird's 'Musical sophistication on Broadway: Kurt Weill and Leonard Bernstein' (167–78), which offers much insight on Bernstein's classical composition and modern dance connections, as well as a persuasive argument for both Bernstein and Weill as 'crossover' artists who happily blended classical and vernacular idioms in their work and who were directly influenced by the theatrical experimentations taking place in the 1940s. For a detailed account of the making of the musical and film versions of *West Side Story*, see Keith Garebian, *The Making of 'West Side Story'* (Toronto: Toronto University Press, 1995).

The cinematic work of Kenneth Branagh also features in later chapters on film adaptations of Shakespeare (see chs 7 and 8), but for readers particularly interested in the relationship between *Love's Labour's Lost* and the American musical, helpful analyses and cogent arguments can be found in articles by Michael Friedman, Kelli Marshall, and Ramona Wray in various volumes of the journal *Literature/Film Quarterly*. This is a journal that quite frequently includes articles that discuss soundtracks and musical scores to films for those interested in this aspect of film adaptations of Shakespeare. Later chapters on the topic of film music will offer specific recommendations for further reading on that subject, but for those keen to pursue the connections with music video made in the closing sections of this chapter, a useful source is John Mundy, *Popular Music on Screen: From Hollywood Musical to Music Videos* (Manchester: Manchester University Press, 1999).

Those wishing to follow up the discussion of Julie Taymor's *Titus* (2000) begun here might like to know that the DVD version of the film includes a commentary on the musical score by its composer Elliot Goldenthal.

5

Shakespeare in the Opera House

she will sing the song that pleaseth you
1 Henry IV, III.i.211

Opinion has often been fiercely divided between those who think that Shakespearean drama, in its bold gestures, set-piece speeches, vivid characterizations, and frequent relish of spectacle and event, lends itself readily to opera, and in particular to the set-piece effects of aria and duet, and those who feel that opera's attempts to adapt the Bard's words to musical drama can only ever effect a form of mutilation or abuse. Whichever side you fall in the argument, the inescapable fact is that Shakespearean adaptations have flourished in the opera houses of Europe, the USA, and beyond, from the seventeenth century onwards, producing, at least in the work of Verdi, some of its acknowledged masterpieces, and, at the very least, some central works of the canon.

Gary Schmidgall, who has published widely on the topic of the relationship between literature and opera, suggests that Shakespeare's plays might actually lend themselves more readily to operatic conventions and traditions than others, because of their conscious organization and 'orchestration' (1977: 6). There is something, he suggests, in Shakespearean dramaturgy that is peculiarly open to musical interpretation and adaptation, nowhere more so than in the heightened atmosphere and arena of operatic performance: 'Opera has to do with heights. Exaggeration is part of its essence . . . The world of opera is one of high relief, magnification, escalation' (1977: 10). We might identify, therefore, in Shakespearean dramaturgy something comparable to the shifts between recitative and aria that early opera and semi-opera experimented with, an equivalent scale of moves between normal speech and the heightened registers of declamation. Whether or not we accept Schmidgall's thesis, there can be no doubt that composers have found in the Shakespearean canon a rich treasury of operatic plots and inspiration. Anthony Holden (2004) has estimated that there are more than 200 operas with a Shakespearean connection; a recent entry in *The Oxford Companion to Shakespeare* put the estimate at nearer 300 (Dobson and Wells 2001). In a determined effort not to reduce this study to a series of lists, I should stress from the outset that this chapter makes a very limited selection from this range of possibility to make its argument. As a result, there is no time for a detailed study of operas such as Richard Wagner's rendition of *Measure for Measure* as *Das Liebesverbot* ('The Ban on Love'). This 1836 opera retained the part of Angelo, but excised the part of the Duke entirely. In an early example of what I will later argue is a nineteenth-century operatic tradition of according greater prominence to Shakespearean female roles during the process of adaptation, Wagner made his Isabella the author of the bed-swap trick, and he resolved the problematics of Shakespeare's resistance to closure at the end of his play by having Isabella declare a long-standing love for Lucio.

Opera appears to have a recurring interest in focusing on the love plots of the Shakespearean source plays. Hermann Goetz's *Die Widerspenstigen Zähmung*, an 1874 version of *The Taming of the Shrew*, concentrates on presenting a highly romanticized version of the Katherine–Petruccio encounter, and Hector Berlioz's 1862 *Béatrice et Bénédict* effects a similar narrowing of the focus of its intertext, *Much Ado About Nothing*, concentrating on the eponymous lovers rather than Shakespeare's complementary plotline of Hero and Claudio's disrupted wedding. Having observed this investment in the theme of romantic love, it might therefore seem surprising that, in comparison to the long-standing interest of ballet and classical symphony in the ultimate love story of *Romeo and Juliet* analysed in earlier chapters, that play's presence in the opera house is limited, at least in terms of the now established performance canon. We have Vincenzo Bellini's *I Capuleti e i Montecchi* (1830), although this was based on Italian sources of the story rather than the Shakespearean playtext, and Charles Gounod's *Roméo et Juliette* (1867), but otherwise the streets of Verona remain surprisingly empty of operatic travellers. There may, of course, be simple practicalities to address when interrogating this fact. Operatic leads tend to be older performers than is traditional in the theatre; there are practical reasons of voice, range, and depth that occasion this fact, and the added matter of the physiognomy of an opera singer, whose lung capacity has to be considerable, also affects the possibility for casting a convincing pair of star-crossed young lovers. Shakespearean opera reached its zenith in the late nineteenth century, which was the moment in theatre when demands for naturalism were at their most dominant, so these difficulties in achieving a realistic youthful appearance for Romeo and Juliet were doubly problematic. This may in part explain the decision to set what has otherwise proved to be such a rich source of musical inspiration aside in favour of other plays as source material for operatic adaptation and performance.

As will be discussed in more detail below, opera has often challenged the assumptions of the literary and Shakespearean canon when selecting texts for adaptation. There are multiple operatic versions of *The Merry Wives of Windsor* available, by Antonio Salieri, Otto Nicolai, Giuseppe Verdi, Ralph Vaughan Williams, and others, which have created their own veritable performance history and to which we will return both in a discussion here of the 'feminization of opera' and in the following chapter's case study of Verdi. In the twentieth-century Western theatre, naturalism no longer held sway, but neither did the romantic or lyrical comedies seem as rich a field for interpretation for those composers shaped by the interests of Modernism in the possibilities of discord, a-rhythm, and dissonance. For these reasons, in more recent decades we find other Shakespearean plays coming into view in terms of their operatic potential: in 1966 Samuel Barber premiered (unsuccessfully, it should be added) his *Antony and Cleopatra* in New York, and 1978 saw Aribert Reimann's Berg and Schoenberg-influenced *King Lear*.[1] Reimann's opera is a fascinating example of how operatic interpretation, like the classical symphonies discussed in chapter 2, is shaped by the theatrical and performance history of the plays being adapted and also by the critical arguments and intellectual positions of the time.

In the 1960s and 1970s critical readings of Shakespeare were dominated by heavily politicized interpretations of the plays, influenced in part by Eastern European scholars, including Jan Kott, and by theatre practitioners such as Jerzy Grotowski (see Kott 1965). Modern-dress productions and cultural relocations of the plays became commonplace, and several benchmark Royal Shakespeare Company productions were performed in this mode, including David Warner's interpretation of the Prince of Denmark as a radicalized undergraduate in Peter Hall's 1965 production of *Hamlet* (see Dawson 1995: 132–46), Peter Brook's 'absurdist' *King Lear* (1962), and his circus-inflected, sub-Freudian *A Midsummer Night's Dream* (1970). Darker readings of cuspy comedies like *Twelfth Night* also began to emerge with regularity in the playhouses, and even the grimmer tragedies like *King Lear* became more apocalyptic in performance. Brook's aforementioned production, filmed in 1971, was hugely influential in this respect, offering as it did Eastern European political analogues to events in the play. Brook's interpretation also influenced theatrical appropriations of Shakespeare's tragedy, in particular Edward Bond's *Lear*, which premiered in the same year as Brook's film version (see Leggatt 1991: 70). This charged creative atmosphere clearly fed into Reimann's composition, which has been described as 'unremittingly dark' (Schmidgall 1990: 256). There is little distinction in his opera between supposedly 'good' and 'bad' characters, since he cast all three sisters in the soprano range, deliberately resisting a temptation to separate Cordelia from the others. For similar reasons, Reimann made little orchestrational differentiation between the settings and locales of the opera: as Schmidgall notes, 'Lear's *whole world* is inclement, darksome, and aleatory' (1990: 257). One of the most intriguing and resonant decisions of this opera is to have the Fool as a storyteller; this is not uncommon in reactions to viewings of the play, where the Fool's frame-breaking Merlin prophecy at iii.ii of the text version now identified as *The Tragedy of King Lear* establishes a particular relationship with the audience; but it reveals Reimann as a subtle reader and an adapter alert to the text's current potential, both performative and scholarly.

Music, song, and dance, and their attendant metaphors, have a strong presence in the Shakespearean canon. One of the playtexts most alert to acoustic experience and possibility is *The Tempest*. It should come as no surprise, therefore, that several *Tempest*-inspired operas exist – including one semi-opera from the late seventeenth century, *The Enchanted Island*, based on a play by William Davenant and John Dryden, that was itself a considerable reworking of Shakespeare's 1611 playtext. The Swiss composer Frank Martin produced his Schoenberg-influenced *Der Sturm* in 1956; and in 1985 American composer John Eaton deployed the full range of technological advances to produce a fusion piece, involving both taped electronics and a jazz trio alongside a more conventional operatic libretto by Andrew Porter (cf. Holden 2004). These transformations and musical sea-changes are thankfully ongoing, and 2003 saw the Royal Opera House premiere of Thomas Adès's *The Tempest*. At the time of writing, this work was about to enjoy a revival as part of a retrospective on this innovative young composer. Adès, like Reimann, is alert to theatre history in his very contemporary take on *The Tempest*. His Ariel is a female soprano, one stretched in her sound-world to the very edges of the register. The sexual ambivalence that this recognizes in the role, its potential androgyny, stretches back to the singing boy actors of Shakespeare's time, while also acknowledging nineteenth-century traditions of casting female actor-singers in the part. In the source play Ariel is a singing and acting role, and the various musicians and composers who contributed to late seventeenth-century productions of *The Enchanted Island* respected this point by making it the only hybrid acting-singing-dancing part in a theatre tradition of semi-opera that tended otherwise to separate out its actors' roles from its singers and dancers.

In its first production, Adès's *Tempest* was influenced both by surrealist art and by the idiom of the circus that finds its own provenance in early twenty-first-century Western theatre practice and the work of Vsevolod Meyerhold. His opera is as much a product of the critical positions of its time as the works of Verdi or Britten or Purcell. The critical context in which Adès composes is the era of postmodernist theory. This is the world of Shakespeare as a cultural commodity, a figure and concept endlessly reworked, recycled, and adapted, be it in 'big-time' global versions (Bristol 1996), or in smaller, more localized individual appropriations; that can be registered not least in the libretto for Adès's opera by Meredith Oakes, described (not altogether favourably) by Anthony Holden (2004) in his opening night review in terms of postmodern pastiche. The adaptation and appropriation of Shakespeare, in the opera house, as elsewhere, is, it seems, ongoing, and not merely a site of historical nostalgia and re-enactment but of response to contemporary times and issues.

As if to prove the point about Shakespeare's position as a cultural and commodifiable presence in the opera house, there is even one nineteenth-century opera in which he features as a character. Ambroise Thomas's 1850 *Le song d'une nuit d'été* gives the role of William Shakespeare to the lead male tenor of the company. His female soprano counterpart is, intriguingly, Queen Elizabeth I, proof were it needed that John Madden's 1998 film *Shakespeare in Love*, in which Gwyneth Paltrow played a cross-dressing Viola and Judi Dench won an Oscar as an outspoken proto-feminist Virgin Queen, followed in a long line of 'biopics' of Shakespeare, if not in film, then on the stage. In a strange blend of Shakespeare's life with his art, Falstaff appears in that opera as the Keeper of Richmond Park, evoking his link to the park and its deer herd in the Herne the Hunter scenes of *The Merry Wives of Windsor*, a Shakespeare play that, as mentioned, had a surprisingly vibrant history in the opera houses of Europe. But it is the role of Elizabeth I that is key to the claims for the feminization of Shakespearean subject matter as a consequence of the practices and conventions of opera, especially in the nineteenth century, when the form might be regarded as having reached a zenith, that I want to make here.

In her influential monograph *L'opéra, ou la défaite des femmes* Catherine Clément (1989) argues that opera as a genre is all about the 'undoing of women'. Certainly, opera's investment in the tragic mode seems to create a disproportionate amount of female death and suffering on its stages; *Dido and Aeneas*, *Madame Butterfly*, *La Traviata*, and *La Bohéme* all run the gamut from suicide to terminal illness. In terms of Shakespearean adaptations, we may detect more of the same; *Macbeth*, *Othello*, *Hamlet*, and *King Lear* have all been the subject of multiple operatic productions and revisions, and each features poignant examples of female victimhood. In its eighteenth- and nineteenth-century manifestations, opera as a genre appears consciously to highlight or even exacerbate the tragic focus on the suffering female form (see, e.g., Loraux 1987; Berry 1999; Rutter 2001). Ambroise Thomas's 1868 *Hamlet*, for example, makes considerable alterations to its Shakespearean hypotext in order to increase the focus on Ophelia's madness and eventual demise. In Thomas's version, the libretto for which was written by Michel Carré and Jules Barbier, who went on to work on Gounod's *Roméo et Juliette*, Hamlet abandons Ophelia because of her father's involvement in a conspiracy against him. In this version, the usually loquacious Polonius is reduced to a single speech, but he does live to see his daughter buried. At the end of the play Queen Gertrude survives to witness her son's coronation as King of Denmark. Only Claudius and Ophelia meet the end determined for them in the source, and this reduction in corpses consequently heightens the emphasis on Ophelia's tragic death.

Thomas's opera is strongly female-focused throughout – an aspect pointed up early on by the opening chorus celebrating Gertrude's new status as Claudius's queen – and his plot changes are in part designed to ensure that Ophelia's mad scenes become the central set-piece of any performance.[2] This chimes both with operatic traditions of the time and with the nineteenth-century interest in the trope of women and madness. The Victorian period's morbid fascination with the relationship between femininity and hysteria led to a heightened cultural interest in the figure of Ophelia. She was endlessly represented and reworked not only in the theatre and grand opera houses but in the arts in general, in prose, poetry, painting, and music. Susan Basnett suggests that these same cultural emphases not only inflected interpretation and readings of Shakespeare in the nineteenth century, but had a direct impact on theatrical performances of *Hamlet*:

> What fascinated readers in the nineteenth century was the theme of a woman driven mad for love, and performances emphasized the tragedy of Ophelia's madness, Ellen Terry went so far as to visit a madhouse in

order to acquire first-hand knowledge of the symptoms of madness before she first played Ophelia. As the paintings also show, there was a strongly visual quality to nineteenth-century perceptions of Ophelia, which meant that the role appealed to actresses with a strong pictorial style of performance.[3]

Thomas's redirection of focus in his *Hamlet* opera to concentrate audiences' minds on the sufferings of its young female protagonist is therefore a direct response to, and reflection of, the specific critical and cultural interests and theatrical traditions of his own time.

The pictorial quality of opera in performance and its interest in tableaux undoubtedly encouraged it to accept influences from the visual culture of any given period, and many composers worked with their visual imagination to the fore when composing music for operas. The visual arts in general must therefore be added to the multi-directional lines of influence between the arts of theatre, literature, criticism, and music already being argued for in this study. Undoubtedly, performative pragmatics are also at play in such decisions and alterations. Roles such as Ophelia and Gertrude provide showcases for *prima donnas* and lead sopranos in any company; in Thomas's *Hamlet*, for example, Gertrude's beautiful monologue at iv.vii.138 ('There is a willow grows aslant a brook') fittingly becomes a moving aria. But the femino-centric impulse in late eighteenth- and nineteenth-century opera is also reflective of the impact and influence of European Romantic theory on theatrical and operatic practice. It was very much the stage tradition in Romantic era theatre for the heroine to take centre-stage, and nowhere is this more legible than in the stage history of *Othello* and its multiple operatic versions in the nineteenth century.

An intriguing and ambivalent figure though she is in the seventeenth-century playtext, in stage performances of Shakespeare's *Othello* Desdemona, played as she was in the early modern theatres by a boy actor, was a supporting role to the central tragic duet played out between Othello and Iago. In terms of stage time alone, Desdemona's is a far smaller role than either the Moor's or his Ancient's. The introduction of professional female actors, and therefore the presence of a literal female body, on the commercial playhouse stages of London from the 1660s onwards altered responses to the role, as the multiple engravings depicting the bedroom murder scene of the play produced in this period testify. In this visual history of stage performance, an emphasis upon the suffering of the female body in the play becomes a defining feature (see Howe 1992). This reading of the play continued to influence performances throughout the

eighteenth century, although it is noticeable that in this era of high moral-
ity and 'sensibility' Desdemona's complex sexual agency in Shakespeare's
text was played down in favour of offering the example of a chaste female
victim of the male protagonists' jealousy. In this way the sexual mores of
a given period also contribute in a direct way to the adaptation of Shakespeare both on the stage and on the page, since this wholly more chaste
version of Desdemona was undoubtedly that promulgated in several
European translations of the Shakespearean canon in the Romantic
period. Related moral impetuses encouraged the excision of the character
of Bianca from most stage productions of the play in the eighteenth and
nineteenth centuries, an excision which operas saw fit to honour and
repeat.

Gioacchino Rossini's 1816 opera *Otello, ossia il Moro di Venezia* made
Desdemona very much its focus. Rossini's librettist, Marquis Francesco
Berio de Salsa, actually based his text for the most part on a 1792 version
of the story by Jean-François Ducis. This version was performed more
than seventy times at the Comédie Française between 1799 and 1852, and
provided the source of many subsequent translations and adaptations,
even one with a happy ending.[4] Ducis's text 'belongs to its heroine', and
Rossini's opera duly followed suit in keeping Desdemona firmly at its
performative core (L. Potter 2002: 162).

It is this newly feminized version of *Othello* that Verdi and his librettist
Arrigo Boito were undoubtedly heir to in the latter part of the nineteenth
century when they came to adapt Shakespeare's tragedy for the opera
houses of Milan and Paris. In their version, the role of Desdemona is
considerably expanded, and this occurs despite their controversial decision to open the opera not in Venice, but at the point where Shakespeare
opens his second act, in Cyprus, as Othello's embassy disembarks having
survived the terrors of the storm at sea. As James A. Hepokoski notes:
'With the dazzling suddenness of a conjurer's gesture, the convulsive
world of *Otello* appears before us in full boil. It is the most aggressive
initial gesture in opera' (1987: 1). Of course, this new opening enabled the
opera to start in the heightened atmosphere and elemental conditions of
the storm, a huge spectacular set-piece of the kind much loved by nineteenth-century audiences, and one which effected its own conflation with
the dramatic opening of another storm-soaked Shakespeare play, *The
Tempest*, but the decision might have had the adverse effect of reducing,
rather than amplifying, Desdemona's role. For it is famously in her bold
and self-willed statements before the Venetian Senate in Act I that Shakespeare was able to provide his audiences very rapidly with proof of the

agency of his heroine; not only has she married according to her own emotional will, and not her father's ('I do perceive here a divided duty', I.iii.180), but she refuses to be a 'moth of peace' at home while her new husband is dispatched to Cyprus (I.iii.256). By omitting these forceful exchanges, Verdi and Boito ran the risk of downplaying Desdemona's role. In practice, however, these cuts and the reapportioning of some of these lines to the love duet of Act II, enabled them to offer up a less forceful, more Madonna-like character, one who has the function throughout of being an emblem of chastity and piety. This emblematic quality to their Desdemona is perhaps best exemplified in the addition of one of the opera's several tableaux-choruses, the so-called Homage Chorus in Act II. Here in an idiom of pastoral and Marian worship, a chorus of children's voices sings in praise of Desdemona:

> *T'offriamo il giglio, soave stel,*
> *che in man degli angeli fu assunto in ciel,*
> *che abbella il fulgido manto e la gonna*
> *della Madonna*
> *e il santo vel.*

> 'We proffer lilies, tender flowers,
> by angels borne to heavenly bowers,
> which ornament the gleaming mantle
> and gown of the Madonna gentle
> and her holy veil.'[5]

Certainly, the Verdi–Boito Desdemona dominates the central ensemble pieces of the second and third acts, and in the fourth act she is accorded not one but two swan-songs, the 'Willow Song' directly incorporated from Shakespeare, but also the exquisite 'Ave Maria': 'prega sempre, / e nell'ora della morte nostre' ('pray for us always / and at the hour of our death'). Here too the influence of Rossini's non-Shakespearean opera can be registered, since he had inserted a 'preghiere' at this moment in the action.

It is clear from letters exchanged between Boito and Verdi during the lengthy and drawn-out period of the opera's composition (it took more than six years to come to fruition) that Boito's libretto was strongly influenced by the Romantic lyrical focus on Desdemona: 'On the lyric side, the principal character is Desdemona's; on the dramatic side, the principal character is Jago.'[6] In this statement we can register the influence of the main European Romantic translations of Shakespeare with which we know Boito was working, both the German version by August Wilhelm von Schlegel and the prose rendition by François-Victor Hugo (son of the French novelist). The impact of these versions on the Verdi opera's rendering of Jago/Iago is something to which we will return in more detail in the next chapter. In the case of Desdemona, however, it is, undoubtedly, the idealized, deified version of nineteenth-century tradition that drives the Verdi–Boito interpretation:

> Desdemona is not a woman, she is a type! She is the type of goodness, of resignation, of sacrifice. Such beings are born for others, unconscious of their *own self*! Beings that partly exist and that Shakespeare has put into poetic form and has deified by creating *Desdemona, Cordelia, Juliet,* etc. etc. – these are types perhaps that can only be compared to the Antigone of the ancient theatre.[7]

Shakespeare's inclusion of the intensely private scene between Desdemona and her servant Emilia at iv.iii, in which she delivers the 'Willow Song' is further evidence of her character's relationship to voice and song in the play. Lois Potter makes the intriguing point that, fittingly, in the nineteenth century it was actually singers rather than actors who became most renowned for their portrayals of Desdemona (2002: 65).

The interest in the female roles in Shakespearean drama in this period did not lead to an exclusive focus on the tragedies. The comedies and so-called late plays also provided a rich source for femino-centric operatic adaptations and interpretations. As Schmidgall points out, a quick trawl through the titles of Shakespeare-inspired operas in the period proves instructive, in terms not only of identifying which plays and genres occasioned most interest, but also of the feminizing impulse visible as a driving force behind many of these adaptations (1990: 276): we find, for example, several *Rosalinds* in place of *As You Like It*; for *Twelfth Night* there are examples of operas entitled *Viola* and *Cesario* (and, indeed, *Malvolio*, a name by which the play was commonly known even in the seventeenth century); *The Winter's Tale* is reworked twice as *Perdita* and once as *Hermione*; and three out of five operatic versions of *King Lear* carry the title *Cordelia*. Such interests and drives can also serve to challenge the mainstream canon of Shakespeare as established by more conventional theatre histories. Both in the theatre and in terms of general readership, scholars would be hard-pressed to make a case for *The Merry Wives of Windsor* as a central Shakespeare text; yet in opera it is predominant: from Salieri's *Falstaff* in 1799, which created a soprano role for the character of Anne Ford, through Otto Nicolai's *Die Lustigen Weiber von Windsor* (1849), and Verdi's late masterpiece (for which Boito also served as librettist) *Falstaff* (1893), through to Ralph Vaughan Williams's archetypical English pastoral of 1929, *Sir John in Love*, opera has found reason to return again and again to the green environs of Windsor.[8]

The character of Falstaff is of course a crucial factor in these recurrent revisionary impulses: the value placed on his role in operatic terms is evidenced by its further expansion in operatic renderings of *Merry Wives* via the incorporation of scenes from the *Henry IV* plays. Gustav Holst's single-act operatic interlude based on the tavern scenes of the history plays, *At the Boar's Head*, was a major influence on Vaughan Williams's operatic venture, as was Elgar's previously discussed symphonic study or tone poem *Falstaff*. As ever, tradition breeds tradition; once established as part of the operatic canon, it was a self-fulfilling prophecy that *The Merry Wives of Windsor* would be rewritten, restaged, and persistently reinterpreted by each new generation of performers and composers. Nevertheless, in the context of an argument about the feminizing impulse in operatic interpretations of Shakespeare, the surprisingly gender-balanced stage community offered by this play cannot be ignored. The neighbourhood setting of Windsor, unusual in itself in the context of the Shakespearean canon, means that we witness in stage productions of the play the quotidian friendships and rivalries of this world, and in the accompanying discourses of gossip, exchange, and slander, women play a vital role. The women's Windsor network of friendship and exchanges of confidence, which enables them to play practical jokes on the egotistical and bombastic Falstaff, in turn provides several rich roles for the sopranos and mezzo-sopranos of any operatic community.[9]

Verdi's *Falstaff* is a particularly fine example of these ideas in operation. The opera's dramaturgy is built around a structure of contrast and juxtaposition between male and female voices and environments. The 1.i setting of the Garter Inn consciously emphasizes the male voice, in particular the power of the baritone playing Falstaff. The scene is one of noise, tumult, male banter, rivalry, and invective, and quickly establishes a tone and mood of jealousy and competition that will be important for the rest of the opera. Verdi critic James A. Hepokoski once again offers an engaging account of this opening musical and dramaturgic gambit:

> Few operas begin with such a rush of activity as that which launches Verdi's last opera, *Falstaff*. Gone are even the traces of the familiar overtures, preludes, *introduzioni*, and introductory choral tableaux of his previous works; all have been relinquished in favour of a sudden plunge into headlong activity. (1983: 1)

By contrast, i.ii takes place in the pastoral calm of a garden, and offers a distinctly female alternative, not least in vocal register. Here the orchestration is far more delicate and creates an atmosphere of gossip, chatter, and intimacy, a world of shared confidences rather than egotistical rivalry. It is this female willingness to share that will immediately puncture Falstaff's plans, since Alice and Meg readily confer over the love letters he has sent them. The result is a beautiful echoing duet as they read the letters and uncover Falstaff's multiple infidelities; this in turn develops into the wider shared grouping of the quartet in a dialogic pattern of stichomythic exchange and interlinked lyrics:

MEG: *Gli stessi versi.*	'The same verses.'
ALICE: *Lo stesso inchiostro.*	'The same ink.'
QUICKLY: *La stessa mano.*	'The same writing.'
NANNETTA: *Lo stesso stemma.*	'The same crest.'[10]

The wit, humour, and inventiveness of the women, as they describe Falstaff variously as a wineskin, a barrel, a cannon, and a whale, set the tone for their agency and the importance and impact of female intelligence in the drama that unfolds:

> MEG: *Un flutto in tempesta*
> *Gittò sulla rena*
> *Di Windsor codesta*
> *Vorace balena.*
>
> 'A stormy wave
> has cast up
> that voracious whale
> on the shores of Windsor.'

No passive madonnas these; they offer a striking counterpoint to the Verdi–Boito idealization of Desdemona, and appear to have been influenced both directly by Salieri's equally active version of femininity in his *Falstaff* and more broadly by the tradition of 'strong women' in Italian comic opera. Not only is Salieri's Mistress Ford an independent-minded and inventive individual whose thought patterns we see clearly presented in bold assertions to her female friends and in numerous telling asides to the audience – 'Ohibò, ohibò! Senz'entrare in processi, senza mettersi in man di tribunali, l'aggiusterem da noi' ('Now, now! There's no need for trials and courts, we can do things ourselves.') – but he is careful to create a perfect gender balance in his presentation of two witty servants; one, Bardolf, the put-upon assistant to Falstaff, and the other, Betty, who serves the Windsor women. This pair have central parts in the plotline and serve as linking narrators of sorts for the audience.[11] It is in these balancing acts of both dramaturgy and the disposition of character and action that we clearly see the gender consciousness of opera at work.

It is an aim of this study to emphasize that while the influence of Shakespeare on music has been considerable, the domain of musical interpretation, not least opera, has had its impact in turn on the performance and understanding of many Shakespeare plays. Nowhere is this more in evidence than in the performance history of *The Merry Wives of Windsor*, a play which, as we have seen, has partly secured its place in the canon by dint of its popularity in operatic versions. The play's most recent Arden editor, Giorgio Melchiori, has observed that in the nineteenth century stage productions were consciously 'operatic', starring as they did actor-singers such as Elizabeth Lucia Vestris, a notable Ariel and, as already mentioned in this study, a significant nineteenth-century Desdemona and Oberon (see also Wells 2002: 261). Vestris made a significant Mistress Page in an 1824 production for Reynolds in which she sang not only lyrics introduced from *A Midsummer Night's Dream* (the two plays were seen as intrinsically linked in this period, with their 'fairies' and forests, even though, as Phyllis Rackin has recently noted, in *Merry Wives* 'the fairies who appear in the woods outside the town are town children in masquerades' (2005: 63)[12]), alongside songs from other Shakespearean plays and poems. This, as we have seen, provided a direct template for the work of opera-composers at least in England in the early part of the twentieth century, not least Gustav Holst and Ralph Vaughan Williams. The production was a huge success, and led to a long association with the part of Mistress Page for Vestris. In 1839 when she joined her husband Charles Matthews in managing Covent Garden, Vestris's 'operatic' *Merry Wives* had a very successful run of more than a month and was later revived in 1844 at the Haymarket with the same cast (Melchiori 2000: 93). Melchiori further credits the Verdi–Boito opera with establishing the play as a 'Falstaff' one in the popular consciousness (2000: 93, 101). In turn, the twentieth century saw productions that re-conceptualized the play in terms of Viennese opera and 1950s rock music. The history of *The Merry Wives of Windsor* is, it seems, inextricably bound up with Shakespeare's musical afterlives, not least operatic.

As noted at the start of this chapter, it would be impossible, foolhardy even, for an academic study such as this to attempt to be comprehensive in its study of Shakespeare and opera. What is enlightening, however, in the context of a wider argument about the need to contextualize and historicize musical responses to Shakespeare as much as the plays themselves is to offer up certain composers and operas as case studies. To that end, the next chapter will focus on two seminal but aesthetically antithetical composers of opera, Giuseppe Verdi and Benjamin Britten, and consider their operatic versions of Shakespeare in the context of their own cultural, theatrical, and literary inheritances.

Notes

1 There was a sustained interest throughout the twentieth century in Shakespeare's plays as source material for opera. As well as those discussed in detail in this chapter, there were operatic adaptations of *King Lear* (e.g., Italian Alberto Ghislanzoni's *Re Lear* (1937) and Aulis Sallinen's Finnish *King Lear* (2000)); *Hamlet* (Humphrey Searle's English/ German co-production from 1968, which he also adapted as a suite for baritone voice and orchestra); two German versions of *Romeo and Juliet* (Heinrich Sutermeister, 1940; and Boris Blacher, 1950); an operatic *Love's Labour's Lost* (by Nicolas Nabokov, cousin of the author Vladimir, premièred in 1973); Ernst Bloch's *Macbeth* (1910) and *Puck* by Marcel Delamoy (France, 1949), based on *A Midsummer Night's Dream*; as well as Stephen Oliver's 1991 *Timon of Athens* (another example of a composition that developed out of incidental music, in this instance for a BBC video of *Timon of Athens*: see Jowett 2004: 100 for a fuller discussion of this interesting piece). Many of these examples are listed in M. Cooke 2005a. In her insightful article on literary opera, or opera with a narrative source, in the same volume, Caroline Harvey also mentions Shakespeare-derived works such as Luciano Berio's *Un re in ascolto* (1984), which borrows the figure of Prospero from *The Tempest* and Ermmano Wolf-Ferrari's *Sly* (1927) (2005: 56–7).

2 In a less than enthusiastic review of a 2003 revival of Thomas's opera at the Royal Opera House in Covent Garden, London, Anthony Holden (2003) reflected on the feminocentric aspect to Thomas's reworking of Shakespeare's plotlines.

3 Basnett 2004: 61. On the nineteenth-century fascination with the figure of Ophelia, see Showalter 1991. It is also intriguing to note that Kenneth Branagh's nineteenth-century *mise-en-scène* for his 1996 film version of the play revisited this stage history of Ophelia, depicting her in a padded cell (see Sanders 2000).

4 See L. Potter 2002: 60–1. Incidentally, Lord Byron wrote in a letter to Samuel Rogers on 3 Mar. 1818, after seeing the production in Venice, that the pair had 'crucified' the play; the letter is reproduced as Appendix 3 in Busch (1998: ii. 765).

5 The translations provided here are those taken from the accompanying book let to Verdi and Boito (1994).

6 Boito to Verdi, Milan, 24 Aug. 1881; in Busch 1998: i.112.

7 Verdi to Giulio Ricordi, Genoa, 22 Apr. 1887; in Busch 1998: i.301–2.

8 There were ten major operatic versions of the play between 1761 and 1929. Others include Adolphe-Charles Adam's *Falstaff* in Paris in 1856 and Michael Balfe's music to a libretto by S. M. Maggioni in 1838. Melchiori (2000) also lists musical and operetta versions, including J. P. Webber's *Falstaff* (New York, 1928), C. S. Swier, *When the Cat's Away* (Philadelphia, 1941), and James Gilbert's *Good Time Johnny* (Birmingham, 1971). In 2006 the Royal Shakespeare Company added to this list by commissioning a new musical version of *The Merry Wives* from Paul Englishby for their Complete Works Festival.

9 On the female agency demonstrated by the Windsor women of the play, see, e.g., Rackin 2005: 62–70; and Wall 2003; and Helgerson 1999. Thankfully, this historicized and nuanced critical version of the play is replacing a previous tendency to dismissive

accounts exemplified by Graham Bradshaw's description of it as 'not only very inferior but also uncharacteristic – un-Shakespearean in a precise sense' (he makes the claim in the process that Verdi's *Falstaff* is more Shakespearean than Shakespeare!; in Hepokoski 1983: 160).

10 The translations used here are those provided in the booklet that accompanies Verdi and Boito (2001).

11 Melchiori also links these servant characters to comic operatic conventions (2000: 91).

12 Roy Aycock argues for Verdi's own self-conscious conflation/connection of the two plays in *Falstaff* (cited in Hepokoski 1983: 30).

Further examples and reading

This chapter has necessarily been highly selective in terms of the Shakespeare operas it has focused on. Excellent sources for additional lists and information include Irina Cholij's entry on 'Opera' in *The Oxford Companion to Shakespeare*, ed. Michael Dobson and Stanley Wells (Oxford: Oxford University Press, 2001); and Gary Schmidgall's studies, *Literature as Opera* (Oxford and New York: Oxford University Press, 1977) and *Shakespeare and Opera* (New York and Oxford: Oxford University Press, 1990). For those interested in twentieth-century opera as a phenomenon, *The Cambridge Companion to Twentieth-Century Opera*, ed. Mervyn Cooke (Cambridge: Cambridge University Press, 2005a) is a rich source, and includes considerable discussion of Shakespeare-connected material, especially in Caroline Harvey's essay on literary operas, 'Words and Action', as well as important contextual material. The volume provides a timeline for the first performances of new twentieth-century operas, which is a treasure-trove for those interested in Shakespearean operas. Another helpful source for examples prior to and including the twentieth and twenty-first centuries, is the list of 'Composers inspired by Shakespeare' available on the 'Shakespeare in Europe' website created at the University of Basel, Switzerland <http://pages.unibas. ch/shine/musiccompsz.html last changes July 2004>, last accessed 25 July 2006). Examples can be identified there of operas based on, e.g., *The Winter's Tale* (*Perdita* by Carlo Emanuele Barbieri, 1865); *The Comedy of Errors* (Henry Rowley Bishop, 1819); *The Taming of the Shrew* (John Braham, 1828, and Vittorio Giannini, 1953); and *Pericles* (Celia and Louis Zukofsky, 1963). The site is not flawless, and falsely claims some operas based on alternative sources (William Walton's *Troilus and Cressida*, e.g., which reworks Chaucer; and Camille Saint-Saëns's *Henry VIII*, which is based on a Calderon de la Barca play), but it is an invaluable source of reference material nevertheless. To confirm details of productions prior to 1990, Bryan N. S. Gooch and David Thatcher, *A Shakespeare Music Catalogue*, 5 vols (Oxford: Clarendon Press, 1991) is a superlative reference.

For detailed readings and specific contextualizations of the Verdi–Boito *Otello* and *Falstaff*, readers are directed towards the volumes in the Cambridge Opera Handbooks series by James A. Hepokoski, *Giuseppe Verdi: Falstaff* (Cambridge: Cambridge University Press, 1983) and *Giuseppe Verdi: Otello* (Cambridge: Cambridge University Press, 1987). Hepokoski's careful situating of the operas in terms of both the literary-critical histories and performative contexts of the plays as well as his expert musical analysis strikes a chord with my own attempt to historicize Shakespearean musical adaptations and appropriations in this study.

This chapter makes an extended case for the influence of European Romantic ideas and the Continental translations of Shakespeare's texts produced in that period on the versions of his plays found in nineteenth-century opera, in particular the work of Verdi and Boito. Related arguments about symphonic and orchestral responses to Shakespeare were made in chapter 2. James A. Hepokoski's Cambridge Opera Handbook on *Otello*, mentioned above, offers a detailed account of this phenomenon in relation to the Verdi–Boito opera; but for those readers interested in the interaction between Shakespeare and Romanticism, the authority is Jonathan Bate, whose seminal studies *Shakespeare and the English Romantic Imagination* (Oxford: Clarendon Press, 1986) and *Shakespearean Constitutions: Politics, Theatre, Criticism, 1730–1830* (Oxford: Clarendon Press, 1989), are now complemented by an edited anthology in the 'New Penguin Shakespeare Library' series, *The Romantics on Shakespeare*, which is organized according to play, and which reproduces material by A. W. von Schlegel, J. W. von Goethe, and Ludwig Tieck among others (Harmondsworth: Penguin, 1992).

Editions of Shakespeare's plays are thankfully becoming far more alert to the complex history of Shakespearean adaptation, and are recognizing the two-directional lines of influence this often creates, rather than always assuming the Shakespearean source as the governing authority in the relationship. Giorgio Melchiori's edition of *The Merry Wives of Windsor* for the Arden 3 series (London: Arden/Thomson Learning, 2000) is a fine example of this approach, including as it does an extensive account of the operatic and musical history of the play (pp. 80–109). Arden 3's new *Hamlet*, ed. Ann Thompson and Neil Taylor (London: Arden/Thomson Learning, 2006) is similarly sensitive to the adaptational afterlife of that play in music, poetry, and prose, and Juliet Dusinberre's Edition of *As You Like It* (London: Arden Thomson Learning, 2006) is equally alert to the musical afterlife of Rosalind and the Forest of Arden.

6

Giuseppe Verdi and Benjamin Britten: Case Studies in Shakespearean Opera

> He sings several tunes faster than you'll tell money. He utters them as he had eaten ballads, and all men's ears grew to his tunes.
>
> *The Winter's Tale*, IV.iv.184–7

As the previous chapter's discussion of Shakespeare in the opera houses of nineteenth-century Europe indicated, Giuseppe Verdi is canonical in any account of Shakespeare-inspired opera, and it is therefore to two of his three Shakespearean masterpieces, *Macbeth* and *Otello* (the other being the previously discussed *Falstaff*), that this chapter will turn first, before offering a complementary case study of a very different line of operatic inheritance by considering the versions of *A Midsummer Night's Dream* produced by Henry Purcell at the turn of the seventeenth century and by Benjamin Britten in the later twentieth century.

I Verdi's Shakespearean Melodramas

Verdi's *Macbeth* (1847, revised 1865) was his earliest foray into the Shake-spearean canon, and while this opera is viewed by some as adhering more to operatic conventions and traditions than his late Shakespeare operas, *Otello* and *Falstaff*, there are strategies contained within its musical regis-ter and its dramaturgy that are fundamental to Verdi's particular style of adaptation.[1] While Gary Schmidgall chooses to praise this opera on the grounds of its 'fidelity' to Shakespeare (1977: 182), a dubious claim at the best of times, since authorial intention in the often conflicting or editorial-ized texts of Shakespeare's plays is unstable ground for the literary critic, what seem most fascinating to me are those moments where we can trace Verdi's personal creative input. It is where he chooses to make cuts or alterations to the plotline of the received play, or where operatic conven-tion fuses with Shakespearean dramaturgy to offer a new and transforma-tive set of possibilities that the opportunities for discussion and analysis seem richest.

Verdi is now regularly associated with creating a space for acting on the operatic stage and for offering a blend of acting and music rarely seen on the stages of early operatic theatre. In the works of Purcell, for example, there was a strict division, rarely crossed, between actors and singers, and these traditions persisted well into the eighteenth century. Verdi is also linked to an 'aesthetic of simplicity', credited with a stripping back of plots familiar from classical texts of various kinds, dramatic or prose-based in origin (Schmidgall 1977: 184; Abbate 1991). His *Macbeth* is no exception; several of the scenes and characters in the Shakespearean playtext which offer the audience a sense of a world outside the claustrophobic experiences of the Macbeths themselves are expunged. We never see King Duncan except as a silent participant in a procession across the stage when he and his retinue first arrive at the Macbeths' Scottish residence; gone is the pathos and spectator empathy established by the 'temple-haunting martlet' scene (I.vi.4; the phrase is actually Banquo's, but is part of a pastoral response to the Macbeths' castle residence that unsettles audience members aware of the fate that awaits the Scottish monarch).[2] Not only does this increase the emphasis on the Macbeths, but it potentially expands the space for audience identification with the couple, which is in accordance with the heightened pathos of many Romantic versions of Shakespeare, and a practice already witnessed in the Verdi–Boito version of Desdemona in *Otello*.

Verdi's libretto for *Macbeth* was written not by Boito, but by Francesco Maria Piave, and lacks much of *Otello*'s verbal dexterity, but it is similarly shaped by Romantic era translations of Shakespeare. The 1830s had seen two prose versions of *Macbeth*, plus one verse translation, in Italian, and the demonic and Satanic emphases in the opera, especially in the weird sisters' scenes, are undoubtedly heavily influenced by them.[3] These reach a dramatic climax in the third act of the opera. Here, unlike in the other acts, where there are multiple and carefully juxtaposed scenes and episodes, Verdi and Piave opt for one fluid movement. This fluidity of staging provides a striking parallel to the kinds of central plateaux that Peter Holland has identified as a crucial part of the dramaturgic architecture of Shakespearean plays, particularly those written with open-air amphitheatre performances in mind, since these were commonly staged without act breaks, and as a result produced their meaning through a practice of scenic flow and heightened juxtaposition (1997: 4). This finds a ready parallel in Verdi's operas, nowhere more so than in his *Macbeth*. In the specific instance of the third act, the uninterrupted flow of action results in a scene which blurs, almost to the point of deliberate confusion, the supernatural invocations of the weird sisters and their 'polta infernal' ('hellish brew'), and the actions and inspirations of Lady Macbeth. After a scene of apparitions and prophecies, which includes a ballet by the witches – one of the markers of Verdi's working within more traditional conventions than he would in his later ventures into Shakespearean adaptation – Macbeth faints. When he wakes, he is back in his castle and back in dialogue and duet with his wife. The unstoppable forward motion of this act mirrors their joint understanding at the end of this scene that more bloodshed will inevitably follow.

There are other crucial and telling moments of juxtaposition achieved by Verdi and Piave. Act IV begins with a chorus of Scottish refugees. This constitutes yet another pertinent example of Verdi using the chorus to reflect and in some ways extend the function of the speeches by characters in Shakespeare's play, like those of Ross and the Old Man, or Lennox and the Lord (see, e.g., II.iv and III.vi), which speak emblematically of the fate of their nation in the face of Macbeth's usurpation of the crown. The semblance of these scenes to operatic duets is also suggestive. Bernice Kliman has written of the 'choral' aspects to the play, and the specific commentary provided by characters including the ill-fated Lady Macduff and her children: 'The choral segments, which affirm a moral society, readjust the audience's values' (1995: 5). Though Verdi cut scenes and speeches involving the Macduffs, he brilliantly retains their choric function through the specific generic possibilities of opera.

Act IV opens with a scene of remarkable shifts of register, moving forward from the choric plaint of the refugees for their 'Patria oppressa!' ('Down-trodden country!') to Macduff's moving aria on the murder of his wife and children: 'Possa a colui le braccia / Del tuo perdon aprir' ('Oh Lord, and if he escape me then, / Extend thou thine arms to him in pardon').[4] This is a fine example of Verdi's deliberate relocation of a central scene of pathos in the play to an offstage position, thereby reducing the audience's exposure to the full horror of the Macbeths' crimes. This is directly akin to the distancing from the character and fate of Duncan achieved in the first act. Macduff's aria is juxtaposed with the strong martial orchestration that announces the arrival of Malcolm at the head of a troop of English soldiers. This movement in turn brings onto the stage and into the opera a sense of advancing soldierly might that will now carry through to the close. The initially jarring register of grief and might eventually gives way to an emerging sense of political unity and unity of action in the duet between Macduff and Malcolm, which finds its final realization in a climactic chorus. This large ensemble scene is followed immediately by the disturbing bedchamber intimacy of Lady Macbeth's sleep-walking confession, watched onstage only by the Doctor and her lady; their interventions offer in their contrasted baritone and soprano responses reactions of horror and pity that go to the heart of tragic convention:

> MEDICO: *Oh terror!*   'Oh, horror!'
> DAMA: *Ah, di lei pieta, Signor!*   'Mercy on her, oh Lord!'

The musical orchestration of IV.ii is also remarkable, containing as it does Lady Macbeth's fractured song-speeches, full of unanswerable questions (and unanswered – her isolation here is palpable by comparison with Macduff's supported grief in the preceding scene) and a seemingly endless re-enactment of the moment of Duncan's murder. This is underscored by the repeated notes of a sighing alto oboe 'Chi poteva in quel vegliardo / Tanto sangue immaginar?' ('Who would have thought the old man / To have had so much blood in him?'). Lady Macbeth's delivery is also in stark contrast to her earlier assertive and swelling arias, which were full of the imperative mode and underlined by apposite orchestration from the string section:

> *Vieni! t'affreta! Accendere*
> *Ti vo'quel freddo core!*
>
> 'Come! Hie you hither!
> I would set your cold heart aflame!'

As with the expansion and, to a certain extent, de-ambiguizing of Desdemona's role in *Otello*, the stripping out of other scenes and characters from the earlier sections of *Macbeth* creates a heightened focus on Lady Macbeth – though, as Kliman points out, any actor can make Lady Macbeth 'the nerve-centre of the first half of the play' (1995: 1), and in this respect Verdi and Boito were again responding to theatre tradition. The effect, however, is further exacerbated by the fact that the complicated rhythms and registers of the opera tend to come in Lady Macbeth's arias, rather than in those of her husband. Verdi's stated wish for a 'brutish and ugly' soprano who might deliver the role in a 'diabolical' rather than 'angelic' register is a key to the orchestrating, and therefore pivotal, role he accords Lady Macbeth in the tragic events which unfold (Schmidgall 1977: 183). It is telling that he regarded the two crucial moments of this opera as the Macbeths' duet in I.ii and the sleep-walking scene itself (Schmidgall 1977: 191). Duet is deployed throughout as a rich signifier – the stichomythic, shared rhythms of the Macbeths' earlier exchanges gradually give way to isolation and lonely arias; the split is already becoming visible by the start of Act II, when Macbeth enters the stage deep in thought according to the stage directions – *Macbeth penseroso, seguito da Lady Macbeth* – and his wife's opening gambit is: 'Perché mi sfuggi, e fiso / Ognor ti veggio in un pensier profondo?' ('Why do you keep alone / and why do I see you ever sunk in sorriest fancies?'). This lays the ground for Macbeth's appallingly detached response to the news of his wife's death in Act IV: 'La vita . . . che importa? / È il racconto d'un povero idiota; / Vento e svono che nulla dinota!' ('Life, 'tis no matter! It is a tale told by an idiot; / sound and fury signifying nothing!').

If onstage events in Shakespeare's *Macbeth* are here relocated offstage, some of Shakespeare's deliberately offstage events – in particular, Macbeth's anti-climactic and marginalized death – are brought decisively onstage and into the audience's sights in Verdi's version. As previously observed, musical adaptations of Shakespeare are frequently shaped not only by the critical responses to the texts in their own era but also by dominant theatrical practice. Nineteenth-century theatrical interpretations of the role of Desdemona undoubtedly affected both Rossini's and Verdi's operatic versions of *Otello*. Similarly, English actor-manager David Garrick's seminal eighteenth-century productions and performances of the eponymous role in *Macbeth* held sway well into the nineteenth century, and his influence can be clearly registered in the Verdi–Piave opera. Garrick had famously added a lengthy onstage delivery of a dying speech by Macbeth, and this was preserved by actors playing the role more than a century later. There was, therefore, considerable pressure on Verdi, still at an early stage in his career when he composed *Macbeth*, and therefore less empowered to resist external pressures than when he came to work on his late Shakespearean operas, to include a version of Garrick's interpolated speech in his operatic score. We can read this overtly as a case of Verdi being pressured to conform to tradition, since when he came to revise *Macbeth* for performances at the Paris Opéra in 1865, a substantial revision in many respects, he removed this speech, reverting to a more sparing treatment of Macbeth's demise that is far more akin to the extant Shakespearean playtext. Ironically, what now tends to pertain in contemporary revivals is the performance of a conflated edition of the two versions, thereby reducing our ability as audiences to take from the two versions an insight into Verdi's career progression as a composer.

It is, of course, interesting to consider which Shakespearean plays Verdi was drawn to for the purposes of operatic adaptation. He intended, but abandoned, a *King Lear* (*Re Lear*) apparently because of an anxiety about over-complex plotting (Schmidgall 1985), and it is noticeable that his triad of Shakespeare operas all have a highly focused setting, his *Otello* even more so than the source, due to his decision to excise the opening scenes in Venice in favour of a wholly Cypriot location. *Macbeth* and *Otello* are chamber operas in some respect; in the case of *Macbeth*, what Verdi chooses to excise actually emphasizes and increases the focus on the claustrophobic interior of the Macbeths' castle and their marriage. Even in the lighter-hearted comic opera of *Falstaff*, the plotline of *The Merry Wives of Windsor* appears to have been attractive to Verdi partly because of its contained setting in the neighbourhood and environs of Windsor. In the unusually domestic tragedy of *Othello*, Verdi found further rich possibilities, and once again it is in the process of transformation and the acts of revision, his 'fidelity-in-betrayal', that we find the best witness to his musical creativity and operatic innovation.

In his review of the Verdi–Boito *Otello* for the *Anglo-Saxon Review* in March 1901, George Bernard Shaw (under the somewhat dubious pseudonym of Corno di Bassetto) famously declared: 'the truth is that instead of *Otello* being an Italian opera written in the style of Shakespeare, *Othello* is a play written by Shakespeare in the style of Italian opera' (Busch 1998: ii.737). The intense, compressed time scheme of the play, the almost primeval rivalry between its central male protagonists, its conscious blend of intimate domestic interiors and grand ceremonial public space, its tragic onstage death of its innocent heroine, and its key image- and metaphor-soaked speeches, all seem to lend themselves to the heightened atmosphere and register of opera. More than that, as G. Wilson Knight (1960 [1930]) recognized in his 1930 essay 'The *Othello* Music', this is a play that directly invokes notions of music, harmony, and discord at crucial moments in the dialogue and action.[5] Wilson Knight pays attention to the operation of particular words in the aural register of the play, suggesting that grand, single terms such as 'Propontic' and 'Hellespont' 'with their sharp, clear, consonant sounds, constituting defined aural solids typical of the *Othello* music' give a distinct sonic quality to the earlier speeches in the play of its eponymous protagonist, and that it is this control of language, this 'music', that Iago works upon most purposefully in subsequent scenes and exchanges: 'As ugly and idiot ravings, disjointed and with no passionate dignity even, succeed Othello's swell and flood of poetry, Iago's triumph seems complete' (1960 [1930]: 117).

Iago certainly describes his own plot in terms of the bringing of musical discord to the aesthetic beauty of the relationship of Desdemona and

Othello: 'O, you are well tuned now / But I'll set down the pegs that make this music' (II.i.200–1). These are lines that Boito consciously reworks in his libretto for *Otello*: early on Jago declares: 'I vostri infrangerò soavi accordi' ('I'll untune the strings that make this music'), a line he repeats later for added emphasis. Song also has literal agency in this play. This can be witnessed in Iago's corruption of Cassio's reputation via the communal pressures of the *brindisi*, or drinking song, in Act II; as David Lindley describes it: 'Popular music is Iago's persuasive means to entice Cassio with the illusion of conviviality and belonging to the crowd,' and Verdi's opera underscores this idea further by making the drinking song one of the central performances of the Chorus (2006: 152). Similarly, Desdemona's melancholic and solitary 'Willow Song' prefigures her own tragic fifth-act demise in a manner that serves as a pointed contrast to her earlier sense of union with her new husband: 'the mutual music of love turns into the solo lament of Desdemona singing a lyric of desertion' (Lindley 2006: 151). Once again the opera seems to underscore these readings of the play, since the 'Willow Song', now doubled in intensity via its coupling with the 'Ave Maria', offers its own poignant contrast to the beautifully integrated lines of the love duet that Desdemona had shared with Othello in the opening act:

> OTELLO: *E tu m'amavi per le mie sventure,*
> *Ed io t'amavo per la tua pietà.*
> DESDEMONA: *Ed io t'amavo per le tuo sventure,*
> *E ti m'amavi per la mia pietà.*

> OTELLO: You loved me for the dangers I had passed,
> And I loved you that you did pity them.
> DESDEMONA: I loved you for the dangers you had passed,
> And you loved me that I did pity them.

One oft-cited relationship between Shakespearean verse and the discursive and musical world of opera is that between arias and soliloquies. Since both are set-piece moments of delivery, usually by a single character onstage, offering the audience what might seem akin to moments of insight or confession, Gary Schmidgall has suggested that they provide the core of the 'synonymy' between Shakespearean language and music (1990: 3). Certainly the strategic dramaturgic placement of soliloquies at pivotal points in the plays offers an analogue to the use of aria in opera dramaturgy. Schmidgall finds equivalent resonance in what he terms the 'dramaturgy of outcry' or apostrophe; for example, the opening line of the Chorus in *Henry V*: 'O for a muse of fire' (1990: 40). This and other set-piece speeches such as Henry V's St Crispin's Day call to arms, or encapsulatory addresses such as John of Gaunt's deathbed 'This sceptered isle' speech in *Richard II*, are, however, declamatory moments that might seem more analogous to recitative than the reflective space of aria. What Schmidgall sees as the defining aspect of this synonymous relationship between Shakespearean language and opera is, however, the auditory nature of much early modern drama. It was consciously designed to be heard, and auditory prompts stirred the imagination of spectators.[6] It is no coincidence that the culmination of the development of the embedded role and function of the aria in operatic dramaturgy is often felt to be most concretely displayed in the work of Verdi. Verdi wrote for the stage, and not just for musical effect; he understood the specific demands of the performative context: 'I would not want the theatrical world to be forgotten' (quoted in Schmidgall 1990: 64). Verdi's is musical drama, then, melodrama in the literal sense of the word.

As already noted, much nineteenth-century opera was strongly influenced by the ideas and practices of European Romanticism and their particular application to the transmission and reinterpretation of Shakespeare, although in turn it must also be acknowledged that the conventions and practices of nineteenth-century opera made a considerable contribution to understandings of and stagings of Shakespearean drama at this time. Part of this process of cultural, historical, and theoretical transmission and interaction can undoubtedly be traced in the work of translation, constituting as translations do specific acts of interpretation which directly affected the readings offered by certain composers and librettists. As Ton Hoenselaars has noted, translators have a 'key position in the cultural context of the transmission, reception, and reinterpretation of Shakespeare' (2004: x). In the Romantic period, particular versions or translations of Shakespeare's plays become canonical, in particular the Schlegel–Tieck translation in Germany, and in France the prose rendition of the *Complete Works*, completed between 1852 and 1865, by Victor Hugo's son, François-Victor, a version which acknowledged its own debts to the Schlegel–Tieck edition. Though translators at this time laid great store by finding equivalences in the second language into which the Shakespearean verse was being translated, such claims belied the now accepted truth that any act of translation is itself a creative, interpretative act – in short, an act of editing. These translations, then, provided the context for the Romantic Shakespeare which many nineteenth-century composers and librettists were responding to in their own cultural productions, not least Verdi and Boito.

Verdi's personal library at the Villa Sant'Agata is evidence that he had access to several seminal Italian translations and works of literary criticism: the work of Giulio Carcano and Andrea Maffei, who were close friends and whose work was much influenced by German Romanticism, in particular the ideas of Goethe, Schiller, and Schlegel, and the first complete Italian translation of Shakespeare by Carlo Rusconi, which appeared in print in 1835. As Hans Busch notes, 'There is thus no doubt that Verdi read Shakespeare in the German romantic tradition' (1998: i. p.xxxix). Arrigo Boito worked painstakingly on Shakespeare in the original English, but also extensively in mediated or filtered versions such as the Schlegel–Tieck and Hugo editions. These filtrations had a decisive impact on his libretto, especially at the level of character psychology. James Hepokoski has suggested that the Verdi–Boito Otello is undoubtedly shaped by the work of the Romantic translators: 'Boito's and Verdi's Otello skilfully blends elements of August Wilhelm Schlegel's widely read "savage" interpretation of the character with François-Victor Hugo's more elevated, ennobled Moor.'[7] The mediating and shaping effect of the arts of translation can nowhere more be felt than in the depiction of Iago, or Jago as he becomes in the opera. He forms the undoubted core of the action, a fact testified to by Boito's previously quoted observation that if Desdemona is the lyric part of the opera, Jago is the dramatic part.[8] Iago's several smaller soliloquies, which serve as twisting, ambiguous verbal confessions to himself and audiences for the play – as well as structural punctuation, marking as they often do scene ends, a fact which has contributed to critical accounts of Iago as the director of the action – become in the stripped-back version in the opera a single heart-stopping aria: Jago's 'Credo' in Act ii.

Cognates of the infinitive *credere* ('to believe') are littered around the libretto text of *Otello* as if to underline the fact that this is a story about belief and false belief and the willingness of the mind, not least Otello's, to believe what it wants: 'Credo leale Desdemona / e credo che non lo sia' ('I believe Desdemona to be loyal / and believe her not to be so'); 'Impura ti credo' ('Unchaste do I esteem you'). But nowhere does the term carry more negative, yet assertive, qualities than in Jago's aria. Left alone on the stage as Cassio goes in search of Desdemona, he declares to himself and the overhearing audience:

> *Credo in un Dio crudel*
> *Che m'ha creato simile a sè*
>
> 'I believe in a cruel God
> who has created me in his image.'

He continues in this vein, not only calling on Satan to assist him in his enterprise against the Moor, but talking of his tangible sense of the primeval slime from which he came: 'sento il fango originario in me' ('I feel the primeval slime within me').[9]

The careful dramaturgic placement of the 'Credo' before the homage chorus to Desdemona in Act II is a juxtaposition that merely serves to point up these two characters as opposed emblems of good and evil. The Satanic frame of reference so clearly evoked in Jago's aria also locates this version of the Othello story in a Romantic context. While Shakespeare's playtext undoubtedly flirts with notions of the relationship between Iago and the Devil, not least in the scene in which Othello and Iago swear their unbreakable oath to one another onstage (III.iii), these associations are usually presented as being the perception of those around him, in particular Othello ('demand that demi-devil / Why he hath thus ensnared my soul and body?', v.ii.307–8), and therefore any firm association is left to members of the audience to make. In the German Romantic tradition of Goethe and Schiller, however, the association became more explicit and far less ambivalent than in Shakespeare, just as Desdemona's 'divinity' became unquestionable. This line of influence is confirmed by one particular letter from Boito to Verdi in which he chooses a particular translation of Shakespeare (Rusconi's) because it reveals Jago's 'evil mind' in a more explicit fashion than the source playtext.[10]

The obvious literary parallel, one which was frequently made by commentators and reviewers in the nineteenth century, was between Iago and Mephistopheles, more precisely the Mephistopheles of Goethe's play *Faust*. It is no small coincidence that Arrigo Boito's most successful involvement in opera up until this point had been his well-regarded production of *Mefistofele* in 1866. Demonic interpretations of Iago had dominated stage productions of *Othello* in the period prior to Boito and Verdi's creation, and were explicit both in the Schlegel–Tieck and the Hugo translations, and we see a conflation of these influences in the remarkable 'Credo'. The aria has a power that Verdi was certain would receive a strong and positive reaction from opera audiences, even while he feared that other aspects of their collaborative composition might be criticized: 'This Credo is most beautiful, most powerful; and Shaespearean [*sic*] in every way,' he wrote, assuring Boito that 'In Shaspeare's [*sic*] country they will reproach us for omitting the first act, but they aren't going to hold Jago's Credo against you.'[11]

In the light of arguments made elsewhere in this study about the influence of literary criticism on the musical adaptations of any given culture and moment, it is intriguing to note the recurrence of very similar ideas about Iago's character and function in the play in G. Wilson Knight's previously cited essay 'The *Othello* Music': 'Iago is thus utterly devilish . . . He is a kind of Mephistopheles, closely equivalent to Goethe's devil, the two possessing the same qualities of mockery and easy cynicism' (1960 [1930]: 114). We might begin to wonder whether the musicality located by Knight in the language of the play was itself shaped by Verdi's opera; Knight's language in this passage certainly links him to the critical theories of German Romanticism which were the dominant influence on the Verdi–Boito collaboration. His account of Desdemona effects similar links with a *fin-de-siècle* and potentially operatic reading of Shakespeare.[12]

In the midst of their lengthy and revealing correspondence on the process of composing *Otello*, it is possible to see Verdi and Boito worrying about the climax to their opera on several occasions. In one letter, in the midst of celebrating the brilliant and dramatic climax they have achieved in Act III, Boito fears that they have damaged the potential ending of the opera overall.[13] Ultimately, Verdi deployed a brilliant musical innovation on the by now established strategy of deploying *leitmotifs*, recurring musical phrases in opera, a technique heavily influenced, as was observed in comments in preceding chapters on the genres of ballet and musical, by the theories and practice of Richard Wagner. Joseph Kerman has summarized Wagnerian *leitmotif* in these terms: 'the repetition of musical fragments with symbolic intent' (1989: 131). These *leitmotifs* offered the audience recurring themes and encouraged them to connect moments within the drama to each other. The Wagnerian *leitmotif* is, in Kerman's evocative account, a 'small, flexible figure designed for frequent detailed reference and for spinning into a complicated symphonic web' (1989: 131). It is a model that has had considerable influence on film soundtracks, but in Verdi's hands Kerman identifies a considerable shift of practice and effect. Rather than the small, fragmentary nuggets of reference alluded to above, Verdi opted for full-scale lyric repetition, not least in *Otello*, where it is both the lyric and the associated music of the kiss, 'un bacio ancora' ('one more kiss') that clusters around Otello throughout the opera, most tellingly at the point of murdering Desdemona and on the brink of his suicide.

The musical passage that recurs, that swells up one last time in the closing moments of the opera, actively reminds us of the earlier love duet between Otello and Desdemona;[14] like the 'Willow Song', it serves to remind us of absence and loss, for this is no longer a duet, and there is no longer anyone to return his wish for a kiss, of itself an action that requires two participants. Intriguingly, Kerman suggests that Wagner may also have been Verdi's inspiration in this regard. The 'hinge-theme' of the kiss in *Otello* has its most obvious counterpart in the *Liebestod* of Wagner's own opera of tragic love, *Tristan und Isolde* (1989: 134). Since this particular Wagnerian composition will be the focus of detailed discussion in a later chapter on contemporary and hybrid film soundtracks (see chapter 8), I will say no more on this subject here, but opt instead to end this section as Verdi does *Otello*, with a reminder that themes recur in rich patterns in opera, music, and theatre, and that memory as well as expectation plays a crucial role in the experience.

II   Shakespeare Dreamings: Britten, Britain, and Purcell

In previous chapters on jazz, classical symphonies, and ballet, we registered the strong presence of *A Midsummer Night's Dream* in the canon of Shakespearean musical adaptations. A number of theories have been advanced for that continued and diverse presence. Undoubtedly, the play's popularity on the public stage since the time of its inception encourages and lays the foundation for a rich and diverse afterlife in terms of borrowings and appropriations, be it in the form of painting, musical, dance interpretation, or film. In the instance of balletic adaptations, it was noted that experience in choreographing the fairy scenes in specific theatre productions of the play led to several full-scale dance interpretations by the likes of Sir Frederick Ashton and George Balanchine. In this chapter I will continue to trace this two-directional flow between stage Shakespeare and his interpretation in other media and genres, but this time in the context of opera.

As we saw in chapter 3, contemporary theatre productions of *A Midsummer Night's Dream* allude or refer with as much ease to Felix Mendelssohn's score for the play as do ballets and films in their already intertextualized and referential (if not necessarily deferential) position of generic adaptation. Such allusions can be serious or parodic in intention and effect, or even a conscious hybrid of the two positions. But *A Midsummer Night's Dream* was undergoing adaptation and reworking almost as soon as it was first staged in the early modern period. Even during the period of commercial theatre shutdown in England in the 1640s and 1650s, the so-called Interregnum period of civil war and (brief) republican government, 'drolls' – short, invariably comic, entertainments, containing hybridized and cannibalized versions of the 'Pyramus and Thisbe' play-within-a-play

– were being performed illicitly at the Red Bull Theatre in London and elsewhere (see Wiseman 1998).

When public commercial theatre in London officially reopened with the advent of the Restoration, the two newly formed theatre companies at Lincoln's Inn Fields and Drury Lane, under the auspices of William Davenant and Thomas Killigrew, found themselves with a dearth of new dramatic material for performance, and in the early years at least relied heavily on a policy of revivals and reworkings. They were especially reliant on the Jacobean and Caroline repertoire they had inherited, including works by Ben Jonson, James Shirley, Francis Beaumont and John Fletcher, and one William Shakespeare, but they were keen to adapt these works to accord with the new political and cultural tastes of their age. Neither Davenant nor Killigrew was averse to the adaptation, reworking, supplementation, and in some cases wholescale revision of the playtexts in their company's possession.

One playwright in the pay of the Restoration theatres, Nahum Tate, has gained a distinct reputation as an adapter of Shakespeare's playtexts: he reworked *Richard II* (under the title of *The Sicilian Usurper*), *Coriolanus*, *Richard III*, and *King Lear* among others.[15] Restoration rewritings have not fared well at the hands of literary critics and theatre historians. As Curtis Price notes: 'The adaptations are now considered to be the low point of late seventeenth-century English drama. In rewriting Shirley or Beaumont and Fletcher, hack playwrights filed down irony, sharpened up sex and horror, and laid on a thick coating of pathos' (1984: 28). It might be fairer to think of these adapters as responding to the commercial demands, as well as the fashions, moral and otherwise, of the time, a mode in which we far more readily consider the work of a postmodern adaptor such as Baz Luhrmann. Restoration writers were producing 'proximations', to use Gérard Genette's resonant phrase, relevant to their own cultural moment as much as any contemporary appropriator (Sanders 2006: 20). This was a society and culture emerging from a bloody civil war and, for those of royalist sympathies – many of whom made up the audience for the public theatres, which had after all been reopened at royal command – a long period in the political wilderness, often in self-imposed Continental European exile. That context sheds light on Tate's all-too-readily mocked alterations to the plotline of his adaptation of *King Lear*, where there is famously a 'happy ending' as well as a love interest for Cordelia in the form of Edgar. In the seventeenth century this play already had an unstable textual identity, which made it ripe for alteration and adaptation by subsequent generations (see Taylor and Warren 1983). When we think of Tate as a writer who had faced censorship of his work – his version of *Richard III* had been deemed too controversial to be staged in the decades following a civil war and the temporary dismantling of the British monarchy – our readings of his adaptations may shift ground a little (see Fischlin and Fortier 2000: 66–7).

It is, therefore, as an era of free, if not uncontroversial, adaptation that we need to think of Britain in the late seventeenth century, as well as being an age of transition, musically, theatrically, and politically. The 'sexed-up' aspect of several late seventeenth-century reworkings of Shakespeare can in part be attributed to the advent of the professional female actor on the commercial stages of London in the 1660s. A new focus on the female body swiftly followed, and there was a new impetus for increased or expanded female roles as well as ones that focused on the female form (Howe 1992: *passim*). Elizabeth Barry's delivery of the Nahum Tate-authored epilogue to his adaptation of Shakespeare's *King Lear* in her role as Cordelia indicates the newly femino-centric theatrical context for that version, as well as reflecting the commodifiable celebrity status of Barry herself in the theatre of the day. In other Shakespearean adaptations, related responses to the new playing conditions of the Restoration period can be seen in the creation of additional female parts and storylines. In Dryden and Davenant's *The Enchanted Island*, a much revised and itself adapted version of *The Tempest*, this stretches to the creation of a sister, Dorinda, for Miranda (Thompson 1995: 168–9). Dorinda is interestingly one of the few 'acting' characters apart from Ariel (for which there is obvious precedent in the extant Shakespeare script), to sing – she has a brief aria – a fact which adds to our understanding of her as very much a late seventeenth-century creation.

But the transitional nature of the Restoration and late seventeenth-century stages can be registered in musicological as well as interpolational aspects of the operatic and semi-operatic versions of Shakespeare which were undertaken at this time. There had famously been a prohibition on public performances of plays during the Civil War and Interregnum periods, and this had led to a considerable degree of inventiveness on the part of playwrights, theatrical entrepreneurs, and performers and composers during the 1640s and 1650s when the prohibition remained in place. Several of these playwrights and composers had remained in London during this time, rather than joining high-profile aristocrats in exile on the Continent, and some plied their trade as schoolmasters and personal tutors. Schools and academies became suitable cover for theatrical performances in a 'non-professional' environment, and enabled playwrights such as James Shirley to continue to write. Similarly, the salon gatherings at composer and musician Henry Lawes's London residence became the driving force behind much poetic and quasi-theatrical composition in the period, not least by women, including such notable writers as Katherine Phillips and Margaret Cavendish, Duchess of Newcastle (see Chalmers 2005). As noted in relation to the 'Pyramus and Thisbe' performance of the mechanicals in *A Midsummer Night's Dream*, drama appeared during this time in the form of drolls performed illicitly in quasi-theatrical sites such as taverns. The Interregnum period was, then, a space of prohibition but also, ironically, a space of liberation, a site of free play and experimentation, and opera was key to that process. Opera did not emerge fully formed in England out of that experimental moment, however; it was the product of a complicated combination of factors, including not least the influence of the masques and entertainments of the early Stuart courts. Masque combined spoken drama, spectacle, dance, and music in a kind of total theatre that is readily recognizable in modern opera. The 'semi-operas' of Davenant and, after him, Purcell can be viewed in their mix of lyrical music and recitative to be a covert means of staging drama in the period of prohibition and indicative of the emergent musically dramatic form of opera.

It is as this complex and, as yet, not fully evolved combination of and encounter between the spoken and the sung, the acted and the danced, the aural and the visual, that Henry Purcell's operatic works and those of his contemporaries can best be understood (see Price 1984). Their work was directly influenced by the theatrical developments of the day, since many of them wrote music for the theatre, for use in more conventional stagings of plays by Shakespeare and others. Purcell, for example, had set music for one of the lyrics in Nahum Tate's adaptation of *Richard II*, performed in 1680 at the Drury Lane Theatre, as well as setting songs for productions of plays by Dryden, Southerne, and Lee. Purcell's music also featured in Thomas Shadwell's 1678 version of *Timon of Athens* when it was revived at Drury Lane in 1695.[16] Certain Shakespeare plays, in particular *Macbeth* and *The Tempest*, proved popular choices to which to add songs and additional music for their late seventeenth-century performances.[17] From this kind of experiential vantage point, it was, perhaps, equally inevitable that Purcell would progress to more full-blown efforts to accommodate Shakespearean plays to musical drama and the operatic form. In strictly generic terms, his *Dido and Aeneas*, with a libretto by Nahum Tate, is his only full-blown, all sung opera, one which, incidentally, was first performed at a Chelsea all-girls boarding school run by the

Theatre Royal in an interesting advancement on the Interregnum prac-tices in educational establishments described above (Price 1984: 225). But his Shakespearean works, not least *The Fairy Queen*, must be seen as crucial to a history of opera, particularly one concerned primarily with Shakespearean afterlives.

The Fairy Queen is, frustratingly, an example in which the adaptor of the text remains unidentified, although both Dryden and Settle have been advanced as possible contenders. It is interesting to consider what might have drawn Purcell to *A Midsummer Night's Dream* as a source. Unlike today, its performance history in the Restoration period was an unsettled one – Pepys described being left unimpressed by a production in his diary entry of 29 September 1662 (quoted in Price 1984: 322) – but it is a play that in its early Stuart manifestations had possessed a strong musical content, including various fairy songs, Titania's lullaby at ii.ii, and the mechanicals' bergomask at court following their performance of 'Pyramus and Thisbe', and Purcell may well have been drawn to this aspect of its performance language and identity. If this was the case, though, it seems odd in light of that fact that most of Shakespeare's songs are expunged or abandoned in favour of new compositions. *The Fairy Queen* is a remarkable example of compression and concision in response to its Shakespearean source-text and attendant expansion on the operatic side. The mechan-icals' play comes not as a fifth-act comic climax to the proceedings, but is part of the woodland rehearsal scene in the opera's central movement. The entire opening scene in Duke Theseus's court is also cut, and char-acters including Egeus and Hippolyta sacrificed in the process. The death threat to Hermia, which hangs over the comedy in Shakespeare's play, is also excised. It is the fairy scenes of the *Dream* to which Purcell and his adaptor were drawn. The operatic aspects of the performance are all designed as entertainments and masques staged by the fairies for different onstage audiences, including Bottom, and in the final act by Oberon for Theseus and his entourage – thereby substituting for the mechanicals' play in structural terms and offering a far more magical and exoticized climax, and a resistance of comedy at the close.

Purcell's Oberon is undoubtedly the heart of his *Fairy Queen*, and it is this fact which has led many commentators to observe the spectral pres-ence of his early baroque experiment in English and Shakespearean opera in Benjamin Britten's own 1960 operatic adaptation of *A Midsummer Night's Dream*. Gary Schmidgall has observed that 'Purcell haunts Britten's fairy scenes', and this haunting can be attested to not only at the level of char-acterization but in the dramaturgy and musicology of this Britten–Peter

Pears collaboration (1990: 289). One of the most obvious structural analogues with Purcell's *Fairy Queen* is Britten's decision to start his opera in
the forest and omit almost entirely the first act of Shakespeare's play.
Unlike Purcell, he does not expunge the marriage of Theseus and
Hippolyta entirely, but he does compress the waiting time for their nup-
tials and relocate their references to it to his final act. As with Purcell,
Egeus and the death threat to Hermia are removed entirely, and the focus
is instead on the magical, sexualized space of the wood. Britten and Pears
of course performed and recorded their own individual version of *The
Fairy Queen* as a miniature baroque opera with the Shakespearean acted
sequences entirely omitted and in which they reversed the running order
of Purcell's 'entertainments', choosing to commence with Oberon's birthday entertainment, commonly referred to as the 'Masque of the four
seasons'.[18]

Like so many of the musical interpreters discussed in this study, Britten
and Pears were influenced by the current critical theories of their day. In
the decade that preceded the first staging of this opera as part of the intimate gathering of the Aldeburgh Festival (this is a chamber opera in the
true sense of the term when compared with the grand La Scala spectacles
of Verdi), the dominant readings of Shakespearean comedy were those
that identified festive structures and referents within the plays. This was
critical theory as influenced by the emergent discipline of anthropology
in the early part of the twentieth century and the attendant studies of
social structures and mythologies. The work of C. L. Barber, in particular
his seminal work *Shakespeare's Festive Comedy* (1959), which includes a
chapter on *A Midsummer Night's Dream*, was influential in this regard.
Barber associates *Dream* not only with midsummer fertility rites but also
with the sexual games of Mayday celebrations (1959: 119–62), and Britten
and Pears's opera, with its saturnalian forest focus and heightened sexuality, appears to respond to these contemporary critical framings of the play.
Philip Brett notes that:

> Until after the second World War it was common to refer to plays like *A
> Midsummer Night's Dream* as Shakespeare's 'romantic' or 'lyrical' come-
> dies. Productions emphasised the magical qualities of the play, its fairy
> enchantment and illusion and its romance.[19]

He goes on to observe that even the stage design for the first Aldeburgh
performances of the Britten opera seemed stuck in that performative
convention, describing the effect as tantamount to 'camouflage'. In practice, however, Britten's hard-edged version of the forest was far more

indebted to those 1950s Structuralist critics who sought to challenge that version of the Shakespeare comedies and to redefine them as 'saturnalian' rather than romantic.[20]

Similarly in their creation and realization of Oberon, baroque, seventeenth-century, Purcellian, and absolutely contemporary influences on the Britten–Pears partnership can be registered in a potent mix. One of the most overt acknowledgements of operatic traditions in the English baroque style is in their decision to accord the part of Oberon to a counter-tenor voice. Purcell was part of a seventeenth-century tradition that made regular use of the potential of the counter-tenor voice and range. As well as being influenced by English court practice – in 1633 the singers of the Chapel Royal featured six counter-tenors, including the aforementioned Henry Lawes – Purcell was interested, as were contemporaries such as Matthew Locke and Nicholas Lanier, in Italian and French developments in this area (Giles 1994: 44, 50).[21] There is even some critical speculation as to whether Purcell was himself a counter-tenor. Whatever the truth of those claims or hypotheses, his work created remarkable space for the counter-tenor voice. By the time of Verdi's experimentations with the baritone, however, the counter-tenor voice had long fallen out of favour and largely out of use in mainstream conventional opera. The revival was not to begin until the mid-twentieth century, not least through the pioneering work of Sir Michael Tippett and Britten himself. Both composers worked with one singer in particular, Alfred Deller, for whom the part of Oberon in the Britten–Pears *Dream* was specifically composed. As Brett rightly notes:

> The casting of Oberon as a countertenor sent Britten back for his models to his beloved Purcell. In Oberon's first set piece 'I know a bank', we hear echoes of the fantastically elaborate style of Purcell's 'Sweeter than roses' which Britten had once arranged for Pears to sing.[22]

But there are equally important theatrical precedents for this interpretation which deserve acknowledgement alongside the Purcellian lines of influence. The nineteenth-century stage tradition had actually been for female actors to play the role of Oberon, one of the most famous being the previously mentioned actor-singer-manager Elizabeth Lucia Vestris in her 1840 production of the *Dream*. As a result of this standardized practice, a certain kind of androgyny, or even ambivalent sexuality, became readily associated with the role. As Williams notes: 'A woman fairy king would have addressed the patriarchal Victorian culture in complex, fascinating ways' (1997: 93). The practice of feminizing or ambiguizing the role persisted into the twentieth century when Julia Neilson played the role for Herbert Beerbohm-Tree in 1900, and even when not cast as female, the part of Oberon appears to have retained its liminal potential: 'Androgyny marks the major Oberons from the 1930s from Gielgud through Helpmann to the countertenors for whom Benjamin Britten wrote the role . . . in his 1960 opera' (Williams 1997: 188–9). It is this sexual ambiguity in the role that Angela Carter so brilliantly responds to in her own Shakespearean-soaked late novel about the theatre, *Wise Children*, where the masculine authority of the actor Melchior Hazard is explicitly challenged by his decision to play the role of Oberon in a film version of *A Midsummer Night's Dream* (itself a thinly veiled version of the 1935 Reinhardt–Dieterle epic discussed in chapters 2 and 3) (Carter 1992: 124–37). Britten and Pears were well aware of this potentially radical and certainly oppositional stage history of the role of Oberon when they created him as a counter-tenor. Several critics have remarked on the complex relationship that exists between Oberon and his fairy assistant Puck in their opera, and how equivalent power games and sexual dynamics are also played out elsewhere in Britten's oeuvre, not least in operas, both earlier and later, such as *Billy Budd* (1950–1) and *Death in Venice* (1973), themselves adaptations of canonical texts by Herman Melville and Thomas Mann respectively.

As well as being inherently drawn to adaptation in his work, Britten was alert to the theatrical and indeed cinematic inheritances of the source-texts to which he turned. In *A Midsummer Night's Dream* this can be seen most clearly in the recitative role created for a young actor playing Puck. The declamatory, frequently parodic delivery of the performer is deliberately reminiscent of child-actor Mickey Rooney's recitative delivery and aesthetic in the same 1935 Hollywood spectacular motion picture version of the play directed by Reinhardt and Dieterle to which Carter's *Wise Children* alludes. This film was itself intertextual in its relationship with previous theatrical, balletic, and musical versions of the *Dream*, heavily reliant as it was on Mendelssohn's 1827 Overture for its score. Britten's use of the symbolic quality of child performers in his work is well catalogued by other critics, and is particularly to the fore in his deployment of the chorus in *Dream*. This was no grand choric style in the wake of Verdi, but he used local schoolchildren to provide children's voices. For Britten this deliberate defamiliarization of operatic choric practice served to point up both the strangeness and the potential innocence of the fairy world of his opera, though also its potential sexualization; as did his orchestration, which bears the direct hallmarks of the influence of Eastern musical traditions and instrumentation in his work, in particular the use of Balinese instruments, including the gamelan, and the equation of those sounds with ideas of the supernatural, strangeness, the dissonant, exotic, and 'other'.[23] Notions of dissonance and the dangerous side of exoticization in turn reflect back onto Britten's use of children in his operatic *Dream*.[24]

It is not only in the interpretation of Puck and the attribution of the childrens' chorus that Britten's skill with parody can be seen in this opera. The mechanicals' performance of 'Pyramus and Thisbe', which is in Shakespeare's playtext a witty parody of outmoded theatrical styles as well as of Arthur Golding's overwrought English translation of Ovid's *Metamorphoses*, becomes in Britten's dextrous hands an opportunity to send up a version of Italianate opera from which his own radical and experimental practices could not be further removed (M. Cooke 1999b: 143). As in Shakespeare's *Dream*, the brilliant trick of this meta-theatrical, or meta-operatic, moment is that it serves to highlight the technical and artistic achievements of what precedes it. Parody as a tonal register in the Britten–Pears *Dream* might have been even more to the fore had they retained the overt allusion and deconstruction of the familiar bars of Felix Mendelssohn's 'Wedding March' that appear in an earlier preliminary sketch of the score (M. Cooke 1999b: 138), but in the end there obviously seemed no need for such an overt recognition of the fact that this was opera that looked decisively to a pre-Mendelssohn moment. Britten's and Pears's *Dream* looks to the origins of opera in England. Puck's recitative delivery and Oberon's ambivalent, haunting aural counter-tenor voice related directly to those first halting experimentations in semi-opera and musical drama in the mid-seventeenth century, and to the considerable achievements of Henry Purcell in the form that emerged from them.

Notes

1 Schmidgall suggests that in *Macbeth* we see a Verdi 'still tangled in the traditional influences of old conventions' (1977: 181).

2 The recurring use of processions across the stage in this opera also deserves discussion. In addition to the movement of Duncan's retinue in I.ii, there is that of the eight kings, including Banquo (who tellingly featured in Duncan's retinue, and therefore serves as a visual reminder to the audience of this earlier kingly or ceremonial procession), in the Act III apparitions, and finally the procession that marks the coming demise of Macbeth himself in IV.iii, when Malcolm's troop of English soldiers pass over the stage, attired for the purposes of camouflage in the leaves and verdure of Birnam Wood, further instances, undoubtedly, of Verdi's rewriting of Shakespeare in the context of operatic dramaturgy and possibility.

3 Ironically, *Macbeth* as a performed play was little known in Italy when Verdi wrote his opera. Busch notes that 'In the early nineteenth century Shakespeare was so little

known in Italy that Verdi's *Macbeth*, which was premiered in Florence in 1874, preceded the 1st Italian performance of Shakespeare's play by several years' (1998: i.p.xxxix). Again we witness the genuine possibility of reverse flows of interpretation, from Verdi's opera to the Shakespeare playtext. Certainly we will see this to be the case in the Goethe-influenced versions of Iago that predominated in Europe in the Romantic period and much of the nineteenth century.

4   The translation is by Peggie Cochrane, and taken from the booklet to Verdi and Piave (1976).

5   An intriguing footnote to this is provided by the fact that the 'Pomp and Circumstance' phrase that Edward Elgar borrowed for his marches also derived from the playscript of Shakespeare's *Othello*.

6   For a brilliant recent analysis of this auditory context and environment for the plays' receptions, see B. R. Smith 1999. A bridging link between early modern dramatic soliloquy and the operatic aria may be found in the 'ayre' which became popular on Jacobean and Caroline stages, in particular in plays by Richard Brome and James Shirley which were song-heavy in their design. Such plays became popular in late seventeenth- and early eighteenth-century adaptations which added their own songs and music and contributed to the process of musical adaptations and additions to Shakespeare from which opera in its nineteenth-century manifestations clearly derives. On the use of the 'ayre' in Caroline drama, see Ingram 1958.

7   James A. Hepokoski, 'Otello as *Dramma Lirico*', in the CD liner notes to Verdi and Boito (1994). See also his extended discussion of this topic in his Cambridge Opera Handbook on the opera (1987: 165–87). Hepokoski also makes a thrilling case for the influence of specific actors' interpretations of the role of Othello himself on the Verdi–Boito opera. Theirs is, he argues, a blend of the extreme passion and problematic 'primitivism' of Ernesto Rossi's mid-nineteenth-century interpretations of the role and the more idealized version of the Moor promulgated in the productions of Tommaso Salvini (1987: see esp. 167–9).

8   Boito to Verdi, Milan, 24 Aug. 1881; in Busch 1998: i.112.

9   The end of the 'Credo' also reworks lines from Macbeth's 'Life is but a walking shadow' soliloquy, a passage which is clearly marked up in Boito's personal copy of the Hugo translation of the play (Busch 1998: i.163 n. 1).

10 Boito to Verdi, Quinto, 10 May 1886; in Busch 1998: i.216.

11 Verdi to Boito, Genoa, 11 Mar. 1889; in Busch 1998: i.368.

12 Again Hepokoski is suggestive on this subject, noting that the 'groundwork for the Romantic *ottocento* conceptions of her character was again laid by Schlegel. Saintly images abound' (1987: 178).

13 See Boito to Verdi, Milan, Monday, 18 Oct. 1880; in Busch 1998: i.25.

14 On Verdi's fondness for the practice of 'groundswells', see Kerman and Grey 1989.

15 On Tate's controversial adaptation of *Richard II*, which was banned after just two performances, see Shewring 1996: 30–6.

16 Purcell set the masque of Cupid and Bacchus for this production, itself an interesting substitute for the play's 'Masque of Amazons' which was retained but moved to earlier in the play; see Adams 1995: 339. Interestingly, this production also included an interpolated subplot featuring Timon's rival mistresses, Melissa and Evanda, a further indication of Restoration interest in increasing female presence on its stages (Price 1984: 90).

17 See Kliman on the popularity of musical additions to productions of *Macbeth*, not only in Dryden's operatically enhanced version in the Restoration, but throughout the eighteenth and nineteenth centuries (1995: esp. 18–19, 24).

18 Both Pears and counter-tenor James Bowman, who had appeared in Aldeburgh productions of *A Midsummer Night's Dream*, took part in this production.

19 Philip Brett makes this claim in his thought-provoking CD liner notes to Britten and Pears 1990 [1960].

20 Ibid.

21 European exponents of the baroque counter-tenor tradition would include the Italian Alessandro Stradella and the French composer Jean-Baptiste Lully.

22 Ibid. 9.

23 M. Cooke 1999c: 173, 176. On notions of the exotic with particular reference to Britten, see also M. Cooke 1998a; Brett 1994 and 1993.

24 Recent biographies of Britten have suggested that children are far from innocent agents in Britten's operas, such as his Henry James adaptation *The Turn of the Screw* (1954); see Carpenter 2003 and Bridcut 2006. In a further variation on this theme and Britten's self-conscious intertextuality in his work, the tenor Ian Bostridge, in his CD liner notes to Britten 2005, which includes his recording of Britten's 'Nocturne', which ends with a setting of Shakespeare's Sonnet 43 ('When most I wink, then do mine eyes best see'), observes that Britten consciously evokes Pyotr Tchaikovsky's *Pathétique* Symphony in this setting, and in doing so draws analogies between his own sexual attraction to young men and Tchaikovsky's (the *Pathétique* was dedicated to his nephew with whom he had been infatuated since he was a child). See also Wells 2002: 397 on the 'Nocturne'.

Further examples and reading

On Shakespearean adaptation in general on the late seventeenth-century stage and on the development of semi-opera in England at that time, see Sandra Clark, 'Shakespeare and Other Adaptations' and Todd S. Gilman, 'London Theatre Music, 1660–1719', in *A Companion to Restoration Drama*, ed. Susan J. Owen (Oxford: Blackwell, 2001), pp. 274–90 and 243–73 respectively. On Henry Purcell's specific interactions with that genre, see Curtis Price, *Henry Purcell and the London Stage* (Cambridge: Cambridge University Press, 1984). While for obvious reasons this study has concentrated on the Purcell work with a specifically Shakespearean connection, his operatic forays into the literary canon more generally are significant. Both *Dido and Aeneas* and the John Dryden–Purcell collaboration *King Arthur* are valuable examples of his work in this respect. Semi-opera and early modern manifestations of musical theatre are enjoying something of a revival in terms of twenty-first-century performance, and interested readers will find much of note in contemporary reviews of opera and related performances in newspapers. My own work is indebted to Anthony Holden's scholarly and combative articles in *The Observer*.

Verdi and Wagner dominated nineteenth-century operatic tradition in terms of both practice and theory. For insightful comparisons of their styles and agendas, see Carolyn Abbate and Roger Parker (eds), *Analyzing Opera: Verdi and Wagner* (Berkeley: University of California Press, 1989). On the specific issue of the *leitmotif*, much critical ink has been spilt; a useful overview of the issues can be found in Joseph Kerman's *Opera as Drama*, 2nd edn (London: Faber, 1989). Those readers interested in the specific literary influence of the Wagnerian *leitmotif* will find Timothy Martin's detailed analysis in *Joyce and Wagner: A Study of Influence* (Cambridge: Cambridge University Press, 1991) very useful indeed. As recommended in the preceding chapter, for a detailed study of the Verdi–Boito *Otello*, the obvious starting point is James A. Hepokoski's erudite and engaging study in the Cambridge Opera Handbook series, *Giuseppe Verdi: 'Otello'* (Cambridge: Cambridge University Press, 1987).

On Benjamin Britten, an excellent starting point is *The Cambridge Companion to Benjamin Britten*, ed. Mervyn Cooke (Cambridge: Cambridge University Press, 1999a). Especially useful in this context is the chapter by the editor himself on 'Britten and Shakespeare: *A Midsummer Night's Dream*' (pp. 129–46), which includes detailed discussion of the textual adaptation of Shakespeare's play undertaken by Britten and Pears for their production. Cooke was able to look at Pears's marked-up copy of the Penguin edition of the play which is housed in the Britten–Pears Library at Aldeburgh, Suffolk; for the portal to this and related resources, see <http://www.brittenpears.org>. See also William H. Godsalve's *Britten's 'A Midsummer Night's Dream': Making an Opera from Shakespeare's Comedy* (London and Toronto: Associated Universities Press, 1995).

7

Symphonic Film Scores

Mark how one string, sweet husband to another,
Strikes each in each by mutual ordering
                                                    Sonnet 8

One of the most vibrant arenas in which the encounter between Shakespeare and music is currently being staged is undoubtedly film, and in
particular the creation and composition of film scores. As Hans Eisler and
Theodor Adorno predicted as early as 1947, the musical element in soundtracks has become a crucial commodity in the film industry's marketing
of any movie, in particular in the youth and teenage market where, as we
shall see in the following chapter on contemporary and hybrid film scores,
the 'hip soundtrack' is often a central means of marketing a film as well
as encouraging a lucrative sales afterlife in the form of accompanying
merchandise, not least CDs and MP3 downloads.[1]

This intense and productive relationship between Shakespeare, music,
and film has, however, been there from the very start of motion picture
history, from the inception of this new technological genre in the form
of silent movies to the equally novel interpretative and creative possibilities that the transition to 'talkies' opened up. As one of the most influential scholars of film music, Claudia Gorbman, has noted: 'Music signifies
in films not only according to pure musical codes, but also according
to cultural musical codes and cinematic musical codes' (1987: 2–3).[2]
This chapter will consider some of these cinematic and cultural significations in relation to particular films and their scores, focusing on the
work of William Walton, Dmitri Shostakovich, and Patrick Doyle,
among others.

These scores fall, as the title of this chapter suggests, into the category
of 'symphonic' music. As Kathryn Kalinak notes, the investment of
Hollywood filmmakers in the commissioning of symphonic and orchestral music to score their films was a direct inheritance from nineteenth-
century theatre, in which, as we have seen, music was a vital component

in any production: 'The classical Hollywood film score relied largely on the resources of the standard symphony orchestra with unusual instruments added for particular effects' (1992: 13). As that quotation from Kalinak makes clear, 'classical' in a Hollywood film context has a particular and precise reference to a specific era and style of filmmaking, and that is why, although in some circles, as we saw in chapter 2 on 'Classical Shakespeares', the term 'classical' might be used as an easy designation for orchestral, symphonic, and, indeed, choral music of this kind, in the context of film theory and cinematic analyses the term is in danger of being misleading. In this chapter, therefore, film scores that rely on conventional symphonic and orchestral structures for their effects will be designated simply by the label 'symphonic'. Walton, Shostakovich, and Doyle, while not all writing music in the 'classical' era of Hollywood studio theatre, were producing these kinds of symphonic film scores for their commissioning directors, and hence the connections and comparisons I wish to draw between them in this chapter.

As well as exploring the specific semiotics of musical composition in particular films, the example of Doyle's work for Kenneth Branagh will provide a means to examine the conscious intertextuality of much of this film music, the allusion to and awareness of other film scores in its compositional style and effects, not least in Doyle's case Walton's epic scores for Laurence Olivier's screen Shakespeares or Nino Rota's theme-driven musical accompaniment to several of Franco Zeffirelli's Shakespeare films. This intertextuality invariably extends beyond reference to other film music and draws into its frame the influence of other media and generic practices in relation to music and performance, in particular opera.[3] Defining elements in film soundtracks prove to be the sub-Wagnerian principle of *leitmotif*, already discussed in the context of opera (see chapters 5 and 6), and theatre itself, especially in its nineteenth-century manifestations.[4]

One particularly influential strand of nineteenth-century theatre in this regard is melodrama, with its precise codes and conventions. Gorbman has argued persuasively that 'the classical Hollywood film *is* melodrama – a drama with music' – and suggests that a film soundtrack's function as an identifier of location, period, character, and even emotion, can be linked directly to the practices of theatrical melodrama:

> Melodrama called for music to mark the entrances of characters, to provide interludes, and to give emotional colouring to dramatic climaxes, and to scenes with rapid, physical action. Musical cues appear abundantly in 'acting editions' of British melodrama. From them we can

see that the clichés of film music arose directly from those of melodrama. (1987: 34)[5]

The first silent motion pictures were clearly the transitional space and medium in which this relationship between theatre melodrama and its dramaturgy of 'hyperbole, excess, excitement, and "acting out"' (Brooks 1995: p. viii) and the new technology of film was bridged. In many silent films music is a key signifier of mood and the required thought associations needed to identify the 'villain' or moment of high tension (the stereotypical damsel in distress tied to the railway tracks by the moustache-twirling 'baddie') or comic slapstick. In the work of Buster Keaton and Charlie Chaplin and the considerable body of silent films that adapted Shakespearean material, music was a key component in the production of meaning; it participated in what Jeff Smith has memorably termed the 'mutually implicative structure of music and image' (1998: 156). The importance of music to the experience of film, not least silent film, is indicated by the common practice of early cinema houses of employing live pianists to play along with screenings. Gorbman suggests that this was a practice directly tied to nineteenth-century theatre and its emphasis on spectacle and sound as opposed to dialogue (1987: 34).[6]

In previous chapters, I have indicated the considerable influence of ballet, opera, and classical symphonies on nineteenth-century theatrical stagings of Shakespeare's plays, and nowhere is this more evident than in the stage history of *A Midsummer Night's Dream*. Productions of that play established the accompanying Incidental Music of Felix Mendelssohn, as well as interpolated balletic sequences, as required elements in any performance, as important in terms of audience expectations as – if not more than – Shakespeare's seventeenth-century dialogue. The full effects of this hybridization of influence can be registered in one of the earliest sound-supported Shakespeare films, Max Reinhardt and William Dieterle's 1935 *A Midsummer Night's Dream*. This film has already been explored in terms of its use of dance (see chapter 3). Reinhardt was an established theatre director in his German homeland when he was forced into exile in the United States by the rise of fascism in Europe in the 1930s. It was perhaps inevitable that once resident in the USA he would venture into the new technological playground of motion pictures. His film *Dream* is heavily influenced by a Hollywood Bowl theatre production of the play that he had directed in 1934; the film includes several of the stars of that production (Williams 1997: 177).[7] Although the casting of James Cagney as a working-class Bottom and child star Mickey Rooney as a Huckleberry Finn-like Puck is intriguing, my main subject here is the musical and choreographic choices that Reinhardt and Dieterle made for their film spectacular. Recorded at the height of the US Depression, the film has often been read in terms of expensive escapism, with its emphasis on fantasy and its extravagant *mise-en-scène* involving real redwood trees being uprooted and the importation of a frightening tonnage of topsoil into the Hollywood studio to re-create the Athenian woods of the play.[8] Despite being a direct contemporary of Bertolt Brecht, none of the influences of that playwright and screenwriter's 'Epic Theatre manifesto' or its desire to make the mechanics of production visible are evident in Reinhardt and Dieterle's escapist and consciously romanticized aesthetic.[9] In practice, though, the fairy ballet sequences and the goblin orchestra of the film offer a rather dark and unsettling version of fantasy, one more akin to Northern European traditions of fairy-tale than the gauzy-winged flower fairies of the Victorian stage. Nevertheless, Reinhardt and Dieterle were steeped in the tradition of nineteenth-century pictorialized and musically enhanced versions of *A Midsummer Night's Dream* and their extensive use of Mendelssohn for the soundtrack was part of this consciousness.

While nineteenth-century theatre history, and its links with ballet in particular, is one crucial key to the influences and allusive register of early Shakespearean film scores, so, too, is nineteenth-century opera, not least in its Wagnerian manifestations:

> Based on the Wagnerian principles of motifs and *leitmotifs*, a theme in a film becomes associated with a character, a place, a situation, or an emotion. It may have a fixed or static designation, or it can evolve and contribute to the dynamic flow of the narrative by carrying its meaning into a new realm of signification. (Gorbman 1987: 3)

According to Gorbman, classical scoring of films was in the Hollywood tradition directly allied to ideas of 'pseudo-Wagnerian orchestration', to the extent that certain kinds of music became shorthand signifiers of what was appearing onscreen: drumbeats to signify Native American tribal practices, for example, in the Hollywood western. In subsequent appearances or rephrasings those musical signifiers also served as a reminder of earlier associations, functioning therefore in a manner directly akin to Wagner's use of the *leitmotif* and deployment of repetition in large-scale operas as 'motifs of reminiscence' (Gorbman 1987: 7, 28). In the western genre, for example, drumbeats of the kind mentioned could signify the approach of Native American characters without ever showing them onscreen.

How much the practice as adopted within the film industry truly resembles or adheres to Wagnerian practice is a highly contested point. Nevertheless, the idea of the *leitmotif* system as an aid to understanding and rapid interpretation in the experience of film-going is clearly at the core of the work of one of the most prominent (though also controversial) recent composers for Shakespeare on film, Patrick Doyle. Doyle's work for actor and director Kenneth Branagh on films ranging from *Henry V* (1989), *Much Ado About Nothing* (1993), *Hamlet* (1996), and *Love's Labour's Lost* (1999; Doyle provided incidental music for this film and selected the main part of the score from pre-existent show-tunes dating from the 1930s–50s – discussed in detail in chapter 4), to the forthcoming Japanese-located *As You Like It*, has attracted its fair share of fans and detractors. James Loehlin has suggested that, despite Branagh's quest for accessible, 'popular' Shakespeare, Doyle's score for *Henry V* ends up contradicting Branagh's onscreen performance at several points in the action, particularly in the post-battle sequences (1996: 144). Even Kenneth Rothwell, not an unsupportive commentator on Branagh's cinematic techniques, notes the disastrous consequences for the 'How all occasions do inform me' soliloquy in *Hamlet* (Q2 Additional Passages, iv.iv.23–57), where Branagh is to be found 'shrieking at the top of his lungs to drown out Patrick Doyle's theme music' (1999: 258). Doyle's music, it should be stressed, is just one component in the overblown interpretation of that particular scene – a military-coat clad Branagh is viewed amid snow-capped mountain tops delivering his speech, and the camera self-consciously pans out further and further to emphasize both epic landscape and subject matter; just as, indeed, the soaring orchestration on the soundtrack swells ever louder and louder, forcing Branagh into an ever-increasing declamatory mode. It should be noted that when this four-hour-plus-long film initially played in cinemas in the UK, a refreshments interval was taken at this point; Branagh presumably wanted the theatrical equivalent of a pre-interval climactic moment, or, forgive the pun, peak, but the truly melodramatic outcome has become a working example of how not to (over)do it.

The emotive manipulations and tendencies to excess which many critics of this film *Hamlet* see in its overall aesthetic are to an extent grounded in Doyle's score. These manipulative aspects are in part a product of Doyle's commitment to a particularly rigid brand of sub-Wagnerian *leitmotif* and of coded significations in his music. Doyle deploys *leitmotif* as a method of character association in the film. 'Ophelia's theme', for example, is deployed in a hybrid fashion, both as a non- or even meta-diegetic signifier to the audience, but also at one point during her very public breakdown before the Danish court as the tune to one of her popular songs of unrequited love, death, and bawdy. These motifs for particular characters, especially Hamlet and Ophelia, link Branagh's film and Doyle's score to other films in the epic genre, in particular the work of David Lean and his widescreen masterpieces such as *Lawrence of Arabia* and *Doctor Zhivago*. Branagh's decision to film in 70 mm widescreen, with all its cinematic connotations of epic scale and grandeur, as well as its specific technological effects on colour and depth of perception, is part of that allusive context to Lean's work and to film epic in general (Sanders 2000: 160). *Doctor Zhivago* (1965) is itself a film adaptation of a Boris Pasternak novel that was inspired by Shakespeare, so the layers of reference are multiple.[10] The allusive framework of Branagh's *Hamlet* also takes place at the level of the soundtrack, since the score to *Doctor Zhivago*, composed by Maurice Jarre, deployed a musical refrain to identify its female protagonist at both onscreen and offscreen moments.[11] In his use of aural refrain in this way in *Doctor Zhivago*, Lean was responding to pre-existent traditions in Russian cinema, with which his Pasternak-authored film clearly aligned itself. In the Soviet context film score composers such as Sergei Prokofiev, Aram Khachaturian, and Dmitri Shostakovich deployed their music as dramaturgic punctuation and as psychological and emotional reminders in the narrative of certain characters and events.

Another important set of influences on Doyle was surely the Shakespearean collaborations of Franco Zeffirelli and Nino Rota, especially the constant refrain of 'What is a Youth?' in the 1968 *Romeo and Juliet* and the deployment of 'Bianca's theme', the ballad 'Let me tell, gentle maiden, let me tell', in the 1967 *The Taming of the Shrew*. Rothwell observes the variations in meaning that this particular ballad accrues as it is used and reused, cited and quoted, throughout the film score at salient moments in the dramaturgy: 'Rota's "Bianca's theme" that so eloquently celebrates the outward beauty of Bianca, as if she were Petrarch's Laura, . . . re-emerges when Kate "surrenders" to Petruc[c]io, the music supports Shakespeare's "chiasmus" motif in which Bianca and Kate gradually exchange roles' (1999: 131). 'Bianca's theme' is first heard as part of the carnivalesque procession that opens Zeffirelli's film, as is a first, faster version of what will ultimately become Petruccio's recurring theme 'What is a Life?'. 'What is a Youth?', sung onscreen as part of the diegesis – that is to say, as part of the internal world of its film – at the Capulet ball, recurs throughout the non-diegetic, overlaid soundtrack (sounds which cannot be heard within the world of the film), initially identifying Romeo as he walks the streets sniffing at blossom like a true 1968 flower-child, but later serving as a reminder of the first encounter between Romeo and Juliet, and thereby underlining the tragic trajectory that is established for them from the start. Tellingly, the refrain also plays, albeit at a far slower tempo, during the dying moments of Tybalt and Mercutio. The lyric of the song sings literally of the ephemerality of youth, love, and life, just as Shakespeare's dialogue insistently reminds us that these 'star-crossed lovers' and their hot-headed peer group cannot endure long in an earthly or secular context.

Branagh, like Zeffirelli, had the express intention of popularizing Shakespeare through the medium of film, and the manner in which he uses that medium in *Hamlet* – in particular his fondness for explanatory flashback – is part of an overall drive to explain, plug gaps, and carry the audience with him. In his commissioned scores, however, there is a question as to what extent 'carrying with' ultimately equates to instructing audiences how to think and feel. Certainly a similar tendency to deploy music as an underscoring, explanatory, supposedly accessible device, particularly on big set-piece iconic speeches, can be found in Doyle's earlier work for Branagh's first venture into filmed Shakespeare, *Henry V.* Throughout this film the audience is highly conscious of the epic orchestration that underlines, and sometimes in terms of volume overlays, the events and exchanges being witnessed. The score for the film was performed by the City of Birmingham Symphony Orchestra and conducted by Simon Rattle, who had at this time a *wunderkind* reputation in classical music that was akin to Branagh's in the classical theatre. There can be little doubt that this score was expected to be a high-profile aspect of Branagh's *Henry V*, and the decision to allow it center-stage at several of the most iconic moments is a product of this understanding of the film as well as being in many respects one of its most obvious flaws. The St Crispin's Day speech at iv.iii.20–67 is a particularly telling example of the fact that music is to some extent an extra character or interpretative frame in this film, often more present than Derek Jacobi's frame-breaking, meta-cinematic Chorus, which is seen at the start standing on an unoperational film set before the doors open on to the medieval *mise-en-scène* of Branagh's performance.

Music plays throughout Branagh's emotional delivery of the St Crispin's Day speech; its volume is modulated, rising exponentially with romantic, soaring strings at several points, and dropping down for emphasis on the lines where Henry addresses his men in a more personal, less stirring vein

– 'We few, we happy few, we band of brothers' (iv.iii.60). Ultimately it soars to a voluble climax in conjunction with the speech, and the crowd erupts into cheers. It is this idea of dialogue and music working in tandem that seems to define most of the Branagh–Doyle collaborations, but it is also in practice what can make Doyle's self-conscious orchestrations and refrains seem far too intrusive, detracting from, even at times drowning out, the speeches in favour of the easy emotional signifier.

Henry V is a complex play in terms of its signifying politics, and Branagh's film has been read by critics such as James Loehlin as oddly contradictory in its wish to represent the horrors of war and yet to protect the film's protagonist-hero from blame or implication, even in its most horrific and personally sponsored acts of violence such as summary executions.[12] Branagh's battlefield is at times an unrelenting image of mud and blood that does much to suggest other historical battlefields to contemporary audiences familiar with the images of Paschendaele, Vietnam, and at the time of the film's release in the UK the very recent memory of the Falklands War. He also famously restored those scenes depicting the less-than-heroic actions of Henry which Laurence Olivier had seen fit to cut in his 1944 patriotic wartime version of the play; yet the romantic effects of the music are a crucial indication that Branagh's directorial decisions often undercut that anti-romantic, anti-war tendency in his script and his *mise-en-scène*.

This can be seen (and heard) in what has become the film's most recalled moment, the so-called 'Non Nobis' sequence, in which, in a lengthy four-minute, 500-foot tracking sequence, a bloodied and downbeat but crucially undefeated Henry carries one of the war dead off the battlefield (see Loehlin 1996: 143). The tracking device allows for a remarkable panorama of the consequences of conflict; Henry passes by angry, mourning French widows, scavengers raiding the corpses of the war-dead, and horrifically injured and maimed individuals. The genuine weight of the body he carries means that he slips and stumbles regularly in the mud, appearing therefore as a vulnerable human being, very different from the shining armour-clad version offered by Olivier at this same point in the proceedings. Yet the decision to allow the solo version of 'Non Nobis' – begun at Henry's command on the battlefield, 'Let there be sung *Non nobis* and *Te Deum*' (iv.viii.123) and sung by Patrick Doyle himself in the role of Court – to swell out into a highly orchestrated and expansive many-part chorus undercuts these personalizing and humanizing moves. What we receive, therefore, in the transfer to the full chorus – which will also recur over the closing credits of the film, further stamping the iconic significance of this sequence on audience memory – is a movement from the personalized and vulnerable voice articulated within the diegetic frame of the battlefield to an overlaid score which, presumably, none of the characters onscreen can hear. The point at the beginning of the tracking shot was surely that Henry shared this touching delivery of the song with his fellow soldiers just as he has shared the battle with them; indeed, Loehlin makes the point that the delivery of the song by Court is significant, as 'it helps to resolve the rift between Henry and his men remaining from the night scene' (1996: 143). The recourse to the epic soundtrack rather than the diegetic mode of delivery undoes much of the interesting work achieved in the earlier part of the sequence, falling back on film soundtrack cliché and the big effect in ways similar to the soundtrack of the Branagh–Doyle collaboration on *Hamlet*. That this was a decision actively taken by Branagh and Doyle for the cinematic context can be witnessed by a comparison with the stage production from which Branagh took his inspiration for the film, and in which he also took the lead role, though this time directed by Adrian Noble for the Royal Shakespeare Company in 1984. When in the production Henry called for the 'Non Nobis', it was delivered onstage by the company of actors in the form of plainchant (Loehlin 1996: 97). Branagh appears then to have taken an active (and to a certain extent counteractive) decision to hype up the musical impact of the 'Non Nobis' sequence on film, in much the same way as cinematic versions of *Henry V* feel compelled to piece out the 'imperfections' of stage performances, which cannot, as the Chorus makes entirely clear from the start, re-create in any realistic way the battlefields of Agincourt.

Doyle's tendency towards epic orchestration and manipulative cadences is often compared to the work of William Walton for Laurence Olivier's screen Shakespeares. It is perhaps inevitable that since Branagh's entire career, in particular his film career, has actively invited comparison with his predecessor actor-director (the choice to make many of the same films, *Henry V*, *Hamlet*, and now also *As You Like It* makes the link explicit and cannot, surely, be explained away by happenstance), his decision to work with a single composer in each instance has led to comparisons between Doyle and Olivier's chosen collaborator, Walton, who wrote scores for all four of Olivier's screen Shakespeares (three of which Olivier also directed).[13] Some scholars have been quick to remind us that Doyle, unlike Walton, did not have an established career as a composer prior to the Branagh commissions (indeed, much of his experience in writing film scores has emerged subsequent to the *Henry V* commission); but it is not on these exclusivist terms that the comparisons are best conducted. Instead, it is telling to test what has perhaps become too easy an elision between Walton's epic orchestrations for Olivier's filmed Shakespeares and Doyle's scores by comparing and contrasting the interpretation of specific sequences and speeches. Despite the almost stereotypical association of Walton's scores with the kind of epic, underlying orchestration I have been describing in Doyle's work, the St Crispin's Day speech in Olivier's version is in fact delivered entirely without musical addition or supplementation. Only once the speech is delivered and we see preparations for battle does Walton's score strike up its strings once more.[14]

Elsewhere the film achieves what is actually a strikingly avant-garde blurring of diegetic and non-diegetic music to complement Olivier's ambitious movements between consciously theatricalized performance in the Elizabethan Globe Theatre and the quasi-naturalistic or realistic potential of the new medium of cinema. Just as Olivier plays with the audience's perception of the real and the performed – the first half-hour of the film is firmly set on the stage of the Globe with the varied interruptions and frame breakings of a boy carrying pre-Brechtian placards announcing the location of each scene, performers forgetting their lines, audience reactions and responses, and bad weather (English rain starts to fall quite heavily at the start of the Boar's Head scenes) – so Walton's music shades in and out of diegetic and non-diegetic modes.

The epic sweep of both music and camera accompanies a panoramic view of London at the start of the film. The opening credits depict a playbill blowing through the city streets – a device repeated at the close of the film in order to achieve a self-consciously theatrical frame. It is a device that has been alluded to recently in other Shakespeare-inspired films, including Tom Stoppard's version of his stage-play *Rosencrantz and Guildenstern Are Dead* (1991) and John Madden's *Shakespeare in Love* (1998). These images of London in Olivier's film, however, soon give way to the diegesis of a Globe Theatre performance with the gallery musicians providing trumpet flourishes and incidental music. This meta-theatrical mode is maintained until the transitional scenes at Southampton Harbour, when a newly 'realistic' Henry addresses the crowd. Prior to this we have seen a consciously theatrical delivery from Olivier, as he acknowledges audience reactions at the Globe, and is even seen coughing backstage as he prepares his voice for onstage delivery. Similarly, it is only from this point onwards that Walton's score moves into its more epic and non-diegetic orchestrations. Even so, just as the Southampton sequence retains a deliberately painted backdrop, Walton and Olivier seem keen to remind the film audience of the artificial and constructed nature of the production; it is really only the battle sequences where this tension is suppressed and the audience is encouraged to receive the experience directly and without the conscious frame breakings that elsewhere define the film's aesthetics.

In the Agincourt scores, the musical score achieves an impressive scale and sense of integration. The diegetic and non-diegetic interactions on the soundtrack are to do with the noise of battle, in particular the sound of the archers' arrows being released into the skies, and the overlaid 'martial' music. In the closing sections of the film, however, Olivier and Walton revert to their previous playfulness. The French court scenes are self-consciously aestheticized and pictorialized, with direct visual allusions to several plates from *Les très riches heures du Duc de Berry*. Walton adds to this framing and distancing effect by having audiences see the choir that sings within the French palace taking instruction from a slightly comic conductor at the bottom of the frame. Just as Olivier takes great joy in mischievously letting the camera draw back from his new French bride's face in close-up after the spectacular imagery and musical accompaniment of their joint wedding-coronation only for the alert audience member to realize that what they are now seeing from a distance is the heavily made-up face of a boy actor performing the part of Katherine in the Globe and that the applause of the French courtiers has seamlessly segued back into that of the Globe spectators, so Walton repeats his comic choir scene another time, thereby allowing the camera to pan up to show the choristers as part of the musical company of the Globe. The camera then pans even further up to show the Globe gallery musicians who started the whole thing off, eventually resting on an image of the theatre's flag being brought down to signal the end of the production. In terms of audience response to these repetitions with variation, the effect of memory is startling; the flag is a potent reminder of the battlefield scenes, and in this way, even in the midst of the most overtly meta-theatrical sequence in the film, the alternative possibilities of cinema are celebrated and advanced. Walton's score and Olivier's film seem to me a far more subtle response to the possibilities of filmed Shakespeare than they are often given credit for being nowadays, and in practice reveal less their similarities with the sub-Wagnerian accessible soundtracks of Patrick Doyle than their genre-aware experimental ventures and intentions.

As already noted, there is a strong critical history which links the use of music in classical film with the conventions of nineteenth-century theatre and indeed early cinema, and it is possible to argue for Doyle's tendency to melodrama as being simply heir to that tradition. It is an important question to pose, however, to what extent the reassertion of those melodramatic signifiers and musical conventions restricts or contains interpretation of Branagh's films? To what extent do his film Shakespeares fall back as a result on the simplistic moral binaries of classic melodrama – good, bad; hero, villain; romance, battle? The orchestration of battle sequences in filmed Shakespeares is an interesting and revealing case study, not least because these sequences are clearly interpolations made possible by the cinematic medium. In his *Henry V*, Branagh strives to confront his audiences with the realities of armed conflict. There are depictions of hand-to-hand fighting in the muddy trenches of Agincourt, which are both powerful and affecting. Initially it is telling that the acoustics for these scenes are entirely based on the diegetic sounds of battle, from clashing shields and armour, and cries of pain as throats are slit and people are stabbed, to, most strikingly, the awesome, dominating sound of the hailstorm of arrows being released by the English archers in frighteningly quick succession. This portion of the battle sequence is also in real time. As with the 'Non Nobis' section, however, Branagh seems unable to trust to his initial directorial instincts for the scene, feeling it necessary to cede not only to slow-motion imagery, which has an oddly distancing and romanticizing effect on the violence being depicted, but to accompanying classical orchestration on the soundtrack. This is yet another notable movement away from diegetic to non-diegetic sound that seems to undermine the 'realism' of what immediately precedes it. Branagh's style here is clearly informed by the work of several of his own predecessors in filmed Shakespeare; the mud and grim realism has much in common with Orson Welles's memorable filming of the Shrewsbury battle sequences for his *Henry IV* film *Chimes at Midnight* (1965), but the slow-motion stylized scenes accompanied by overlaid music are also an act of homage to the work of Japanese director Akira Kurosawa, not least his *King Lear*-inspired *Ran* (1985) and his samurai version of *Macbeth*, *Throne of Blood* (1957) (Loehlin 1996: 141). The mediating effect of other film Shakespeares on each new venture in the field can never be underestimated; Olivier was as conscious of Welles's work as Branagh was of each of them in turn. As well as considering the intertextual frame of reference with other media, then, we need to consider film's self-reflexive allusivity and the effects this might have on understanding and approach when composing scores.

Several critics have commented on aesthetic connections between Roman Polanski's blood-soaked 1971 *Macbeth* and Kurosawa's film adaptations of Shakespeare. Bernice Kliman observes that 'Like Kurosawa, Polanski uses landscape and space emblematically' (1995: 123), and she goes on to suggest that the aesthetic continuum is aural as much as visual: 'Like Kurosawa, too, Polanski uses landscape brilliantly, associating particular sounds with particular places and psychic states: some of the discords of the Third Ear Band sound similar to aural manoeuvres in the Japanese film' (1995: 124). The use of the Third Ear Band is revealing in terms of the film's overall interest in discord and dissonance and the unsettling of its audience from more familiar positions of response to Shakespearean tragedy; Polanski's violent imagery is also part of this conscious unsettling of the spectator's gaze.[15] This experimental, percussive and improvisatory group, founded in the late 1960s by drummer Glen Sweeney, acknowledged inspirations ranging from medieval chamber music to the rhythms of Indian *raga* that contribute further to the intercultural frame of reference already recognized in the comments above about Kurosawa's shaping influence. The discordant, often uncanny tones that accompany the weird sisters at the opening of the film resurface with the violent onscreen murder of Duncan to suggest a community in which a sense of ethics has become truly skewed. But discord is not the entire story of this soundtrack. The band featured Paul Minns on oboe, and the film makes beautiful use of the possibilities of woodwind and strings.[16] The oboe and lute that accompany Lady Macbeth's first appearance onscreen and the preparations of the castle in advance of Duncan's arrival lull audiences into a false position of comfort and festive expectation. It is only as the camera pans out to the hostile environment of the exterior landscape of the castle that the discordant tones return to remind us of Macbeth's bloody intentions towards his king in the wake of the weird sisters' prophecy.

Much rich critical work has been done on the Noh inflections of Akira Kurosawa's film Shakespeares (see, e.g., Massai 2005), but, despite these culture-specific inferences, Kurosawa, like Polanski, was far from averse to making hybrid intercultural references, especially in musical terms. Rothwell (1999: 193) notes his use of classical musical signifiers from the Western tradition, as well as Noh instrumentation and chordal sequences in *The Bad Sleep Well* (1960), his *Hamlet* appropriation. The wedding march in that film score derives, for example, from Wagner's *Lohengrin*, and music from Richard Strauss's *The Voices of Spring* can also be heard on that soundtrack. *Ran* is another intercultural *tour de force* blending Eastern and Western referents with consummate skill. The obvious comparison in Japanese theatre practice can be found in the intercultural stagings of

Shakespeare's plays by director Yukio Ninigawa, who blends Noh and Kabuki practices with those derived from a Western theatrical tradition. This often operates at the level of sound; as Kliman notes of Ninigawa's 1990 production of *Macbeth*:

> Myriad sounds enthralled us: emphatic Japanese speech rhythms, whether brusque or guttural, or whining and pathetic . . . Gongs, Buddhist chants, Western music, and natural sounds of thunder introduced, punctuated, and interpreted. The most startling moment – but one that accorded with the candles that filled the stage for Lady Macbeth's sleepwalking scene – was the *Piè Jesu* lovingly sung as Macbeth lay dead curled in a foetal pose. Startling juxtapositions of divergent theatrical styles shook the audience into attentiveness and awareness. (1995: 147)

All of these examples are brief but rich indications of the possibilities and potential for incidental theatre music and film soundtrack that the late twentieth-century interest in intercultural performance, a movement in which renowned Shakespearean directors Peter Brook and Ariane Mnouchkine were considered major forces, introduced into the realm of Shakespeare-associated music (see D. Kennedy 1993 and Pavis 1996: *passim*).

Undoubtedly our discussion has focused, perhaps inevitably in a book entitled *Shakespeare and Music*, on those films with overtly 'composed' scores. There is, however, an equally strong and important history to acknowledge of Shakespeare films that largely eschew non-diegetic material on their soundtrack: Brook's 1971 *King Lear* is one significant example. As Alexander Leggatt notes:

> Here, apart from the Fool's songs and some strange electronic noises in the storm, there is no music at all – not even for the waking of Lear, where the only symbol of healing and new life is the light on the King's face. In a medium that almost invariably uses music, its absence is striking and self-conscious. (1991: 97–8)

In a film made the same year as Brook's apocalyptic vision of Shakespearean tragedy, the diegetic soundscape of Polanski's *Macbeth* is as central to understanding the sonic framework of that film as the dissonant interventions of the Third Ear Band. *Macbeth*, after all, is a drama that constantly stresses the heard as a resonant signifier – knocking, owls screeching, bells tolling – as opposed to the unstable visions advanced elsewhere ('Is this a dagger which I see before me / The handle toward my hand?', II.i.33–4). More recently still, *The King is Alive* by Kristian Levring (2000), a quite remarkable film about a group of bus travellers stranded in the Namibian desert, who, in the face of their own physical and mental demise, try to perform a version of *King Lear* as remembered by one of their party, is a work that adheres to the so-called Dogme 95 principles. These 'rules' were formulated by a collective of film directors in Copenhagen in 1995, and state not only that individual directors should not be credited but that films should be shot on location, using only props found in that location, and without resorting to artificial light. On the theme of music, the second of the Dogme 95 rules observes that 'The sound must never be produced apart from the images or vice versa (music must not be used unless it occurs where the scene is being shot)'. In this instance the concentration of sound within the diegetic film community adds to an intense appreciation of their isolation and reliance upon each other in the face of a potentially agonizing and lonely death. Here, of course, my analysis of Shakespearean film soundtracks is consciously shading into issues of soundscapes and acoustics, since I consider these an integral element of any film soundtrack; music, diegetic and non-diegetic, is just one element in that more complex matrix in which silence may be as resonant a sign system as composed music.

Titus Andronicus is a play which holds at its centre a profound analysis of acts of articulation and silencing. In the harrowing aftermath of her rape by Chiron and Demetrius, Lavinia, her hands cut off and her tongue cut out, desperately attempts to tell her tragedy to her distraught uncle. Eventually she will resort to a book, Ovid's *Metamorphoses*, to speak of her violent rape by proxy, by pointing with the stumps of her arms to the pages relating to the rape of Philomel by Tereus. In the Ovidian myth, Philomel is transformed into a nightingale who sings of her plight. Julie Taymor's film version of the play, *Titus* (2000), finds a striking equivalent to this idea through her use of music as a signifier on the soundtrack. Elliot Goldenthal's score for this film was discussed in chapter 4 on musicals in terms of its witty pastiche of 1930s big band, jazz, and symphonic musical idioms as part of its eclectic, multivalent referents.[17] In the scenes relating to Lavinia's rape and mutilations, however, Goldenthal opts for a discordant music reminiscent of the early twentieth-century Modernist experimentations of Arnold Schoenberg and others. For the most part, the dissonant music is non-diegetic, available to the cinema audiences as a frame through which to comprehend and decipher events onscreen, signifying as it does the amoral chaos into which the world of Rome has plunged in the play. But at the point of Lavinia's desperation to speak her tragic fate, Goldenthal effects a brilliant blurring of the diegetic and non-diegetic effects of the scene. Asked by her uncle to voice her plight –

'Speak, gentle niece, what stern ungentle hands / Hath lopped and hewed and made thy body bare / Of her two branches' (II.iv.16–18) – she opens her mouth wide in a seemingly futile attempt – tongueless as she is also – to speak. Nothing, it would seem, can come out. But Goldenthal's score ventriloquizes for her at this point; music and image working in eloquent synchrony to loudly, dissonantly, sound the violation that has been wrought upon her body. It is a stunning moment, one that picks up on and extends tropes and images of the mouth elsewhere in the film's visual aesthetics (see Burnett 2003: 276–7). It is also a rich example of how music on film scores frequently articulates the conditions of characters onscreen.[18]

The resonance of silences, gaps in the audible soundtrack, or of soundtrack noises other to or in addition to those produced by vocalists or musicians, remains important to the overall effect of Shakespeare on film, even in those instances where the musical scores of specific screen interpretations of the plays have become inextricably associated with the canon of a major composer. This is nowhere more the case than in the example of Dmitri Shostakovich's film scores for Grigori Kosintsev's Russian-language versions of *Hamlet* (1964) and *King Lear* (1970).[19] The partnership between Shostakovich and Kosintsev was, like so many collaborations mentioned in this study, one with theatrical origins. Through his theatre director friend Vsevolod Meyerhold, Shostakovich had become involved with a theatre group called FEKS (Factory of the Eccentric Actor) which was led by Leonid Trauberg and Kosintsev himself. They were a radical group who aimed to challenge bourgeois theatre associations by asserting the genre's relationship to more demotic arts like the circus, and they were heavily influenced by the possibilities of film within their productions.[20] Through working with Kosintsev on theatre stagings of Shakespeare plays, Shostakovich naturally moved on to score his films. Shostakovich, it should be stressed, was a major composer for film, writing just under forty scores during his lifetime.

It has already been noted in accounting for the influences on Patrick Doyle's compositional practices that in his music for Kosintsev's 1964 *Hamlet* Shostakovich used sub-Wagnerian *leitmotifs*. Ophelia's recurring theme, mostly played on the harpsichord, is particularly resonant with meaning. When we first see her onscreen, she resembles a marionette dancing prescribed, contained movements to the harpsichord, the music of which is deliberately reminiscent of that which played in twentieth-century jewellery boxes, often as the accompaniment to a rigid but turning form of a ballet dancer.[21] These suggestive mechanistic repeats of the harpsichord, into which audiences actively read these connotations, recur later to remind us of this earlier indication of Ophelia's tragic containment by both social expectation and the castle of Elsinore itself, which is prison-like in the spatial semiotics of the film. After the first public display of her descent into mental breakdown, Ophelia runs into the distance towards the vista of the ocean that is framed by the castle windows. A sudden snatch of the harpsichord variations are heard. They will play once more when she returns, now completely broken, for the flower scene which serves as the prelude to her watery death. That death is depicted as an escape from the containment of Elsinore as her soul seemingly floats free over the all-symbolic sea in the shape of a gull.

In the case of Kosintsev's *Lear*, Shostakovich's symphonic overlays have become inextricably associated in the cultural memory with the nihilistic, even apocalyptic tone of the film. Leggatt suggests that 'Shostakovich's music gives the film some of its darkest colouring, especially in the war sequence where his wordless choir becomes "the grief of the whole people"' (1991: 91). At the very end, Kosintsev tellingly cuts Edgar's con-solatory final speech, leaving us instead with the image of this haunted and broken individual walking through a scene of epic desolation and carnage. There is in fact no self-indulgent music at this point; the credits stating blankly 'The End' cut in remarkably fast, and this is indicative of a sparing economy in terms of the use of music for emotional and manipu-lative effect throughout this film. The film begins equally surprisingly, and against the expectation of a Shostakovich score, with a solo clarinet played over the opening credits. At this point the clarinet music is non-diegetic, but it will reappear within the heart of the film, as 'flute' music played by Kosintsev's haunting Fool. This fool, based in part on Shake-speare but also viewed through the prism of Russian cultural experience and the figure of the *yurodivy*, or 'holy fool' such as those who attended the Tsarist regimes, has an enlarged role in the film. He survives (endures?) to the end, outliving his master as opposed to disappearing enigmatically from the script in the hovel scene of iii.vi as he does in the extant Folio version of the play. His recurring tune becomes a plaintive lament over the tragic corpses that litter the scene at the end.[22] Once again the collab-oration between composer and director has theatrical provenance; Sho-stakovich and Kosintsev had collaborated on a stage production of *King Lear* in 1941, and much of the music for the Fool dates from this time (Riley 2005: 105).[23]

The more stereotypical epic orchestrations associated with Shostako-vich and with Kosintsev's screen Shakespeares are in fact reserved precisely for widescreen, emblematic shots of landscape and the all-important disenfranchised and impoverished people who inhabit that domain. The contemporary resonances of this in the era of the stagnating Brezhnev government should not be underestimated, for all the 'primitive' signifiers of the film's setting. The visual part of the film commences with close-up shots of the boots (and sometimes the straw substituting for those boots) belonging to these representatives of the poor who are walking in an as yet unidentified procession or pilgrimage which will ultimately, after several minutes of film and music, itself a mixture of chant and strings, take them to the edges of Lear's fortress castle. The widescreen shot, as well as Shostakovich's score rising to a temporary climax, emphasizes the significance and sheer brute unscalability of this fortress which in the context of Russian mid-twentieth-century politics cannot help but remind watching audiences of the sealed-off fortress of the Kremlin in Moscow. Lear will appear on the ramparts of this castle at two significant moments – at his point of abdication at the end of scenes reworking Act I of the play, and again at the end just prior to his death, when he has seen the ultimate horror of the hanged corpse of his daughter Cordelia framed by the castle masonry.

Elsewhere in the film, Shostakovich reserves his major musical statements for these identifiable moments of climax and for those points when language appears to cede to the visual, allowing diegetic sound instead to do the interpretative or signifying work during most of the scenes of dialogue and verbal exchange. We hear, for example, the sound of hunting horns, the barking of dogs, the crackling of fires that give all-important heat to the cold stone interiors of the various castles and residences of the film's aristocracy, and in the storm the all-pervasive wind and lashing rain. Only towards the very end of these sequences, in order to emphasize the movement towards temporary or momentary climax, as with that first significant arrival of the country's populace at the fortress gates, does Shostakovich allow his score to intrude as part of the meta-diegesis. For example, the cello that plays as Cordelia begins her long walk through the castle antechambers and into exile with her new husband is intended to emphasize the pathos of her situation and that Lear himself has reached a point of no return. Soaring and evocative strains also accompany visual interpolations such as Lear's selection of his retinue of horses, hawks, and hounds to accompany him in his supposed abdication, and the mountainside sanctification of the marriage of Cordelia and France. The handmade cross clearly visible in that last scene served as a potent image of the marginalization of religious practice and ceremony under successive

Communist regimes in the Soviet Union of the mid-twentieth century, and it is no coincidence that both Kosintsev's and Shostakovich's works was regarded as potentially subversive by Joseph Stalin.

Shostakovich's sparing use of musical overlay allows the score of *King Lear* to reserve its emotional impact for epic moments and crux scenes in the film, not least the storm and battle sequences. This is a film that does much of its work by means of the careful juxtaposition of silence and noise. This can be demonstrated in the series of images attached to the blinding of the Duke of Gloucester in the Duke of Cornwall's castle. The horror is created not by over-dramatized musical accompaniment but by the mundane reactions of Regan and Edmund to what they hear. As Gloucester's gruesome cries echo around the castle, these two casually continue to lace their boots and dress themselves. Shostakovich and Kosintsev knew when silence or limited soundscapes could do the work as well as, if not better than, emotional, overlaid orchestration. Theirs is an economy of style that many critics clearly yearned for in Branagh's film Shakespeares.

Early published studies of Shakespeare and music paid only limited attention to the presence of music in a filmed context. In Phyllis Hartnoll's 1966 collection of essays, *Shakespeare in Music*, brief mention is made of Walton's work for Laurence Olivier as well as early Hollywood's use of recognizable classical compositions for its film Shakespeares – such as the use of Mendelssohn in the 1935 Reinhardt–Dieterle *A Midsummer Night's Dream* and the use of Tchaikovsky's fantasy overture for *Romeo and Juliet* in the 1936 film starring Leslie Howard and Norma Shearer. My study emerges in an era when the grounds for understanding the relationship between Shakespeare and film music has shifted on to a wholly new plane of appreciation. Film composers now operate within a recognized profession, one often, though not always, separate from that of classical and symphonic composition. The dominance in modern culture of popular and contemporary music of many shades, from jazz through rock and roll, to rap and hip-hop, has also had massive impact on the development and evolution of the film soundtrack as a factor in, contributor to, and active creator of meaning in the medium. This has had significant results for the particular field of screen Shakespeares, as the next chapter will go on to analyse. In turn, as argued in an earlier chapter on musicals, the pop video has had its own effects on the use and deployment of music in film, in both its non-diegetic and diegetic manifestations. Returning, then, to the concerns of Theodor Adorno in relation to contemporary culture, and in particular to film's deployment of music, which I highlighted in the introduction to this chapter, classical music's presence in many of these more contemporary film adaptations, appropriations, or 'updates' of Shakespeare as brief allusions or quotations might seem to confirm his anxiety that the practice of quotation would fragment classical compositions to such an extent that their use could only ever be parodic or deconstructive. Yet, as I hope the next chapter will prove, the opposite of Adorno's fears seems to me to be the case. Allusions to classical music in the scores for Baz Luhrmann's 1996 *William Shakespeare's Romeo + Juliet* or Tim Blake Nelson's US high school re-vision of *Othello*, *O* (2000), are poignant and enriching contributions to films which value their musical score as a major producer of meaning and effect. Classical music may function differently for the auditors and spectators of these films, but we have to accept that different audiences for filmed Shakespeares are an important part of their musical complexity and significations.

In acknowledging these multiplicities of potential response to Shakespearean film music, we need also to historicize those responses, just as earlier chapters on the musical and opera sought to offer a diachronic account of composition in those genres. A critical study of Shakespeare such as this needs to account for the changing 'audibility' of music in all its forms. Nino Rota's aforementioned score for Zeffirelli's 1968 *Romeo and Juliet* clearly had one set of meanings for the generation who had heard his music for *La Dolce Vita* and who had been witness to the Italianate influences in European cinema in the decades of the 1950s and 1960s. The tune for 'What is a Youth?' signified entirely differently for a British generation born in those heady days of 1968 who grew up knowing it first as the soundtrack or jingle to a rather tacky romantic interlude regularly scheduled on prime time radio under the heading 'Our Tune', in which listeners shared their personal stories of heartbreak on air and chose a suitably apposite song to be played along with it (music as the soundtrack to our lives indeed). I can well remember school classroom screenings of Zeffirelli's film where those of us who recognized the music from its other, 'romantic' context could not help but giggle as it accompanied the tragic passions of the star-crossed lovers onscreen. Zeffirelli's equally ground-breaking youth casting for his young lovers now looks oddly antiquated in its Renaissance costuming when placed alongside Baz Luhrmann's millennial version, and the soundtrack seems equally outmoded.

In time, though, Luhrmann, too, will come to seem a product of his socio-cultural and technological moment, and his 'cutting-edge' soundtrack and special effects will become signifiers of something other, motifs of reminiscence in themselves, not least of former youth for a newly mature audience for whom he was *their* schoolroom Shakespeare. Each generation hears differently: Walton's epic battle soundtracks played in a different mode to audiences in 1944 than they do to a post-Vietnam generation. Cultures have different ranges of audibility, something the brief discussion of intercultural Shakespeare film soundtracks in this chapter can only gesture towards. Musical Shakespeare, then, is as subject to the vicissitudes of time and context as any other version of Shakespeare, theatrical, operatic or, indeed, critical. We just have to keep trying to listen hard.

Notes

1 Eisler and Adorno 1947: *passim*. The phrase 'hip soundtrack' appears on the video jacket to Gil Junger's 1999 adaptation of *The Taming of the Shrew* in the context of a US high school *10 Things I Hate About You*. The film's score, as well as the thematic relationship of music to its narrative, is explored in more detail in the next chapter.

2 The discussions in this chapter and that which follows are hugely indebted to the participants in the exploratory seminar on Shakespeare and Film Music which I facilitated at the 2005 gathering of the British Shakespeare Association at the University of Newcastle. Special thanks to Ruth Benander, Saviour Catania, Kendra Leonard, Lucy Munro, and Heather Violanti for their generous contributions.

3 For a wide-ranging analysis of the relationship between opera and film, see M. Cooke 2005b.

4 See Jeff Smith 1998: 6. As explained in the Prelude to this volume, while the basic idea of the *leitmotif* as it is deployed in film scores is frequently associated with the work and theory of Richard Wagner, in reality the *leitmotif* system as it operates in film is now far removed from any practice in musical drama that Wagner would recognize or acknowledge, hence my preference for the term 'sub-Wagnerian' to indicate these shifts.

5 For a detailed discussion of the theatrical conventions of melodrama, see J. L. Smith 1973 (esp. p. 31). Interestingly, Smith suggests that melodrama endured in the genres of opera and classical ballet (pp. 46–8), and that this in turn transferred to cinema and 'the silver screen' (p. 48). On the importance of discussions of melodrama to film scholarship, see Brooks 1995: p. viii.

6 Eisler and Adorno posit the fascinating idea that music played a quasi-'magical' role in film screenings, offering an antidote to the ghostly, spectral qualities of the soundless cinematographic image or 'walking shadow' (quoted in Gorbman 1987: 40).

7 The production also included a 60-strong ballet troupe (Williams 1997: 178).

8 See Williams 1997: 179; he notes that the forest was created with '67 truckloads of trees and shrubbery . . . [including] a transplanted redwood tree, a pond, and a stream, all arranged over 66 thousand square feet'.

9 See Willett 1992: 37. Interestingly, similar concerns drive the Eisler–Adorno attack on Hollywood film music in 1947, which in 'warding' off the ghostly or spectral effects of film also masked the mechanics and the material facts of the process (Gorbman 1987: 58).

10 Pasternak co-wrote the screenplay with playwright Robert Bolt.

11 Intriguingly, the actor who played Lara Antipova in Lean's film was Julie Christie, Branagh's Gertrude in this film *Hamlet*. This is one Gertrude who is allowed to deliver her descriptive monologue on the death of Ophelia, albeit aria-like to the accompaniment of Doyle's emotive orchestration using the string section, without the film medium's usual tendency to want to visualize Ophelia's death – there is just a fleeting glimpse of Ophelia under water at the very end of this scene, in stark contrast to Olivier's full-blown reconstruction of the Pre-Raphaelite painter John Everett Millais's imagining of this moment, with Gertrude reduced to a presence only as voiceover (cf. Bate 1997: 265–6). Gertrude's speech, 'There is a willow grows aslant a broot', was the inspiration for a musical composition (for a small orchestra) of the same name by Frank Bridge in 1927. For a recording of this piece, see Bridge 2004 in the Discography.

12 Loehlin 1996: *passim*. In this excellent volume that looks at several theatre and film versions of *Henry V* from the seventeenth century onwards, Loehlin uses the playwright John Arden's statement that in *Henry V* Shakespeare appeared to have written a 'secret play within the official one' (quoted p. 1). For Branagh's film version, Loehlin turns that statement on its head to suggest that what Branagh offers, contradictorily, is 'the *official* version of the play disguised as the secret one' (p. 145) and that, for all its anti-war gestures, in the end it endorses war and heroism in problematic fashion, not least aesthetically.

13 I am not including in this count his 1965 *Othello* which was a recording of a stage performance or the television production of *King Lear* in which Olivier played the King in 1983. Both these productions are discussed in Rothwell 1999.

14 Comparable practice might be registered in Nino Rota's score for the Zeffirelli *Romeo and Juliet*, where Mercutio's angst-ridden delivery of Queen Mab is allowed to stand alone, unpunctuated by musical accompaniment.

15 Julie Taymor's *Titus* (2000) clearly shares a number of these aesthetic and intellectual aims.

16 Another band member who played on the Polanski soundtrack was Paul Buckmaster, who had taken part in *Will Power*, the 1974 jazz concert tribute to Shakespeare discussed in ch. 1.

17 Jeff Smith argues that in the 1950s Leonard Bernstein and Henry Mancini were influential in diversifying the classic Hollywood symphonic score with elements of jazz and Latin rhythm (1998: 45).

18 It is worth adding that Taymor's film had its origins in a 1994 stage production for which Goldenthal also wrote the incidental music (cf. Walker 2002). It was also clearly an influence on jazz musician Django Bates's incidental music for the 2006 Globe Theatre production of *Titus Andronicus*, not least in these particular scores involving the silenced Lavinia, where the music frequently 'spoke' for her.

19 The important connection between Russian film and Shakespeare, and Shakespeare's more general resonance in Russian culture from the eighteenth century onwards, can only be glimpsed at in this context. An extremely useful account of the impact of Lenin's admiration for both Shakespeare and the medium of film on twentieth-century theatrical and cinematic practice in Russia is offered by John Riley (2005: 94). As well as Shakespeare's constant presence in the Russian theatre, many works of Russian literature used Shakespearean texts and characters as points of reference: e.g., Ivan Turgenev's *A Prince Hamlet of the Schigrov District* (1854) and Nicolai Leskov's 'Lady Macbeth of Mtensk' (1865), which Shostakovich himself made into an opera. As already noted, Pasternak's *Doctor Zhivago* was also Shakespeare-inspired, and it was Pasternak himself who provided the translation for Kosintsev's *King Lear* film.

20 Riley notes that early productions by FEKS featured clips of Chaplin movies (2005: 5). Through Meyerhold, Shostakovich also became familiar with Sergei Eisenstein, whose

innovative use of music in his scores had a profound influence on Russian cinematic practice.

21 Elsie Walker (2002: 200–1) identifies an allusion to this sequence in the Lavinia scenes of Julie Taymor's *Titus*.

22 Riley (2005) makes important links between Kosintsev's use of the *yurodivy* here and that at the end of Shostakovich's favourite opera, *Boris Godunov*. The 1954 film version of the opera directed by Vera Stroyeva has him sitting among the ruins, awaiting a time of troubles in an image directly akin to the Fool's role at the end of Kosintsev's *King Lear* (p. 105).

23 Many Russian musicians wrote incidental music for theatre or ballet productions of Shakespeare. Shostakovich wrote not only for Kosintsev's 1941 *King Lear* production but also for a 1954 staging of *Hamlet*. He had also been pencilled in to write music for Kosintsev's 1943 stage version of *Othello*, but sadly this particular collaboration never materialized (Riley 2005: 94–5). The significance of the Fool in this film interpretation of *King Lear* finds an intriguing parallel in Akira Kurosawa's Kyoamia in *Ran*. Played by Peitah, a well-known Japanese transvestite performer, this singing, dancing Fool is noticeably allowed to transgress the otherwise rigid visual protocols of sitting and standing in the film's community (Rothwell 1999: 198). Kosintsev was immersed in Japanese culture and acknowledged the influence of Noh practices and the work of Kurosawa on his own (Riley 2005: 103), but here it appears to be Kurosawa's 1985 film which pays its own intercultural homage.

Further examples and reading

There are too many examples of Shakespeare films to list them all here. An excellent source for material on this subject is Kenneth Rothwell, *A History of Shakespeare on Screen* (Cambridge: Cambridge University Press, 1999); now in its 2nd edition (2004). Films of particular note in terms of their scores which I was unable to discuss here for reasons of space include Gus Van Sant's *My Own Private Idaho* (1991), which itself alludes to Orson Welles's *Chimes at Midnight* (1965; known as *Falstaff* in its 1966 US release). In those sections of the film that directly equate to the Hal–Falstaff scenes of the *Henry IV* plays and which feature the film's Falstaff equivalent 'Bob', cod-Elizabethan music plays as if to signify the hyper-reality and intertextuality of these moments. Similarly inventive in its range of referents is Michael Almereyda's *Hamlet* (2000). More 'classical' symphonic scores accompany Oliver Parker's *Othello* (1995) and Michael Radford's *The Merchant of Venice* (2004), perhaps in keeping with the decision of these directors not to update the setting of the plays. Jocelyn Pook's score for the latter is especially interesting in its use of counter-tenor Andreas Scholl to deliver many of the selected song settings. Trevor Nunn's Edwardian *Twelfth Night* (1996) includes several songs within its diegesis, as does the play, delivered in this instance by the film's Feste, Ben Kingsley. That his singing is used as an aural pre-credits frame to the whole film indicates Nunn's sense of the centrality of music as both theme and idea within the play (it famously opens, of course, on a line that refers to music and playing).

I have concentrated for the purposes of this study on film scores, but the world of television adaptation offers similarly rich yields in terms of thinking about music and the process and politics of Shakespearean adaptation. Useful examples include the Andrew Davies adaptation of *Othello*, made for British television in 2001, which relocates the play to the current-day London Metropolitan Police Force and which, like *My Own Private Idaho*, plays with mock-Elizabethan references in its score; the US TV re-envisioning of *Macbeth* as a crime fiction drama, *Scotland PA* (dir. Billy Morrissette, 2001); and the recent BBC series *Shakespeare Retold*, which included updated versions of *The Taming of the Shrew*, *A Midsummer Night's Dream*, *Much Ado About Nothing*, and *Macbeth*.

For those readers interested in some of the ideas of intercultural performance and inter-pretation raised here in the discussions of the work of Akira Kurosawa, an emerging genre of Indian 'Bollywood' interpretations of Shakespeare poses interesting questions both in terms of adaptation and musical scoring. *Omkara*, directed by Vishal Bharadwaj, a Hindi version of *Othello* in which the play's themes of race are re-visioned as inter-caste rivalry, was released in 2006; the same director's *Maqbool*, a version of *Macbeth* set in the Mumbai underworld, was released in 2003. Versions of *Hamlet* and *A Midsummer Night's Dream* are also planned by other Bollywood directors.

For those new to film theory, a reliable guide to analysing the medium of cinema is David Bordwell and Kristen Thompson's *Film Art: An Introduction*, 7th edn (London and New York: McGraw-Hill, 2004). On the study and analysis of film music in particular, see Claudia Gorbman, *Unheard Melodies: Narrative Film Music* (Bloomington: Indiana University Press; London: BFI Publishing, 1987); Katherine Kalinak, *Settling the Score: Music and the Classic Hollywood Film* (Madison: University of Wisconsin Press, 1992); and Jeff Smith's superlative *The Sounds of Commerce: Marketing Popular Film Music* (New York: Columbia University Press, 1998).

There has been a recent upsurge of books and studies of Shakespeare and film. Useful works include *The Cambridge Companion to Shakespeare and Film*, ed. Russell Jackson (Cam-bridge: Cambridge University Press, 2000); Mark Thornton Burnett and Ramona Wray (eds), *Shakespeare, Film, Fin-de-Siècle* (Basingstoke: Macmillan, 2000); Diana Henderson (ed.), *A Concise Companion to Shakespeare on Screen* (Oxford: Blackwell, 2006); Anthony Davies and Peter Holland (eds), *Shakespeare and the Moving Image: The Plays on Film and Tele-vision* (Cambridge: Cambridge University Press, 1994); Lynda E. Boose and Richard Burt's edited collections *Shakespeare the Movie* (London: Routledge, 1997) and *Shakespeare the Movie, II* (London: Routledge, 2003); and Katherine Howard and Thomas Cartelli, *New Wave Shakespeare on Screen* (Cambridge: Polity, 2006). Several articles in Dutton and Howard's 4-vol. edition of *A Companion to Shakespeare's Works* (2003) also deal with Shake-speare onscreen.

8

'You know the movie song':
Contemporary and Hybrid Film Scores

Music and poesy use to quicken you;
The Taming of the Shrew, I.i.36

Discussion of contemporary film scores in the context of Shakespeare and music immediately brings to mind films such as Baz Luhrmann's now seminal *William Shakespeare's Romeo + Juliet* or Tim Blake Nelson's high school *Othello*, *O*, with their high-volume, zeitgeist soundtracks of contemporary songs performed by the voguish bands of the day such as Garbage, The Cardigans, or Black Star. Their anthologizing approach – the bringing together of a range of bands and performers on a single soundtrack, often comprising a medley of songs existent prior to the film's creation – and contemporary frame of reference marks them out as tangibly different from the commissioned orchestral suites by Shostakovich, Walton, and Doyle for films by Kosintsev, Olivier, and Branagh. A deliberate blurring is effected within these films between the deployment of this music in diegetic and non-diegetic contexts – that is, as part of the literal film world being depicted on the screen or as part of the overlaid score, which characters cannot hear but which audiences use as an additional interpretative frame. In the case of the latter, we shade into what Claudia Gorbman describes as the 'meta-diegetic', because the music in these scenes contributes to the interpretation or understanding of what is being witnessed onscreen, rather than functioning as mere accompaniment or backdrop (1987: 30).

There would appear to be a clear division between the highly orchestrated scores written by mainstream classical composers, and invariably performed by large-scale symphony orchestras, and these contemporary soundtracks performed by a range of bands and artists from the realm of popular culture. However, even mentioning the Luhrmann and Blake Nelson soundtracks immediately problematizes that neat division, just as, indeed, so-called symphonic film scores blur into debates elsewhere in this book about classical composition and other musical genres. Where

159

exactly does Felix Mendelssohn's Overture and Incidental Music for *A Midsummer Night's Dream*, for example, leave off being a classical suite and become ballet, or, indeed, in turn become a film score when used by Reinhardt and Dieterle for their Warner Brothers motion picture version of the play in 1935? What role does the soundtrack 'quotation' of Mendelssohn's music play in Michael Hoffman's 1998 film of *Dream*? Is the self-conscious borrowing of Mendelssohn a retroactive move that aids the location of audience consciousness in the nineteenth-century *mise-en-scène*, or is it parodic, asserting that this is an interpretation of *Dream* informed by more than twentieth-century interests and values?[1]

The soundtracks for Luhrmann's *Romeo + Juliet* and Blake Nelson's *O* might be felt to challenge conscious uses of 'period' musical idiom to establish the location of films in favour of immediate cultural relevance. Luhrmann's film retains Shakespearean dialogue but finds modern socio-cultural and visual equivalents to the playtext's vocabulary of swords and codes of honour in late twentieth-century urban gang and gun culture; Blake Nelson abandons Shakespearean text and language almost entirely in his US high school basketball reconfiguration of *Othello*, relying instead on Shakespeare's plot plus allusions at the level of character names such as 'Desi' and 'Hugo', and an equally knowing musical score. Undoubtedly, both soundtracks are assertively 'modern', yet in practice both actually mix and meld references to contemporary song and musical genres, from indie pop to rap and hip-hop, with identifiable quotations from the classical musical domain. It is an awareness of this consciously intertextual, *bricolage* effect of their postmodern scores that proves far more informative about the cultural, intellectual, and aesthetic processes at work and their operation within the context of the films than the label that has too often been rather lazily assigned to them of their being 'soundtracks for the MTV generation'.

The MTV analogy deserves more detailed analysis, for it suggests a target audience not simply accustomed to a fast-moving, high-volume, musical backing track to their days and affairs, but one that is highly literate both in reading visuals mediated through a musical or auditory frame – the pop music video being the prime example of a form that has honed and perfected these skills – and which is accustomed to the hybridity of reference that can place opera alongside hip-hop in a sequence of juxtaposition spread across a matter of minutes or seconds onscreen. Several of the Shakespeare films examined in this chapter make the MTV analogy explicit, such as Gil Junger's inclusion of a snippet of the programme 'The Real Thing' as part of his teenage protagonists' prime time viewing in the postmodern take on *The Taming of the Shrew*, *10 Things I Hate About You*. Luhrmann's *Romeo + Juliet* deploys the small screen mediation of the tragic events depicted in his film at several points in the narrative, even giving the Chorus to a television newsreader. The 'MTV generation', then, for want of a better phrase, is a visually literate, quotation-literate audience, one well accustomed to the high-speed practice of intertextual or co-textual reading. Junger, Luhrmann, and Blake Nelson, and their musical directors and collaborators, were able to exploit these skills when creating their Shakespeare adaptations and soundtracks. They are quick to pick up on the semiotics of diegetic and non-diegetic blurrings of the kind that appeared so avant-garde in Laurence Olivier's 'meta-theatrical' film of *Henry V* in 1944, and to develop those possibilities when devising their scores.

Many contemporary film scores which adopt the anthologizing approach do not commission new songs or lyrics for their films but take great delight in selecting tracks from an existent corpus which they consider to be relevant, resonant, even apposite, in their application to the themes and concerns of the film being made. Film theorists most often refer to these as 'compilation scores,' and the George Lucas-directed film *American Graffiti* (1973) is regarded by many as pioneering in its use of existent songs in this manner in order to create a 'dichotomy between musicality and narrativity' that is productive of meaning (Jeff Smith 1998: 154, 172–7).

This chapter will explore the idea and process of the compilation score at work in both *O* and *10 Things I Hate About You*. In an earlier chapter on musicals, the postmodern knowingness of Tommy O'Haver's 2001 *Get Over It* was invoked on similar terms; there the songs of Neil Sedaka and Elvis Costello are placed in productive juxtaposition alongside the idiom and conventions of the popular stage musical. Selections of songs for soundtracks in this way do dual work in Shakespearean adaptations, contributing on a surface level to a film's youth aesthetic, while also having deeper resonance at the level of punning reference or sustained analogy with the source-text. Having stated that such songs are rarely specifically commissioned for these films, however, it is important to stress that Luhrmann's *Romeo + Juliet* is a rather different case. The bands that he and his musical director Nellee Hooper hired to provide the film's vibrant, hybrid score contributed songs with lyrics and themes that were directly allusive to the plotline and dialogue of Shakespeare's play, as well as the action of Luhrmann's film.[2] For example, Gavin Friday's 'Angel' plays when we first see Juliet in her angelic fancy dress for the Capulet ball. Several songs, such as Kym Mazelle's rendition of 'Young hearts run free', underscore the youth emphasis of the movie, while others, such as Stina Nordenstam's 'Little star' or One Inch Punch's 'Pretty piece of flesh', directly rework lines from the play (see i.i.28, ''tis known I am a pretty piece of flesh'; and iii.ii.22, 'Take him and cut him out in little stars'), adding to the layered referentiality of the film.

'Pretty piece of flesh' first occurs as part of Luhrmann's astonishing quasi-operatic opening sequence, which had cinema audiences reeling from the first minutes of watching. We move from a TV news report to a high-octane, high-volume operatic chorus on the soundtrack which overlays images of skyscrapers, helicopters, and giant religious statuary, establishing at high speed many of the crucial frames of reference for this very modern take on Shakespeare's tragedy. The operatic element helps to establish tragic expectation, as does the double delivery of the Chorus's predictive prologue, an effect further exacerbated by flashing up the words of that prologue onscreen. The Chorus tells any audience for play or film how it will all end: 'A pair of star-crossed lovers take their life' (Prologue, 6). In a move not dissimilar to the zoom in from the aerial urban skyscrapers of New York to the specifics of a West Side street in *West Side Story*, Luhrmann's camera then hones in on the specific event of a gas station *contretemps* between two rival groups, the Montague boys and the Capulets, led by self-proclaimed 'Prince of Cats', Tybalt. Images of the Montague boys are ushered onscreen to the diegetic accompaniment of One Inch Punch, to whose song they are singing along in their open-top car.

The hybridity of references in this opening sequence is a key to Luhrmann's aesthetic throughout: we have the operatic or symphonic directly juxtaposed with the contemporary, and the epic juxtaposed with the highly localized. Luhrmann's decision to divide his gangs along ethnic lines in a further nod to *West Side Story* has interesting implications for the soundtrack, since the rap-orientated delivery of a phrase like 'Da boys' at the moment when we witness men onscreen who clearly have a WASP identity alerts us to the need to read beyond surfaces in this film.

The hyperreal editing and hyperreal soundtrack combine in their effects; not only do we have multiple blurrings between the supposedly diegetic and non-diegetic – for example, the action frequently pauses in this opening sequence for credits identifying who the characters are to flash up on screen in a typography deliberately reminiscent of daytime TV soap operas – but there are multiple intertextual visual allusions and spoofs. These allusions function simultaneously in parodic, yet entirely celebratory ways. This is one of Luhrmann's great skills as a director, as well as being a brilliant reworking of the deployment of the rhetorical figure of the oxymoron which is a governing linguistic feature of Shakespeare's play. In this opening sequence, alongside Shakespeare, opera, television soap, and newscasts, war films, westerns, especially spaghetti westerns, and musicals are all evoked with an ironic humour amid shocking scenes of violence. The deployment of hybridity and postmodern allusiveness in Luhrmann's work is not always parodic, even here, where the humour is undoubtedly foregrounded. Elsewhere the allusive nature of both film and score finds a remarkable romantic and tragic depth, nowhere more so than in Luhrmann's candlelit tomb scene at the end of his film, the spectacular setting for Romeo and Juliet's tragic demise.

Luhrmann's tomb scene has already received the benefit of many column inches, but in the context of this study I want to argue for its diverse, hybrid aural semiotics, which bring into play in a multi-faceted way a complex field of Shakespearean allusion and the potential for multiple modes of 'recognition' in audiences, readers, and listeners alike. James Loehlin describes the *Romeo + Juliet* deathbed scene as 'completely isolated and self-contained' in visual terms (2000: 129). Luhrmann's decision to cut the role of Paris from the tomb scene, as well as the Friar's interventions, heightens the focus on, and effectively isolates, his star-crossed lovers. In the same way, his strongly interventionist directorial decision to make both Romeo and Juliet recognize that the other is alive for one brief, impossible moment, only to realize in that exact same moment that theirs is now, for certain, a doomed love, since Romeo has consumed the vial of fatal poison in the mistaken belief that Juliet is really dead, heightens the tragic register for frustrated film audiences who witness all the misunderstandings taking place and yet can do nothing, are powerless, as it were, in their cinema seats. Luhrmann was actually following in a long line of adaptations of Shakespeare's play when he selected this alternative happening in the tomb scene. Late seventeenth-century adaptor Thomas Otway first introduced the change, but it became fully incorporated into theatrical tradition when actor-manager David Garrick adopted his interpolation in the eighteenth century. Garrick also added a seventy-five-line dialogue between the couple to further heighten the pathos (Levenson 1987: 20), and it was this version of the script that was performed, with little revision, until 1843 in English theatres (Levenson 1987: 31), and which influenced Hector Berlioz when he composed his dramatic symphony based on the play. Luhrmann, ever alert to his artistic inheritances, is aware of these theatrical and classical musical precedents when he makes his decisions about how to film the tomb scene, and it directly affects his choice of music at this point in the soundtrack.

For all its suggestions of containment, Loehlin's essay makes significant reference to Luhrmann's deployment in the tomb scene of the 'last phrases' of Wagner's *Liebestod* from *Tristan und Isolde*. This extra-textual, and indeed extra-filmic, reference offers a series of competing interpretative frames for understanding that ensures that the spectator is an active participant in the production of meaning and serves to challenge the surface isolation and uniqueness of the couple onscreen. Loehlin rightly observes that the Wagnerian musical referent implicitly associates Romeo and Juliet with a 'mythic medieval past of chivalry', as, indeed, did their earlier fancy dress costumes, knight and angel respectively, at the Capulet ball (2000: 129). The operatic lyrics effectively being 'quoted' at this point serve to reaffirm the motifs of water and drowning that have clustered around the couple throughout: 'Juliet's violent suicide is washed over by the ecstatic love-death of Isolde, swooning in bliss on the body of her love: *"ertrinken, versinken – unbewußt – höchste Lust!"* ("To drown, to sink – unconscious – highest pleasure!")' (Loehlin 2000: 129).[3] The star-crossed lovers' first sight of each other in the film is achieved through the watery mediation of a fish tank; they later embrace passionately underwater in an attempt to avoid the surveillance cameras on the Capulet estate; and there are numerous other aquatic frames for actions and events in the film. It is clear, then, that Luhrmann's recourse to *Tristan und Isolde* at this particular moment in the screenplay might be related to the dominance of sub-Wagnerian theories and the wider practice of *leitmotif* and repetition in film scores that I discussed in the previous chapter.

Shakespeare ensured that audiences understood the fate that lay in wait for Romeo and Juliet via the doom-laden and prescriptive prologue, delivered by the Chorus. This is supplemented in Luhrmann's aesthetic by his deployment of the drowning motif. Our first onscreen glimpse of Juliet is underwater; she is, in the terms of tragic expectation, already dead, or fated to a death. This is echoed when we see Romeo's head underwater at the party, as he attempts to rouse himself from the drug-induced state occasioned by the pills given him by his loved-up friend Mercutio. These linked images serve to underline the shared tragic trajectory of the pair from this moment on. Romeo will meet Juliet in the succeeding frame.

In a book whose title, *Opera as Drama*, deliberately acknowledges the shaping influences of Wagner's essay 'Oper und Drama', Joseph Kerman has spoken of the 'elaborate symmetries' of *Tristan und Isolde*, and the 'dense symphonic web' woven by Wagner's use of *leitmotif* in his opera (1989: 162). Observing the way in which these references and repetitions accrue, and thereby build sympathy and identification with character or event on the part of spectators, Kerman remarks on the skilful manipulation of musical and dramatic effect that this constitutes: 'The last 80-odd bars of the score are rather closely repeated from the height of the love-duet in Act 2' (1989: 175). He adds that an audience recognizing that link, remembering the earlier delivery of those musical phrases, will also register the utterly transformed context for this repetition. There are, significantly, new words this time round, and this is no longer a duet but a song delivered by Isolde alone, transfigured as she is into a state of acceptance of union in death, a common trope in Romantic tragedy. This for Kerman moves far beyond simple echo effect or refrain:

> From the purely musical point of view, the effect of the 'Liebestod' – Wagner called it 'Verklarung' – is unlike any effect obtainable by the use of leitmoti[f]s. It is more like the recapitulation of a Beethoven symphony movement . . . It is more like the return of the music for the kiss at the end of Otello – a grand climactic repetition summing up the drama in a single gesture, rather than a momentary detail, however striking. (1989: 176)

We discussed Verdi's use of the 'un bacio' motif in his *Otello* in chapter 6, but there are clearly ways in which Luhrmann, by citing Wagner on the soundtrack at this particular moment, introduces into his allusive frame something more than just the well-established, and even hackneyed, convention of *leitmotif*. What is most telling, perhaps, is the way in which Wagner's synthesis of the Isolde myth has seeped into our cultural consciousness and become an archetypal image, at least in Western artistic traditions.[4] The informing context for Luhrmann is, then, one of romantic tragic myth and archetype, a tradition in which Tristan and Isolde, Romeo and Juliet, and Othello and Desdemona, are predominant examples. The choice of the 1865 Wagner *Liebestod* is multiply significant, since, as Jill Levenson points out, Wagner actually gave this name to 'the myth which informs the fiction of Romeo and Juliet', adding:

> Although the meaning of this term shifts – love-in-death, death-in-love, love's death – it refers to a specific narrative format and psychological event . . . By linking passion with death the *Liebestod* myth sets the limits of desire at the highly charged point where lovers feel that they have transcended ordinary human experience, driven to union which means dissolution of self, a permanent metamorphosis. (2000: 2–3)

Luhrmann's deployment of the aural framing device of Wagner's *Liebestod* begins at the moment when Romeo approaches the enclosed tomb area, a containment signified by the heavy entrance doors through which the camera, and by extension the audience, perceives chinks of light from the welter of burning candles inside, but fades away for the scene proper. The music re-emerges on the soundtrack immediately following Juliet's gunshot suicide, thereby neatly framing the sequence in a manner that appears to support Loehlin's 'contained' reading of this scene. However, just at this moment, the audience is directed towards a wider frame of reference, as a flashback montage of the couple's brief and passionate relationship is placed onscreen: the fleeting nature of the images seems to recapitulate the Friar's pithy earlier summation of their romance's trajectory: 'These violent delights have violent ends' (II.v.9). Even in this use of montage, that ultimate medium of cinematic possibility, though, we can register a Wagnerian and operatic sphere of influence informing Luhrmann's directorial practice. Kerman describes one crucial Wagnerian technique as 'the long passage of plot résumé, during which some major character relates the course of previous action with the liberal assistance of *leitmoti[f]s*' (1989: 174). Luhrmann's flashback montage sequence fits this description well. This study has placed great emphasis on the multi-directional flow of influence between performed and musical Shakespeares, indicating a rich reverse flow of influence from musical adaptations such as opera and ballet into commercial playhouses and theatre practice, as well as from source to adaptation. The medium of film is no exception to this rule, and is influenced in its responses to Shakespeare not only by the vast archives of theatre and performance history but by other media which have engaged in the adaptation, appropriation, and interpretation of the Bard. That Luhrmann's film should turn to sung Shakespeare, and in particular the genres of opera and musical, should not perhaps surprise us, since his small but impressive body of work demonstrates ongoing artistic encounters with both forms. If *Moulin Rouge* (2001), Luhrmann's musical film, which was influenced by contemporary pop culture, Hollywood film musicals, the Indian Bollywood cinematic tradition, and opera, among other things, demonstrated a clear line of connection to Giaccomo Puccini's Parisian *fin-de-siècle* opera *La Bohème*, which Luhrmann went on to direct on Broadway soon after wrapping up the filming of *Moulin Rouge*, so does *William Shakespeare's Romeo + Juliet* bear the traces of his interest and directorial background in the diverse arenas of dance, disco, opera, music video, television and film advertisements, and musical.

There is, however, a set of important questions raised by Luhrmann's creative practices, concerning recognition, and the depth or extent to which any specific act of recognition is made by members of the cinema audience in response to his film. In the tomb sequence of *Romeo + Juliet*, does Luhrmann expect his audience to comprehend, assimilate, and apply the wealth of intertextual references I am suggesting are potentially at play in his soundtrack citation of the *Tristan und Isolde Liebestod*? Does it deepen their understanding or potential response to what they are witnessing if they do? Perhaps the first set of questions to pose concerns the nature of recognition. For some members of the audience who are entirely unfamiliar with opera, let alone the specific canon of Wagner, the *Liebestod* refrains might signify something 'operatic' or 'classical', and that may well be a mode or genre they can relate to a sombre or serious tone, perhaps thereby enabling Luhrmann to underscore the tragic nature of what he is placing onscreen at this moment. As well as being a generic signifier in this way, the semiotic may have cultural overtones. Opera and classical music have elite connotations for the urban, youth audiences that were the demographic for this film; is a statement being made that young, passionate love deserves to be valued in society in a way that so many of Romeo and Juliet's adult mentors – from their parents to the Friar – have failed to recognize? Is there an authenticating strategy at work in Luhrmann's invocation of classical music at this moment?

Elsewhere in the score a classical musical idiom has been deployed for parodic effect; Mozart's Symphony no. 25 plays in the hyped-up and hyper Capulet household pre-ball and, as it switches on and off with the opening and closing of Juliet's bedroom door, is clearly associated with the extravagant excesses of Lady Capulet, a point underscored by the speeded-up film of her movements. Juliet is, by contrast, silent. Here, then, the symphonic music serves as a comic grotesque signifier. There is undoubtedly a social and cultural levelling effect at work in Luhrmann's hybridized aesthetics. Postmodern Shakespeare fights for space in *Romeo + Juliet* among the advertising hoardings in his Verona Beach locale. But there is also a telling point about the ways in which his potential target audiences receive information and may well have received their Shakespeare and even their opera, through commercial media such as advertising jingles, film trailers, and billboards.

Loehlin's citation of the watery lyrics of Wagner's *Liebestod* and their specific relevance for Luhrmann's version of Romeo and Juliet's love story suggest that, at least for those members of the audience familiar with and able to recognize the Wagnerian reference, a deeper, less archetypal,

more specific allusion is in operation. It is with this idea of multiple potentials in play that I think we can best understand and account for the effect
of these allusive frames of reference in contemporary film scores. They
function differently for different members of the audience, offering for
the critic what linguistic scholars helpfully refer to as spectrums of recognition or clines of allusivity.[5] There is a distinct playfulness in the
operation in Luhrmann's work of multi-layered processes of quotation,
citation, allusion, and recognition. His interpolation of opera in the closing
sequences of his film, in a score which is otherwise invariably described
as resoundingly 'contemporary', and which even when it does venture
into classical allusion, as in the Mozart example, is perceived as doing so
in a parodic register, is an indication that many of our (my) comfortable
labels of 'classical' and 'contemporary', elite and popular, simply will not
hold. It must be stressed, however, that symphonic music is as much part
of Luhrmann's score as the Nellee Hooper-produced songs that are more
readily remembered. Luhrmann's long-term collaborator Craig Armstrong provided much of the incidental symphonic and orchestral music
for the film; indeed, in a telling move, music from the soundtrack was
released on two contrasting CDs, the first volume of which contained the
'pop' songs produced and commissioned by Hooper, and the second of
which featured the Wagner *Liebestod* alongside Armstrong's orchestral
and instrumental arrangements. Sometimes these orchestral arrangements were of the same 'pop' songs that featured in the first volume,
thereby creating an effect of developmental refrain even within the CD
format.

Another memorable sequence in Luhrmann's film, where he brings all
these multiple frames of reference, citation, and allusion into play, in part
via his use of music and the all-important blurring of the relationship
between diegetic and non-diegetic material that is so intrinsic to his style,
is the so-called sonnet scene. This is the moment when Romeo and Juliet
first encounter one another in the potent atmosphere of the Capulet ball.
David Lindley has persuasively argued that in the play itself the heady
combination of dance and music would have had strong connotations of
dangerous romance for early modern audiences (2006: 131). Remakes of
Romeo and Juliet have certainly made this scene a central part of their aesthetic, from Zeffirelli's Italian Renaissance version with the set-piece
delivery of Nino Rota's 'What is a Youth?' in his 1968 movie, to the
tension-ridden basketball court 'dance' in *West Side Story*.

The heart-stopping, time-stopping encounter of Tony and Maria
(Romeo and Juliet) in *West Side Story* is achieved through cinematic special

effects. They appear to become still points of focus in the swirling blur of the dancers onscreen. Shakespeare's play achieved a similar suspension of real time and rhythm via the audible effects of a shared sonnet between his two lovers. Romeo and Juliet speak a quatrain each on first meeting, deploying and echoing images of love and religion, an encounter that enacts the very experience they are undergoing:

> ROMEO: If I profane with my unworthiest hand
> This holy shrine, the gentler sin is this:
> My lips, two blushing pilgrims, ready stand
> To smooth that rough touch with a tender kiss.
> JULIET: Good pilgrim, you do wrong your hand too much,
> Which mannerly devotion shows in this.
> For saints have hands that pilgrims' hands do touch,
> And palm to palm is holy palmers' kiss.
>
> (I.v.92–9)

They then share the third quatrain before the ultimate act of linguistic coupling is achieved through the rhyming couplet that Shakespeare used so self-consciously throughout his sonnet sequence and his regular use of the sonnet for dramatic effect in his plays (Bate 1997: 279):

> ROMEO: Have not saints lips, and holy palmers, too?
> JULIET: Ay, pilgrim, lips that they must use in prayer.
> ROMEO: O then, dear saint, let lips do what hands do:
> They pray; grant thou, lest faith turn to despair.
> JULIET: Saints do not move, though grant for prayers' sake.
> ROMEO: Then move not while my prayer's effect I take.
> *He kisses her.*
>
> (I.v.100–5)

Early modern audiences were attuned to hear these important and signifying shifts of rhythm in Shakespeare's dextrous use of dramatic verse. Luhrmann is all too aware that our modern ears are no longer attuned to 'hear' the rhythm of a shared sonnet; yet he does not decide to relocate the meaning of this crucial encounter of the lovers entirely within the realm of the visual, a charge that is often made against film's handling of Shakespearean versification. Instead, he finds a brilliant modern equivalent for the musicality of *Romeo and Juliet's* lyrical tragedy. He reworks the sonnet encounter in a truly contemporary idiom, through a perfect combination of the visual and the auditory.

Romeo's and Juliet's eyes meet through the glass and water of a fish tank that ostentatiously separates the men's and women's toilets in the

Capulet mansion. There is much to be said here about the visual iconography; the fish tank is entirely transparent, and therefore gives the illusion of two people touching, but they are separated by water and the fluid yet hardened material of glass. The image contributes to the *leitmotifs* of water and drowning that we have already assigned to the film's aesthetic and narrative arc, but it also offers a reimagining of the physical obstacles to their love, the spatial impossibilities of their encounters, which Shakespeare located on the early modern stage via the suggestive visual icon of the balcony at II.i.[6] What plays throughout this encounter in Luhrmann's film is Des'ree's love song 'Kissing you', a track which has since become an anthemic signifier of the work. On the CD liner notes, in a direct nod to the Nino Rota precedent, it is described as the 'Love Theme'; certainly it recurs at salient moments throughout the score and film as a sub-Wagnerian *leitmotif*, though in the transformed guise of Armstrong's orchestral arrangements. The musical motif recurs, for example, in a version for piano and strings when Romeo and Juliet meet in secret following the ball in the courtyard of the Capulet mansion, and when they consummate their marriage in the tragic aftermath of Mercutio's and Tybalt's deaths.

As well as brilliantly and accurately equating the function of the Elizabethan love sonnet with the modern love song – akin perhaps to the decision by Charles Gounod in his opera version, *Roméo et Juliette*, to write this encounter as a madrigal *à deux voix* – Luhrmann uses the delivery of the song and the later orchestral arrangements of it in the score, and within the visual *mise-en-scène*, to achieve the kind of spatial and social depth that Claudia Gorbman has assigned to the function of film music (1987: 16). Throughout the fish tank encounter, Des'ree is performing the song within the walls of the Capulet mansion. This both brings the song into the diegetic world of Romeo and Juliet – they are hearing it as they fall in love, it is the literal soundtrack to their romance – and serves to remind the audience, especially in Luhrmann's careful cutting away from the lovers back to the crowd watching Des'ree's performance, that this is only ever a temporary escape from the pressures of reality and the world outside. Luhrmann repeats this spatial and sonic trope several times, not least in the kiss that Romeo and Juliet steal soon after this encounter in the lift on the margins of the crowded and chaotic ballroom and in their underwater performance of the balcony duet. 'Kissing you' in its variant forms becomes, then, a *leitmotif* of the score, serving as a mnemonic for the couple's love, but also for the tragic impossibility of their romance. It becomes a modern version of, or supplement to, the *Tristan und Isolde* 'borrowing' in the tomb scene.

In the previous chapter, we considered the film theorist Claudia Gorbman's designation of a 'Wagnerian' approach to film scores as one that has an investment in *leitmotifs* (1987: 28). Clearly Luhrmann's invocation of Wagner's tragic lovers not only inserts Romeo and Juliet as characters into a history of literary trope and mythic recyclings, it also, as Loehlin's comments on the watery resonances of Isolde's death indicate, highlights and re-emphasizes his own use of *leitmotif* for the lovers in the film. But the invocation of Wagner, and specifically of *Tristan und Isolde*, does more than that; it asserts a generic frame of reference, the *Liebestod* or mythic archetype of the tragic lovers. By framing his tomb scene so self-consciously with classical allusion, Luhrmann allows his postmodern film to acknowledge its own participation in a tragic and artistic continuum. The previously cited montage of the lovers' past is inherently new and contemporary, part of what has been described as Luhrmann's postmodern investment in hybridity and *bricolage*. But it is also age-old; just as his shocking 'innovation' of having the lovers realize that each is alive before they die is actually a reworking of eighteenth-century theatrical tradition and of earlier cinematic versions of the play,[7] so the nineteenth-century Wagnerian allusion recasts our simplistic responses to the inclusion of the music of Garbage and Des'ree elsewhere in the score.

So, in many respects, it is the intersection or encounter of the so-called symphonic and contemporary in recent filmed Shakespeare that interests me as much as typifying a score as either one thing or the other. And to this end, the other brief example I want to turn to is Tim Blake Nelson's pre-Columbine high school shooting tragedy *O*. Barbara Hodgdon has written recently of this film's 'stunning opening where the *"Ave Maria"* from Verdi's *Otello* . . . plays softly behind an image of white shapes surrounding an oriel window that resolves into doves' (2003: 101). One of this film's visual and narrative *leitmotifs* will certainly be the hawks/doves binary, playing on and reworking as it does the tropes of black and white, light and dark, from the Shakespearean script; literalizing them, for example, in the impressive form of the hawk mascot of the college basketball team, whose needs and triumphs dominate the lives of the college students depicted in the film, and deploying them to metaphorize the rivalry between Hugo and Odin James in the narrative. Hodgdon's account of this opening sequence creates a binary of its own in its working opposition between the classical and operatic qualities of the Verdi aria (often, as we have seen, equated with the Shakespearean soliloquy) and contemporary music in the idiom of rap, which is 'raced black, [and] aggressively subversive of white culture' and provides the 'dominant sound of the film'

(Hodgdon 2003: 101). Rewriting the aria–soliloquy equation, she suggests that rap's 'dialogic, rhythmic linguistic structure functions as a verbal substitute for Shakespeare, but also works to displace the questions of power, racism, and class it verbalizes away from "character" and into sound' (Hodgdon 2003: 101). This is interesting, but in practice the rap and hip-hop music played in the film is actually equated or associated more readily with white college students; it is played in their hall rooms, for example, in an active display of their wish to belong to or 'pass' within a more modern, urban semiotic (see Quinn 2005; Krims 2000). A closer look at the lyrics of the songs and groups featured appears to confirm this reading: several refer to a desire to be part of a social group or gang, and the stringent social codes usually attached to these acts of belonging: 'Let me in the club' by Roscoe, 'Da Rules' by Crush, and 'Who ride with us?' by Kyrupt are a few salient examples. This does, I think, trouble both the easy binary of musical forms offered by Hodgdon's analysis, as well as their assumed racial or ethnic links.

There is also a gender issue at play here – although Hodgdon says that the 'Ave Maria' is performed by the Paris Opera boys' choir, it is in fact delivered by a female soprano, the *prima donna* in the opera from which the recording is made,[8] and this draws attention to the fact that in Verdi's opera the song belongs to Desdemona, an operatic addition to the 'Willow Song' scene of the playtext, as we saw in chapter 5. It is worth noting the tragic expectation that this scene and, by extension, the use of song sets up in both playtext and opera. This would suggest that when Blake Nelson incorporates it so tellingly into the soundtrack for *O*, and specifically into its opening and closing frames, it carries with it certain specific meanings, not least as a generic signifier of tragedy and tragic expectation. This is important to this film, where Odin's final speech is one both about the wish to break free of social stereotyping and yet the crushing realization of those same expectations in allowing a 'white school prep boy' to 'play' him in the way that Hugo has: 'You tell me where I'm from didn't make me do this.' That the 'Ave Maria' returns, the coda of white elitism in Hodgdon's reading but also, surely, the coda of tragic expectation in the framework of this film, at the very moment when Odin fires the last fatal gunshot that will end his life and the hopes that so many around him, not least Hugo's basketball team coach father, have invested in him, merely underlines the analogy.

As noted in previous chapters, *Othello* has long been linked with questions of musicality and dissonance, most famously in G. Wilson Knight's seminal essay on 'The *Othello* Music' (1960 [1930]). In the context of *O* it seems important to realize that Verdi is not simply displaced by rap in the film soundtrack, even though, as Hodgdon observes, the opening sequence of the 'Ave' does give way to the assertive tones of rap, and, in terms of onscreen images, the doves cede to the hawk and the hothouse competitive environment of the basketball arena. Our aural memory of the 'Ave Maria' and its association with Desdemona in the operatic version of the play enables a femino-centric angle of sorts on what might otherwise seem like very patriarchal emphases within the college setting. It also makes us alert to the allusive interpretative framework required to mobilize the full spectrum of this film's possible meanings. *O*'s conscious, emphasized location in the American South and its embedded history of slavery and the civil rights movement protests – this setting is clearly indicated by the mosquito-netted *antebellum* architectural style of the college fraternity houses and the Spanish moss through which several shots are viewed – adds a further troubling interpretative frame to the use, deployment, and appropriation of so-called black culture by the community depicted in the film.

Odin James's initials, O.J., bring to mind another contemporary African-American sports star whose narrative was one of tragic love and murder,[9] and elsewhere the film flirts dangerously with social stereotypes, both musical and ethnic; the scene in which Odin clearly forces his sexual climax on Dessie without her consent is a troubling enactment of racial stereotypes of black male libido. Yet the film is also careful to challenge many of the stereotypes it introduces, bringing to the fore in the storyline of Roger – a reworking of the play's marginalized rich gentleman, Roderigo – the brutal and brutalizing homophobia of much US high school culture, in a way that is perhaps all too easily glossed over with humour in comic film counterparts such as *10 Things I Hate About You*, as well as the stifling impact of social pigeonholing for boys like Odin and Hugo alike. The crushing effects of the values placed on achievement at sports in this culture are seen to play their part in the brutalization of Hugo. Those lyrics of exclusion and belonging on the score point up a genuine faultline in the US social system.

Rap's drowning out of the elitist sounds of opera, then, on *O*'s soundtrack is far from being the whole story. As with the framing effect of the Wagnerian *Liebestod* in Luhrmann's *Romeo + Juliet*, the 'Ave Maria' from *Otello* returns as a specific framing device in the closing scenes of Blake Nelson's film. Once again as an audience we read in ideas of tragic containment, of inescapable structures and paradigms, and social and cultural archetypes, even as the dialogue – in particular Odin's painful assertion that 'where he's from' in terms of ethnicity is not what has brought him to this end – asserts the antithesis to this. There are striking parallels in treatment and method here with the Luhrmann, and both sequences, Luhrmann's Wagnerian tomb scene and Blake Nelson's aria-framed modern adaptation, serve to challenge some of Adorno's influential theories about the disintegrating effect of repetition and quotation from great musical pieces. In his essay 'On the Fetish Character in Music and the Regression of Listening', Adorno speaks about the dangers of the effect of the fragmentary on our understanding, appreciation, and appropriation of musical works. He criticized the focus on specific moments in musical composition either in listening habits – the anthologizing of certain moments or movements from larger operas or symphonies as CD or MP3 'tracks' or on classical radio stations would be modern examples of this practice – or in the twentieth-century practice of 'borrowing' or musical quotation, suggesting that 'the romanticizing of particulars eats away the body of the whole' (1991: 36). Adorno suggests that this kind of quotation or fragmentation can only ever have a disintegrating effect, and it is a quality that he specifically associates with Wagner's compositional methods, in particular the focus on *leitmotif*, a fact that may be important for our purposes:

> Things become vulgarized. Irrelevant consumption destroys them . . . The memorability of disconnected parts, thanks to climaxes and repetitions, has a precursor in great music itself, in the technique of late romantic compositions, especially those of Wagner. The more reified the music, the more romantic it sounds to alienated ears. Just in this way it becomes "property". A Beethoven symphony as a whole, spontaneously experienced, can never be appropriated. (1991: 36)[10]

Many of Adorno's statements hold true for our encounters both with Shakespearean quotations and the use of classical music in advertisements today. In some cases listeners freely acknowledge that they first encounter both Shakespeare and classical compositions by Bach, Elgar, and others via this route. There can be little doubt that both Luhrmann and Blake Nelson adopt a classical musical frame of reference for their modern appropriations of Shakespeare as in part a knowing nod to the fact that their own work is a modern take on a 'classic'. The allusive context indicates and acknowledges that there is a long interpretative history of such 'takes' on Shakespeare, musical, filmic, and otherwise. But in both instances, for the listener who recognizes the specific allusion, the use of Verdi or Wagner does additional work, offering supplementary frames of reference to the tragic genre and its attendant expectations in any audience or recipient of the material and to appreciation of the specific archetypes of doomed romance depicted in each film. In the case of Luhrmann's quotation of *Tristan und Isolde*, it feeds into the water and drowning motifs of the film, just as in Blake Nelson's *O Desdemona's* swan-song aria from Verdi has specific resonance for the fates of Odin and Hugo.

We need to acknowledge the different allusive repertoires of members of the audience for any one film and at any one time. Our own readings and responses might alter as our frame of reference expands or shifts over time; as our listening habits range more widely, we may recognize allusions on a second or third viewing of a film that were not available to us first time around. Music in this respect becomes a means of historicizing our own interpretative practices. Frames of reference for films can be deliberate and envisaged, and I am suggesting that this is the case with the sub-Wagnerian uses of *Tristan und Isolde* and *Otello* in these specific film sequences as 'motifs of reminiscence' and as multiple signifiers. I would argue that they function rather differently from the kind of commodification implicit in Adorno's account of the repetition of musical fragments in contemporary composition.

But associations and resonances can also be happenstance, and that may be as true with soundtracks as with *mise-en-scènes* (see Gorbman 1987: 28). The release of Blake Nelson's film was considerably delayed due to its resonance, which could not have been predicted, with a real-life high school shooting at Columbine in 1999. Several subsequent enquiries argued that the schoolboys in that case were directly influenced in their violent actions by the music they listened to; the soundtrack of their lives was in this instance seen as a crucial factor in their behaviour. The resonance of neither film nor score is a fixed thing; it evolves, changes, and gathers meaning over time, and there is both a diachronic and a synchronic account of soundtracks to be offered in all cases. What is inescapable, however, is the emotive force of music in all areas of life. In a study such as this, where the focus of interest ranges from Duke Ellington to Ralph Vaughan Williams to Dmitri Shostakovich, it would be too easy to be dismissive of the recent tendency in mainstream Hollywood filmmaking to adapt or reconfigure Shakespeare for the teenage market in the form of high school movies accompanied by self-proclaimed 'hip soundtracks'.[11] In such films as these the soundtrack is rarely a work of specific composition, and is therefore different in both scale and approach from the commissioned soundtracks of Walton or Doyle for Olivier's or Branagh's screen Shakespeares. But it would be grossly unfair to suggest that these 'hip soundtracks' ignore their relationship to the Shakespearean source material in favour of direct appeal to the tastes and listening habits of their target population and teenage audience. Often the songs, their lyrics and subject matter especially, and sometimes even the performers themselves, are chosen for their relevance or apposite relationship to both film and Shakespearean subtext. What is also a common feature of this particular genre of films and the relationship of their acoustic accompaniment is the frequent blurring they effect between the diegetic and non-diegetic modes, in ways just as thoughtful and insightful as those I was arguing for in the context of more classical film soundtracks in the previous chapter.

A perfect working example of this tendency is Gil Junger's 1999 *10 Things I Hate About You*, a US high school transposition of *The Taming of the Shrew*, which, as well as creating a star vehicle for then teen-idols Heath Ledger and Julia Stiles as Patrick Verona and Kat Stratford respectively, the Petruccio and Katherine of Shakespeare's playtext, appealed to Shakespeare's brand status in numerous other ways.[12] As well as one sequence in which the resident school 'nerd' woos his partner for the school prom dance via both the words and image of Shakespeare – he leaves an Elizabethan dress in her locker along with an invitation from one 'W. Shakespeare' to the ball – the film includes several classroom sequences involving both the study and adaptation of Shakespeare's sonnets. The film's title is also a subtle allusion to the sonneteering tradition, an older version of the courtship rituals with which it is concerned. That connection is signalled by means of the tagline on promotional material to the film, which paraphrases not Shakespeare, but a later female exponent of the sonneteering tradition, Elizabeth Barrett Browning, transforming her 'How do I love thee? Let me count the ways' from Sonnet 43 of her 1845 sequence *Sonnets from the Portuguese*, into 'How do I loathe thee? Let me count the ways'.

What is frequently fascinating about this film is how Shakespeare, poetry, and music quite literally operate in tandem as part of the high school and teenage courtship rituals being depicted. This is in many respects a quirky modern take on the link between seduction and song present in many of Shakespeare's wooing scenes, from Romeo and Juliet's sonnet encounter at the Capulet ball to the masked encounter and attendant confusions between the dancing Beatrice and Benedict in *Much Ado About Nothing*. This Seattle-based film makes its own convincing point about the centrality of music to teenage cultural identity in the contemporary era, stamping this association from the opening sequence onwards.

In a fine example of the diegetic–non-diegetic blurrings posited as being central to the operations of music in this sub-genre, the opening credits of *10 Things I Hate About You* are accompanied by overlaid music only for it to become rapidly clear that this is part of the film's diegesis, part of an aural competition between the car radio blare-outs of two vehicles temporarily stopped at traffic lights. The film here both enacts and subverts a cliché of the genre – the traffic crossing stare-out is as old as the teenage film, with its provenance in James Dean movies – but that the two rivals are both women here (one being Kat Stratford herself) is a fun twist.

Kat's alternative tastes in music are pointed up both by the sneering condescension of her rival in this sequence and by the lyrics of independence offered by the song she is playing at high volume. Attempting to train Patrick in Kat's likes and dislikes for the purpose of wooing her successfully, Cameron dutifully informs him that she likes 'Angry Girl Music of the Indie Rock Persuasion'. Other feminist signifiers of independence are assigned to Kat throughout the film, not least through the books and writers she is associated with, most prominently Sylvia Plath, whose *The Bell Jar* Kat is clearly seen reading in one indicative framing shot. Her desire to go to university and her refusal to succumb to peer-group pressure on a whole range of issues from music to sexuality is part of her outsider status in the class-ridden, 'herd mentality' world of the US high school, the same hothouse environment that Blake Nelson's *O* investigates through a tragic Shakespearean prism rather than the romantic comedy frame selected by Junger. In one earlier sequence, a coded discussion of Kat's sexuality takes place between Cameron and Bianca when her younger sister denies that she is a 'k.d. lang fan'. The function of music as social identifier and categorizer is painfully to the fore in both film and social group.

It is, perhaps, no surprise that when Patrick Verona, himself an outsider in this hierarchized and ritualized community, arrives after being away for a year that he is matched with the romance-resistant Kat. Nor that he is encouraged to pursue his initially mercenary aim to seduce her via the medium of music; he is given CDs to listen to that are indicative of her taste, and he is encouraged to attend her favourite hangout, the deeply uncool 'Club Skunk'. The club scene is another useful insight into the pivotal role that music plays in the Kat–Patrick courtship – its rhythms and lyrics provide a modern counterpart to the shared rhythms that early modern audiences would have heard in the shared iambic pentameters of Petruccio's and Katherine's early exchanges in *The Taming of the Shrew*. What was being seen onstage was a quite violent argument in which two characters hurl bawdy and invective at each other in an offensive onslaught; what was heard underlying it, though, was the shared pentameter rhythm:

> PETRUCCIO: Come, come, you wasp, i'faith you are too angry.
> KATHERINE: If I be waspish, best beware my sting.
> PETRUCCIO: My remedy is then to pluck it out.
> KATHERINE: Ay, if the fool could find it where it lies.
> PETRUCCIO: Who knows not where a wasp does wear his sting?
>   In his tail?
> KATHERINE: In his tongue.
> PETRUCCIO: Whose tongue?
> KATHERINE: Yours if you talk of tales, and so farewell.
> PETRUCCIO: What, with my tongue in your tail? Nay, come again,
>   Good Kate, I am a gentleman.
> KATHERINE: That I'll try.
>   *She strikes him*
>
>   (II.i.209–17)

The auditory impact runs counter to what the eyes bear witness to; in a trick he repeats with other warring couples such as *Much Ado*'s Beatrice and Benedick or Biron and Rosaline in *Love's Labour's Lost*, Shakespeare lets the audience know that the plot trajectory for this couple will be romantic, even if against their better instincts, through their coupling and harmony in the dramatic verse. A similar kind of instinctual response to the inevitable 'getting together' of the initially ill-fated Kat and Patrick is achieved in *10 Things I Hate About You* via Kat's musical predilections. Her favourite band, 'Letters to Cleo', seen performing in the club scene, later perform a cover version – itself an interesting motif for adaptation more generally in this playfully derivative film – of the Nick Lowe song 'Cruel to be kind', which has obvious cunning and punning links in its title to the plotline of *The Taming of the Shrew*, a modern counterpart to Petruccio's speeches of falconry and horse mastery in the text of the play. In a further blurring of 'soundtrack' and diegesis, Patrick has hired the band for the high school prom in a desperate attempt to please Kat, and they will appear again in the closing sequence of the film when they perform 'I want you to want me' on the school roof as the camera pans away to reveal impressive aerial shots of Seattle. The segue at this point into the credits inverts the opening movement via heard music into the diegetic world of the high school community.

Elsewhere in the film Patrick takes the agency of music into his own hands in his efforts to win Kat's heart and attention. In a fantastically good-humoured parody of the Hollywood musical number (the prevalence of this trope in contemporary film updates of Shakespeare is discussed in chapter 4), he wins a smile from Kat by offering her the self-deprecating performance on the school steps of the 1967 Frankie Valli hit 'Can't take my eyes off of you', accompanied by the school sports' band and tannoy system, before being escorted from the premises by security guards. There are acknowledgements being made here of the link between the teenage Shakespeare films of the 1990s and the audiences for many 1950s and 1960s musical versions of his plays, in particular *West Side Story*, whose considerable influence on Luhrmann's *Romeo + Juliet* has already been discussed. If that musical and its film version identified the importance of the dance motif of Shakespeare's play to a new era of teenage visibility and cultural awareness, so Junger's film essays the centrality of popular musical culture to its youth audience and characters. The high school prom scene is a veritable cliché of US school movies from the 1950s onwards, and as with its approach to Shakespeare, Junger is keen both to acknowledge the precedents and to subvert them.

As in *The Taming of the Shrew*, Bianca is allowed to subvert expectations of her feminine passivity and seize agency in her life, not least when, standing in the centre of the crowded dance floor, she punches the loathsome Joey several times for his hubris and cruelty. The peer group pressures and heartache that surround the occasion of the prom are usefully revealed, just as elsewhere Junger's high school *mise-en-scène*, like that of Blake Nelson's *O*, is reflective and critical of the peer pressures surrounding wealth, status, display, and sexuality in this context. It is telling that the sonnet chosen for adaptation in the classroom sequences is Sonnet 141, a clever exposé of a society that determines its feelings and perceptions purely from surface appearances: 'In faith, I do not love thee with mine eyes, / For they in thee a thousand errors note' (ll. 1–2). Junger's prom sequence is defiantly not the big climax of the film; instead, that is left to a quieter classroom sequence in which Kat tearfully reads aloud her self-penned sonnet about a broken heart before a guilt-torn Patrick, whose acceptance of a financial bribe to woo her has been revealed publicly. Patrick's final act in the art of wooing is to buy Kat, who dreams of playing in a band, a white Fender Stratocaster guitar with the 'filthy lucre' earned from Joey. When she remarks that he may now have run out of seduction techniques, he assures her, 'There's always drums and bass and maybe one day a tambourine.' This is a light-hearted reworking of Shakespeare's own parodic sequences exposing the failure of textbook seductions in his play – witness III.i, where Lucentio and Hortensio compete for Bianca's hand via the textual and sexual suggestiveness of Ovid's *Ars Amatoria* ('The Arts of Love'). Music in this Shakespeare adaptation is, then, a force for good, a forger and statement of identity, an escape route and source of comfort and consolation in the teenage bedroom, and an essential component in the courtship ritual.

In the end, perhaps, 'hip soundtrack' is a rather limited description of the way in which song functions in *10 Things I Hate About You*. Retrospectively, the power of music in the film rests not just in the suggestive nature of the apposite lyrics for the songs selected for the compilation score, which offer explanatory frames for what is being seen onscreen as well as direct roots back to the Shakespearean source, but in entirely wordless sequences as well. This is nowhere more so than in the scene where we see a thoughtful and wounded Kat finding solace, headphones on and guitar in hand, in a music shop, watched over by an equally pensive Patrick (an interesting new take on the Shakespearean standard of the 'overhearing scene'), to the beautiful accompaniment of Joan Armatrading's voice: 'Why do you come here, when you know I've got troubles enough?'. This is no song from the contemporary music charts, no gross or blatant appeal to a teen audience; Junger lets the music speak for itself.

In a related vein, it might be argued that Shakespeare's presence in all these teen market-orientated adaptations is similarly subtextual. Without the full frame of reference, of source-text, allusion, and analogue, these films by Luhrmann, Junger, and Blake Nelson do not collapse – they offer perfectly enjoyable acts of entertainment within their own remit – but, if we can hear the allusive subtexts, the rhythms beneath the surface dialogue, perhaps they can speak to us a little more deeply and with a little more resonance after all.

Notes

1 For further discussion on this topic, see Jones 2004.
2 Hooper produced many of the song versions heard on the score to the film; the additional symphonic music on the score was produced by Luhrmann's long-term collaborator Craig Armstrong.
3 Isolde does not literally drown in the operatic version of the myth, despite its coastal setting in Cornwall. There may be a further layer of reference in all this, however, to Ophelia's drowning/suicide, a potent nineteenth-century idea and image, as we have seen in earlier chapters.
4 A brilliant theatre production devised by the Kneehigh Theatre Company and performed in 2005 and 2006 in various locations offered a profound exploration of this idea, citing Wagner's opera at various times within its postmodern allusive frame.
5 My thanks to Sarah Grandage for ongoing discussions of this topic.

6 Tellingly, Luhrmann knowingly subverts audience expectations in the film of this iconic moment from the play: Leonardo Di Caprio's Romeo climbs up the balcony to Juliet's room only to fall backwards into the mansion pool when he is unexpectedly startled by Miriam Margoyles's comic turn as the Nurse. This Romeo and Juliet will fittingly enact their balcony scene underwater in an effort to escape the prying eyes of the mansion's surveillance cameras.

7 See Loehlin 2000: 129, citing an unpublished paper by Kenneth Rothwell. The film is from 1916 and starred Theda Bara.

8 Blake Nelson's own film credits are misleading in this respect: although it is noted that the production of *Otello* used is performed by the Boys' Choir of the Opéra de Paris, it is in fact the children's chorus for that production that this choir provides. The main company for the production was the orchestra and chorus of the Opéra Bastille, and the singer of the 'Ave Maria' was actually Cheryl Studer.

9 And one whose trial for the murder of his white American wife, Nicole Simpson (he was ultimately, if controversially, acquitted), was persistently and troublingly compared to the *Othello* plotline. See Hodgdon 1997: 23.

10 For an alternative view on repetition, see McClary 1998. Adorno's theories were undoubtedly negatively influenced by the appropriation of Wagner by the Third Reich. Quotation and fragmentation in works by other composers troubled him less. I am grateful to Daniel Grimley for discussion of Adorno's theories.

11 As mentioned in the previous chapter, this phrase derives from the video jacket to Gil Junger's *10 Things I Hate About You* (1999).

12 On Shakespeare's brand status, see a stimulating recent discussion by Sonia Massai (2005).

Further examples and reading

A number of the films discussed in this chapter are marketed to an explicitly youth-oriented audience, so for comparison readers might like to consider the scores to other Shakespearean adaptations in this category: Tommy O'Haver's *Get Over It* (2001), which was discussed in an earlier chapter on musicals, makes some great parodic play both on the boy band phenomenon and the trend for Shakespeare rock musicals, as well as having a very knowing compilation score; Andy Fickman's *She's the Man*, a US high school version of *Twelfth Night* (with its cross-dressing narrative intact) is a recent excursion into this field (2006).

Many of the suggestions for further reading on film scores and Shakespeare onscreen provided in the previous chapter are equally relevant here, but it is worth repeating Jeff Smith's *The Sounds of Commerce: Marketing Popular Film Music* (New York: Columbia University Press, 1998) for its salient discussion of the development of the idea and practice of the 'compilation score'. Many of the articles in the journal *Literature/Film Quarterly* discuss film scores in some detail.

9

Contemporary Music and
Popular Culture

> I do not desire you to please me, I do desire you to sing
> *As You Like It*, ɪɪ.v.15–16

This study began with a 'Prelude' that attempted to stress the qualitative and quantitative differences between adaptation, appropriation, quotation, citation, allusion, reworking, borrowing, sampling, and afterlife in any analysis of the musical interpretation of Shakespeare and his oeuvre. The most fractured and fragmented Shakespearean presence of all is perhaps to be found in contemporary popular music, especially the compressed form of the popular song lyric, to the extent that terms like 'adaptation' seem inaccurate, even irrelevant, when applied to the glancing references or invocations that these frequently involve. It is difficult in the same context to be confident, therefore, about the extent to which these fleeting references or allusions require recognition – 'deep', fully contextualized, or otherwise – on the part of their receiving audiences of their Shakespearean origin or inspiration for the production of their meanings and effects.[1]

In some contemporary song lyrics understandings of particular plays or even the dramaturgic context of particular quotations are of considerably less importance than they might have been for an eighteenth-century setting of one of Ariel's songs from *The Tempest*, or 'Fear no more the heat of the sun', the funeral dirge from *Cymbeline*. Purists might counter that it is equally questionable whether we need as listeners to recognize the Shakespearean source of *The Merchant of Venice* for works such as Ralph Vaughan Williams's *Serenade to Music*, or, indeed, the specific scene from which the lyrics for that piece derive: an exchange between the newly wed Lorenzo and Jessica, now settled in Portia's romance-driven domain of Belmont. It is, after all, a response to the wider topic of music, rather than an interpretation of the sexual, religious, or racial politics of the source play. Nevertheless, it would seem fair to suggest that in many pop and rock appropriations of Shakespeare's names, lines, and play titles the 'borrowings' serve the purpose of standing metonymically for theatrical, and even literary, culture in general, rather than being specific or locally resonant allusions.

Perhaps in these instances it is fair to argue that a 'big-time' version of Shakespeare (Bristol 1996: *passim*) is in operation, one that mobilizes a generalized sense and understanding of Shakespeare's cultural centrality, as opposed to a locally specific and highly analytical frame of reference to a particular play or speech. Examples of this method include Peter Hamill's song 'After the show' (1985), which, as its title suggests, is a rumination on the acting profession, and which, as well as alluding to *Hamlet* and the art of soliloquizing, cites Samuel Beckett's *Waiting for Godot*, another seminal theatre text. Canadian rock group Rush invoked a similar line of association in their track 'Limelight' (1997), where they quote the meta-theatrical observation from *As You Like It*: 'All the world's a stage' (II.vii.139). They used the same line as an album title (1987), but once again it was the general theme of theatricality and stage perform-ance that drove the adoption of the phrase rather than any specific concern with the play or its gender-bending themes. In another Hamill song, 'A way out' (1999) a line from *Hamlet* provided the jumping off point for lyrics that play on the concept of being 'out' of things, and the common-place phrases we attach to this idea: out of stock, out of date, out of love. It would be easy to suggest that in all these cases Shakespeare is merely functioning as part of common parlance, and that there is little specific relevance to the quotations other than a playfulness with language and metaphor.

Yet, in further analysis, Hamill proves to be a songwriter who considers Shakespeare to be a shaping influence. 'A way out' is aware of other Shakespearean drama besides *Hamlet* in its Paul Muldoon-esque run on words: Lady Macbeth's sleep-walking scene in which she attempts to wash the blood of Duncan's murder from her hands is recalled, for example, in the phrase 'Out, damned spot' (see v.i.33).[2] Hamill looks to another meta-theatrical speech from *Hamlet* for a song entitled 'The play's the thing' (2002), which alludes to Hamlet's assertion at II.ii.606–7 that 'The play's the thing / Wherein I'll catch the conscience of the King'. Elsewhere in the lyrics to that track Hamill draws in a wider Shakespearean context as he ruminates on the skill of a play-wright whose dramatic writings still seem deeply relevant to modern culture. The Earl of Warwick's speech from III.i of *2 Henry IV* is quoted at some length:

> There is a history in all men's lives
> Figuring the nature of the times deceased;
> The which observed, a man may prophesy,
> With a near aim, of the main chance of things
> As yet not come to life, who in their seeds
> And weak beginnings lie intreasurèd
> Such things become the hatch and brood of time;
>
> (III.i.75–81)

And the same song also evokes Jaques's set-piece soliloquy from *As You Like It* on the seven ages of man which begins with the 'All the world's a stage' observation and ends with a haunting evocation of old age:

> Last scene of all,
> That ends this strange, eventful history,
> Is second childishness and mere oblivion,
> Sans teeth, sans eyes, sans taste, sans everything.
>
> (II.vii.163–6)

Both these extracts are concerned with the topic of personal time and history, suggesting that Hamill is well read in the Shakespearean canon.

There is some case for arguing that rock and popular music have always sought a form of authenticity and authority from allusion to literary and cultural sources. Progressive rock groups such as Yes and Genesis were deeply self-conscious in their adaptation of literary sources into song, and, as mentioned in chapter 2, the guitarist from the latter group, Steve Hackett, extended that interest during his solo career by composing a fully orchestrated suite for classical guitar inspired by *A Midsummer Night's Dream* (1997). These rock groups were not alone in this impulse; Duke Ellington's motives in adapting or 'riffing' on Shakespeare for the *Such Sweet Thunder* suite he co-created with Billy Strayhorn (1957) have often been described as an effort to stress jazz's cultural significance (Lanier 2004). But authenticating strategies alone cannot adequately explain the presence, however fragmented, of Shakespeare and his dramatic verse in popular music culture.

One connecting thread is surely locatable in the fact that the common subject of much popular song is love, however fraught, thwarted, or beset by uncontrollable passions it might be at various turns. The archetypal form in Shakespeare's era for writing about love was the sonnet, and we have already noted in previous chapters how, in addition to creating his influential sonnet sequence, Shakespeare embedded dramatic examples of the genre in plays ranging from 1 *Henry IV* to *Love's Labour's Lost* to *As*

You Like It. In the last of these, the romantic male lead Orlando is seen pinning sonnets on trees in the Forest of Arden in a wilful satire on the besotted Petrarchan lover of sonneteering convention (see iii.ii.1–10). If sonnets have influenced composers from Gustav Holst to Gerald Finzi to Einojuhani Rautavaara in the twentieth century, they have also enjoyed contemporary popular music settings by groups and performers as diverse as the South African Zulu a cappella group Ladysmith Black Mambazo to former Roxy Music glam-rock singer Bryan Ferry and female vocalist Des'ree. All of these examples were gathered together, along with readings by professional actors of several Shakespeare sonnets as well as other love- and music-related speeches from his plays, for a 2002 CD, the proceeds of which were dedicated to the Royal Academy of Dramatic Arts, the Michael Kamen-produced *When Love Speaks*. Kamen is himself a crossover artist with a backlist in both classical composition and film scores, and the CD features his own high school operatic setting for Desdemona's 'Willow Song' from *Othello*, performed by the eminent soprano Barbara Bonney. This particular setting, which features a clarinet line supporting the female voice, consciously hearkens back to the links between woodwind and the tragic Shakespearean heroine discussed in chapter 2.

The musical examples on this CD are not purely Shakespearean. An example of music contemporary with the playwright himself is offered in a version of John Dowland's 'Come again: sweet love doth now invite', sung by the tenor John Potter, but in the dialogue between tenor voice, lute, baroque violin, double bass, and soprano saxophone – the latter enjoying a striking solo section – Dowland's lyric is made to discourse in a partly modern idiom, one aware of the history of jazz adaptations of early modern texts and music. A similarly heightened sense of intertextuality and intertheatricality feeds the choice of Christopher Marlowe's pastoral lyric '(Come) Live with me and be my love' for Annie Lennox to sing. Known partly for her work with Dave Stewart in the Eurhythmics, her interpretation is informed by the modern technology of synthesizers and manipulated voices. Lennox already has a track record in terms of postmodern encounters with Marlowe, since she appears onscreen in strikingly modern dress singing Cole Porter's 'Every time we say goodbye' in the middle of Derek Jarman's iconoclastic film version of that playwright's *Edward II* (1991; for an excellent discussion of the semiotics of this film, see Bennett 1996: 110–15), but a further knowing allusion to film and to Shakespeare onscreen seems possible in the choice of this song. For it is the same Marlowe lyric that is made into a 1930s big band number for performance at the Victory Ball which we see in full swing (if you will forgive the pun) in the opening sequence of Richard Loncraine's 1995 version of *Richard III*, which was analysed in the context of musicals and cinematic pastiche in chapter 4. Kamen's choices throughout this CD seem to point to the kind of knowing intertextuality and multi-layered interpretation that I have argued governs much of the musical adaptation discussed in this book.

Ladysmith Black Mambazo fittingly adapt Sonnet 8, which is on the theme of music ('Music to hear, why hear'st thou music sadly?'), for their distinctive polyphonic vocal performance (cf. Edmondson and Wells 2004: 168–9). The underlying refrain becomes a phrase from the second line 'joy delights in joy' which seems perfectly suited to their fiercely positive performances, first introduced to the global music community in the midst of the horrors, censorships, and deprivations of South African apartheid when Paul Simon worked with them on his seminal album *Graceland* (1986).[3] Another set of cultural and geographical referents entirely is introduced on to the CD by the performance of Sonnet 35 ('No more be grieved at that which thou hast done') by Delta blues musician Keb' Mo'.[4] The wailing blues guitar and the introspection of his singing style find a genuine kinship with the interiority and inwardness of the sonnet form. The sonnet is a form of debate with the self: 'Such civil war is in my love and hate' (l. 14). Similarly apposite is the encounter between Bryan Ferry's soulful voice and the much adapted lines of Sonnet 18 ('Shall I compare thee to a summer's day?'). The sonnet offers the consolation to the young man that when his physical beauty is wrinkled, the poetry of the sonnets will offer an alternative permanence in their 'eternal lines' (l. 12). That, as we have seen in previous discussions both of jazz and classical song settings, this sonnet has been so frequently revised and reinterpreted appears to bear this point out: 'So long lives this, and this gives this life to thee' (l. 14).

Equally beautiful congruence between poem and performative style is to be found in Rufus Wainwright's interpretation of Sonnet 29 ('When in disgrace with fortune and men's eyes'). The melancholic, almost self-pitying tone of the lines and the 'bootless cries' (l. 3) suits his plaintive, folk-imbued delivery perfectly: 'I all alone beweep my outcast state' (l. 2). The song does not rest on this note of depressing isolation, however. Wainwright's tone lifts and rises as he describes 'sweet love remembered' (l. 13) – these words are beautifully drawn out and extended for emphasis in the song version – and his lone voice now finds itself accompanied and comforted by backing singers and complex instrumentation. The banjo and accordion music on this number were provided by folk performers Kate and Anna McGarrigle, a further indication of the diverse range of musical referents assembled for this response to Shakespeare's verse.

Most telling, perhaps, in terms of the knowing referentiality of the collection mentioned earlier, is the choice of Des'ree to perform a musical setting this time not of a sonnet but of Portia's keynote speech from *The Merchant of Venice*, 'The quality of mercy is not strained' (IV.i.181). That choice both confirms and works playfully against the grain of expectation, in that Des'ree is associated for many with the topics of both Shakespeare and love, since she would undoubtedly be best known to a Shakespeare-aware audience (surely the target population of an enterprise such as this) as the singer of the 'love theme' from Baz Luhrmann's *Romeo + Juliet* (1996). Her song from that film, 'Kissing you', is a track which earlier chapters have located in a deep intertextual framework that includes the work of Pyotr Tchaikovsky, Hector Berlioz, and Nino Rota, among others. Yet she does not sing a sonnet, but instead delivers lines that seem in their plea for mercy imbued as much with the gospel tradition as contemporary popular culture (a combination that Luhrmann was not averse to including in his film score with a gospel choir interpretation of Prince's 'When doves cry').

When it comes to linking Shakespeare and romantic love in the contemporary imagination, the archetypal play, as the above example surely proves, is undoubtedly *Romeo and Juliet*. Stephen Buhler (2002) has been instrumental in indicating the plethora of references to that play and its youthful protagonists throughout twentieth-century popular song. He begins his list of salient examples with the Otis Blackwell song 'Fever', perhaps best known in Peggy Lee's sultry 1958 rendition, complete with cod-Shakespearean dialogue: 'thou', 'givest', 'kisseth'. This song emerged at much the same moment as the Ellington–Strayhorn collaboration in the 1950s, and indicates in its easy allusions a cultural centrality on the part of Shakespeare that may not hold as true today. Nevertheless, there have been many other pop songs that allude to or cite the example of the 'star-crossed lovers', including The Supremes' 'Back in My Arms Again' in the 1960s, and later tracks by lyricist-poets such as Bruce Springsteen including 'Incident on 57th Street' (1973), 'Fire', and 'Point blank' (both on his 1980 album *The River*), Tom Waits ('Romeo is bleeding', 1978), and Lou Reed, whose 'Romeo had Juliette' adapts the tragic love story into one with an interracial theme – the protagonists of this song on his *New York* album (1989) are called Romeo Rodriguez and Juliette Bell (Buhler 2002: 252–6).[5]

Buhler makes the very persuasive argument that all these adaptations are filtered through another music-based response to *Romeo and Juliet* that has already been discussed in this study, the 1957 musical *West Side Story*, especially after its release as an Oscar-winning film in 1961. Springsteen's racially inflected version of the story, like Reed's, is directly inspired by *West Side Story* – his lovers are 'Spanish Johnny' and his Puerto Rican Juliet. Similarly, Waits includes his 'Romeo' song on the album *Blue Valentine* (1978), which contains a typically idiosyncratic and moving version of the Tony and Maria duet 'Somewhere' from that musical. The effect of filtration or mediation can also be registered in the Dire Straits song entitled 'Romeo and Juliet' which appeared on their *Making Movies* album (1980). The filmic and intertextual context was signalled by the album's overall concept of making songs about seminal movies, but it extends to the song itself, where the urban gangland Juliet sings lines from a 1960s Angels song (Buhler 2002: 256). In a manner akin to the specially commissioned lyrics to those songs included on Luhrmann's film soundtrack, Mark Knopfler's words make intricate play with actual verse-lines from Shakespeare's playtext as well as songs from *West Side Story*, in their reference to stars and direct citation of lines such as 'There's a place for us' from 'Somewhere'. The presence of *Romeo and Juliet* in musical adaptation persists and appears in such diverse locations as the Elvis Costello and Brodsky Quartet collaboration *The Juliet Letters* (1993), which is a concept album responding to the considerable archive of personal and intimate correspondence sent to the supposed site of Juliet's balcony in modern-day Verona, and boy band lyrics on love and sonneteering.

Just as in orchestral music the iconic power of particular characters can be registered in symphonic poems such as Elgar's *Falstaff*, Dvořák's *Othello*, and Liszt's *Hamlet*, so we can identify something parallel in what might be termed the 'Romeo and Juliet effect' in popular music. If Shakespeare himself becomes metonymic of literature and the theatre, so the star-crossed lovers stand for passionate love in its fullest sense. They are not the only characters to register a presence in contemporary song lyrics, although they are, as Buhler indicates, by far the most dominant. Hamlet and his female tragic counterpart Ophelia also have their percentage of market share. Former 10,000 Maniacs lead singer Natalie Merchant's beautiful 'Ophelia' (on her 1998 album of the same name) or the folk singer Jewel's reference to the same character's drowning in her song 'Innocence maintained' on her album *Spirit* might usefully be read as part of a wider interest in the newly perceived agency of Shakespeare's tragic heroines in the wake of feminist criticism of the plays (see, e.g. Jardine 1983; Rutter

2001; Rackin 2005).[6] Buhler suggests that the comparable agency of Juliet in twentieth-century versions of her story in song lyrics is also in part produced by feminism. A similar impulse certainly informs the adaptation of the previously mentioned Dire Straits song by The Indigo Girls on their 1992 album *Rites of Passage*. There a female voice articulating Romeo's lines is a conscious act of inversion, and also brings into play a lesbian and gay erotica that finds a remarkable line of connection to the early modern world of the boy actor and the acknowledged homoeroticism of the commercial seventeenth-century stage.[7]

Douglas Lanier has noted a particular interest in Shakespeare stemming from the folk music tradition, detailing several versions of songs from *The Tempest* or songs which allude to them (Lanier 2002: 69). Noting the possible influence or mediation of a particular film interpretation of *Romeo and Juliet*, Franco Zeffirelli's 1968 'flower-power' version, Lanier suggests that this might explain the interest of late 1960s hippy culture in the songs and verse of the Bard. Marianne Faithful performed a version of 'Full fathom five' on a 1965 album *Come My Way*; Donovan sang 'Under the greenwood tree' on *A Gift from a Flower to a Garden* (1968); and folk guru Pete Seeger sang 'Full fathom five' on *Dangerous Songs!?* in 1966. Lanier notes that the latter song is actually a creative amalgam that 'combines Ariel's lament for the drowned father with a rewritten line from *Hamlet*, "to fight, perchance to win; ay, there's the rub"' (2002: 69). But the peace and love movements of the late 1960s are insufficient in themselves to explain Shakespearean presence in folk-song and music more generally. Earlier references to the work of Edward German, Gustav Holst, and Ralph Vaughan Williams (see chapter 2) located their deployment of Shakespeare alongside songs and dances from the folk tradition in the context of the English pastoral movement at the start of the twentieth century and in particular the influence of Cecil Sharp and the English folk revival. As well as exerting its influence in terms of traditions of staging Shakespeare at Stratford-upon-Avon and elsewhere, and encouraging a general identification of Shakespeare's plays with a specific notion and understanding of 'Englishness', I would argue that these developments influence later folk invocations of Shakespearean plays, not just in the work of US artist Seeger but more significantly in the distinctly English derivation of the form performed by Martin Carthy and others. Carthy has a track entitled 'Perfumes of Arabia', an allusion to Lady Macbeth's sleep-walking scene ('All the perfumes of Arabia will not sweeten this little hand', v.i.48–9) on his collaborative 1992 album with Dave Swarbrick, *Skin and Bone*, and many other lyrics which display a knowledge of and interest in Shakespeare, a knowledge no doubt shored up by his involvement in productions at the Royal Shakespeare Company directed by Bill Alexander, yet another example of the interaction between theatrical productions and the world of music.[8]

Other musical genres less 'rooted' in the Warwickshire soil (cf. Halio 1994: 35) than perhaps English folk-song have also found a surprising frame of reference in the Shakespearean canon. Hip-hop's negotiations with the Shakespearean legacy in the form of musicals such as *The Bombitty of Errors* were considered in chapter 4, but it has found additional outlets in the tradition of rap 'duelling'. This is a practice that has kinship with the classical musical tradition of violin duels (itself a musical adaptation of the parries and thrusts of fencing). The tradition was picked up and echoed in US culture both in jazz and bluegrass (recall, for instance, the duelling banjos on the soundtrack to *Deliverance*, dir. John Boorman, 1972), and has now metamorphosed further into the duelling MCs of hip-hop. Several club performances of this kind have modelled their 'battle-scenes' on Shakespearean history plays which consciously structure themselves around the primeval image of warring enemy 'brothers'; compare, for example, the linguistic and physical encounter of Hal and Hotspur in *1 Henry IV*. Films such as *Renaissance Man* (dir. Penny Marshall, 1994) have in turn made artistic capital from this surprising but productive juxtaposition of Shakespeare with rap culture and rhythms. In the end, it comes down to verse patterns and rhythms: be it an aria, a 1930s musical show-tune, or a hip-hop duel, music has found its own rich idiom for responding to Shakespeare.

I began this chapter with the theme of recognition. The extent to which we 'recognize' Shakespeare in all or any of the musical genres and examples explored in this study depends on different kinds of knowledge, sometimes different kinds of shared knowledge or frames of cultural reference. It is a much debated issue in current Shakespeare studies to what extent the familiarity with his plays and verse-lines that might have been assumed by a Vaughan Williams writing for a recital hall audience in the 1920s can still be assumed by a pop lyricist in 2006. Perhaps it cannot be the same, but that does not devalue the attempt to explore Shakespearean resonance in a contemporary and popular cultural context. Perhaps the route of access is simply different and as context-specific as that of Vaughan Williams's post-Great War generation. Audiences, in particular youth audiences, in 2007 are visually and aurally literate, but their access to that material comes not through the commercial playhouses or concert halls but via MP3 downloads and the medium of film. The success and influence of Luhrmann's *Romeo + Juliet* is perhaps proof that Shakespeare retains a resonance for this generation, but one that functions, musically and philosophically, in very different ways from those promulgated by previous generations. In saying this, however, one of the most striking things to come out of this study, speaking personally, is an understanding of the complex web of influence, intertextuality, filtration, and mediation that has shaped the history of Shakespeare in a musical context. Even as I seek to stress the precise historical context of a nineteenth-century operatic adaptation of *Othello* or a twentieth-century folk-song, a Restoration song setting for counter-tenor voice, or a pop song on a film score, I also want to suggest at the same time that everything connects.

Popular music is in the twenty-first century finding a new resonance in a theatrical context. New plays appeared in 2006 that used music not only to provide the temporal and geographical locaters of the production's *mise-en-scène* but as an integral part of their narrative. Michael Pinchbeck and Giles Croft's *The White Album*, which premièred at Nottingham Playhouse, deploys, as its title suggests, the Beatles' album of the same name to tell a story of obsession that takes in the history of the Fab Four, Charles Manson, drug addiction, and the demise of the LP. Tom Stoppard's *Rock 'n' Roll*, which opened at the Royal Court Theatre in London, in a parallel move, features Syd Barrett, former lead singer of Pink Floyd (who died during the play's initial run), as part of both the dramatic narrative and the soundtrack – he even 'appears' briefly onstage in its opening moments – as it moves between Cambridge and Czechoslovakia and between 1968 and 1991 in what amounts to a sustained and heartfelt analysis of the relationship between artistic culture, personal experience, and international politics.

Whether Shakespeare will find a new place in the context of these theatrical fashions and aesthetic movements remains to be seen, but, as a closing example in this chapter on popular music, I want to mention the delightful discovery that in 1964, in a television special entitled 'Around the Beatles', John Lennon, Paul McCartney, George Harrison, and Ringo Starr put on a version of the play-within-the-play from *A Midsummer Night's Dream*, the mechanicals' 'tedious brief scene' (v.i.56) of Pyramus and Thisbe (Williams 1997: 212–13). McCartney played Pyramus, Lennon was Thisbe, Harrison played Moonshine, and Starr was Lion. It was an act of comic appropriation that perhaps assumed a knowledge of Shakespeare on the part of the audience, although the popular, slapstick comedy of Shakespeare's playlet did not necessarily require any serious advanced study. Just as audiences today need not understand all the connotations of Shakespeare's parody of Arthur Golding's Elizabethan translation of Ovid's *Metamorphoses* in the risible verse and even more risible delivery of Peter Quince's amateur actors (although as someone in higher education I suppose there is a sneaking hope that if they do, it will enrich their response), so it is not necessary to make the case that in making their own comic interpretation of this specific moment of Shakespeare's romantic comedy, the Beatles were referring back to the mid-seventeenth-century tradition of 'drolls', although it is a happy coincidence of history. It is enough that what they did in 1964 can send us spinning back to the hybridized and adaptational mode of Shakespearean performance that was the inheritance of Henry Purcell, and that informed and influenced Purcell's own musical compositions on a Shakespearean theme, which in turn influenced Benjamin Britten when he looked to the play just a few years prior to the Beatles, not to write popular songs but for the purposes of modern, experimental opera. Everything connects . . .

Notes

1 For a related argument, see Irina Cholij's entry on 'Pop Music' in *The Oxford Companion to Shakespeare*, where she notes that 'the influence of Shakespeare on anglophone pop music has predominantly been in the quotation of a single line of text . . .' (Dobson and Wells 2001).

2 It appears on a 1999 album called *Live* with a track entitled 'Ophelia'.

3 On the connections between Shakespeare and South African culture more generally, see Orkin 2005.

4 The same artist was chosen to perform the version of 'God bless America' that saw fictional TV US president Jed Bartlett leave the White House in the final episode of the series *The West Wing* that was screened in the USA in April 2006 and in the UK in July of the same year.

5 Lou Reed has responded to Shakespeare elsewhere in his lyrics: e.g., in the song 'Goodnight Ladies' from his *Transformer* album (1972) which uses both in its title and its choric refrain this line from iv.v. of *Hamlet*, where Ophelia in her madness sings of her distress. The musical connections of this particular character, who sings several traditional songs in this scene, many of which, as we saw in ch. 2, were re-set by musicians and composers of subsequent ages, may render her particularly attractive to contemporary artists exploring the Shakespearean canon for material to use and adapt.

6 Former punk singer and performer Toyah Wilcox (who starred as Miranda in Derek Jarman's 1980 film of *The Tempest*) released a song 'Ophelia's Shadow' in 2003, on an eponymous album. In 2007, Natalie Merchant was also one of several commissioned artists who set individual sonnets to music as part of the Royal Shakespeare Company's *Nothing Like The Sun – The Sonnet Project*, a collaboration with composer Gavin Bryars and Opera North. The work premièred at Stratford-upon-Avon in February 2007.

7 The same group also released an album entitled *Swamp Ophelia* in 1994.

8 Carthy also performs a version of the Adam McNaughton song 'Oor Hamlet' (aka 'The Three-Minute Hamlet') sung to the traditional tune of 'The Mason's Apron' in live concerts. This is a jokey synopsis of Shakespeare's tragedy.

Further examples and reading

Examples will appear long beyond the publication of this book, I hope, but for those interested in pursuing some of the topics raised here, an excellent introduction to the perils and pleasures of analysing popular music is Simon Frith, Will Straw, and John Street (eds), *The Cambridge Companion to Pop and Rock* (Cambridge: Cambridge University Press, 2001). On rap and hip-hop, also highly recommended are the following: Russell Potter, *Spectacular Vernaculars: Hip-Hop and the Politics of Postmodernism* (Albany: State University of New York Press, 1995); and Adam Krims, *Rap Music and the Poetics of Identity* (Cambridge: Cambridge University Press, 2000).

On Shakespeare and popular music and popular culture more generally, see Douglas Lanier, *Shakespeare and Modern Popular Culture* (Oxford: Oxford University Press, 2002), and the collection of essays *Shakespeare After Mass Media* ed. Richard Burt (New York: Palgrave, 2002) (which includes Stephen Buhler's essay on contemporary pop responses to *Romeo and Juliet* cited on several occasions in the above chapter). Lanier is currently working on a much anticipated study of Shakespeare and rap culture. Irina Cholij's entry on 'Popular Music' in *The Oxford Companion to Shakespeare*, ed. Michael Dobson and Stanley Wells (Oxford: Oxford University Press, 2001) is a helpful survey of the field, and additional references and contexts may be found in Malgorzata Grzegorzewska's article 'Wooing in Festival Terms: Sonneteering Lovers, Rock, and Blues', in *Shakespeare and the Twentieth Century*, ed. Jonathan Bate, Jill L. Levenson, and Dieter Mehl (London: University of Delaware Press, 1998).

Coda

But shall we make the welkin dance indeed? Shall we rouse the night-owl in
a catch that will draw three souls out of one weaver? Shall we do that?

Twelfth Night, ii.iii.56–8

In conclusion, I should perhaps pay heed to the observation of musicologist Ian Kemp that 'A coda is not the place for new themes' (1992: 69). However, looking back over this study, it occurs to me that one of the major connecting threads between the diverse range of musical compositions and responses to Shakespeare that we have been considering as afterlives and borrowings is the fact that the majority of these works found their inspiration in some way within a theatrical context. Many of the composers we have examined, from Henry Purcell in the late seventeenth century, through Thomas Arne in the eighteenth, and Felix Mendelssohn in the nineteenth, to Ralph Vaughan Williams and Duke Ellington in the twentieth, were commissioned to write incidental music for theatrical performances and productions of Shakespeare plays. This in turn often influenced their further engagement with his canon, be it in the form of song settings or more ruminative responses in music to specific characters, scenes, or speeches, or sometimes with the idea of Shakespeare himself. Other composers such as Hector Berlioz or Franz Liszt found comparable inspiration not by working on specific theatre productions but by witnessing them in performance. They were inspired by the act of spectating plays such as *Romeo and Juliet* and *Hamlet*, and the performances of actors such as Harriet Smithson and Bogumil Dawison, to compose dramatic symphonies in response to those playtexts.

Though it pains me in some ways to observe the phenomenon, it is a simple fact that we do not go to the theatre as often or in the ways that people did in previous generations and eras. Higher education students are now far more likely to encounter their Shakespeare through the medium of film. But it is certainly not the case that the advent of film has seen a downturn of interest in Shakespeare or even in Shakespeare-related music. In the twentieth century the pioneering and hugely influential new medium of cinema responded to Shakespeare not only by adapting a vast number of his stage plays for the screen, but by occasioning a whole new outlet for musical composition, inspiring the work of William Walton and Dmitri Shostakovich, among others. It would be far too simplistic, then, to claim that the waning influence of theatre will necessarily foster the waning presence of Shakespeare in the kind of musical afterlives that have been my subject here. The Bard's influence or presence in film continues today, with popular music soundtracks used to shed light on, argue with, or complement Shakespearean lines and plotlines in some works, as well as occasioning a fruitful encounter between popular and classical modes in several such scores. These routes of access to Shakespeare through film rather than live theatre will undoubtedly alter the relationship that audiences both for these films and the musical compositions have with the Shakespearean source, but the encounter will continue to be productive and revealing.

Perhaps, then, we should look to film, and its sister form of television, for the future of Shakespeare and music. It certainly seems a rich future in that regard. Recent examples of Shakespeare-specific commissions include the work of fusion composer Nitin Sawnhey for a Tim Supple-directed *Twelfth Night* for Channel 4 (2003), a production that was heavily influenced by the tenets and practices of intercultural performance in its interpretation of the play.[1] Having said that, though, it is surely far less common in the modern era to see large-scale musical composition being commissioned for artistic contexts other than film. There have been a handful of modern Shakespeare operas – Thomas Adès's *The Tempest* is one fine recent example. But opera has always, controversially, been the recipient of major funding subsidies. Few working theatres in the West today can afford to maintain orchestras, let alone salaried musicians. There seems little or reduced space, then, for the kind of musical and theatrical encounter that was possible in the nineteenth century and which gave Mendelssohn and others their opportunities. And yet . . . as well as the imaginative use of music in mainstream productions such as those at the Royal Shakespeare Company, including Greg Doran's 1999 *Timon of Athens*, which redeployed the incidental music of Duke Ellington to rich effect, and Katie Mitchell's work with plainchant in her productions of the history plays in the 1990s, there has been a noticeable emergence in recent years of small theatre companies with a genuine commitment to live music in their work.

Several of these companies – for example, Northern Broadsides, Shared Experience, and Kneehigh Theatre – not only encourage the practice of employing actors who have additional skills in playing instruments or singing, enabling them to produce their own music for shows, but they have also demonstrated a marked interest in the practice of adaptation. Shared Experience has established a working identity as a company that adapts novels to a live theatrical experience, with an emphasis on physical theatre, dance, mime, and movement. Kneehigh Theatre have produced some of the most ground-breaking recent adaptations of literary works, ranging from the traditional Cornish myth *Tristan and Iseult* to Angela Carter's highly theatrical novel *Nights at the Circus*. As I write this, they are on tour with a Shakespearean adaptation, a production of *Cymbeline* that forms part of the Royal Shakespeare Company's Complete Works Festival, which has itself already demonstrated an interest in and commitment to the relationship between theatre and music in its jazz-accompanied *Othello*, staged in April 2006, and a specially commissioned project on the sonnets – *Nothing Like the Sun*, created by Gavin Bryars in collaboration with Opera North and other contemporary artists and performers – scheduled for 2007, as well as a new musical version of *The Merry Wives of Windsor*. The incidental music for Kneehigh's *Cymbeline* (composed by Stu Barker and the company; see Kneehigh 2006 in the Discography) was no mere background noise. Dominic Lawton's remarkable delivery of many of these numbers in a fused ska-hip-hop idiom provided the heartbeat of the performance. Nowhere was this more evident than when, in his role as one of Imogen's brothers, he offered a searing rendition of 'Fear no more the heat of the sun', a moment of radical innovation and yet moving continuity with the history of Shakespeare in musical adaptation. Northern Broadsides have a long-established relationship with Shakespeare and have produced versions of *The Merry Wives of Windsor*, *King John*, and many other plays in which music has played a central role in the work of the company, the production of meaning, and the impact of the performance on audiences. In the summer of 2006 the Globe Theatre in London also responded to these trends with the commission of jazz musician and composer Django Bates to compose incidental music for their production of *Titus Andronicus* (dir. Lucy Bailey).

Relationships are changing, then, between audiences and Shakespeare, and undoubtedly between audiences and genres such as the theatre, ballet, and the classical music concert, but new relationships and encounters are emerging at the same time, not least in the context of film and television soundtracks, and the emergent practices of adaptation, sampling, and 'borrowing'. There remains, then, a reassuring sense on my part that there will be a continued afterlife of Shakespeare in music of all forms. Play on.

Note

1 Supple's remarkable intercultural production of *A Midsummer Night's Dream* as part of the Royal Shakespeare Company's Complete Works Festival in 2006 and its commitment to music and dance as part of its performance idiom has already been mentioned in an earlier chapter (see ch. 3, n. 6).

Glossary of Musical Terms

NB: These definitions have largely been derived from those provided in the *Concise Oxford Dictionary of Music*, ed. Michael Kennedy (Oxford: Oxford University Press, 1996). They are intended as guides to readers unfamiliar with the terminology and should in all cases be supplemented by fuller definitions and analyses available in standard music reference books and sources.

acoustics – the study of sound.

alto – highest adult male singing voice (especially in church music) or lowest female singing voice (also known as the 'contralto').

aria – long accompanied song for a solo voice in an opera or oratorio.

ballet – artistic dance form performed to music, using precise and formalized set steps and gestures.

baritone – adult male singing voice between tenor and bass in range.

baroque – movement in seventeenth-century and eighteenth-century literature, art, architecture, and music. Associated with ornate style and formal structures, such as in music the use of developmental variations upon 'grounds'.

bass – lowest adult male singing voice.

bel canto – a lyrical style of operatic singing.

big band – large group of musicians playing jazz or swing music.

blues – melancholic music of black American folk origins.

chaconne – a form of moderately slow continuous variation on a ground bass, used predominantly during the baroque era. Sometimes used to denote an instrumental piece of a particularly austere character using ground bass variations.

chamber opera – a small-scale opera, usually of an intimate quality, calling for fewer vocal and instrumental resources than full-scale opera.

chord – group of notes sounded simultaneously, usually in harmony.

consonance – recurrence of similar sounds to create effect of harmony.

contralto – lowest female singing voice.

contrapuntal – music in counterpoint, which is the art or technique of setting, writing, or playing a melody or melodies in conjunction with another.

counter-tenor – adult male alto singing voice.

crescendo – gradual increase in loudness in a piece of music.

diegetic music – music that takes place within the plot or narrative of a film; for example, when characters put music on a CD player or attend a party at which music is being played or performed live.

diminuendo – gradual decrease in loudness in a piece of music.

dissonance – lack of harmony in the arrangement of musical notes; or the combination of simultaneous sounds of musical notes to produce chords and chordal progression.

dynamics – gradations of volume in music; for example: *forte*, *piano*, or *crescendo*.

folk music – traditional songs and music, often handed down orally through generations; music associated with particular communities or regions.

forte – music played loudly.

gospel music – religious music, of a revivalist nature, which has its origins in the USA in the second half of the nineteenth century.

ground – in music, a short melody, usually in the bass, repeated continually with changing upper parts; a late sixteenth-century innovation, associated with the baroque movement in the arts.

harmony – the combination of simultaneously sounded musical notes to produce a pleasing effect, usually with the effect of consonance.

hip-hop – urban youth music and attendant subculture of graffiti art, break dancing, and rap poetry. Often involves rap with an electronic backing, though it has also pioneered the use of electronic sampling of existent sounds and music to create new works.

incidental music – in the theatre, music written especially for a dramatic performance; in theatre and film more generally, music that accompanies the action or provides atmosphere at particular moments in the action.

jazz – type of music of black American origins, characterized by improvisation, syncopation, and a regular rhythm. Typically played on brass or woodwind instruments.

key – in music, adherence to notes from one of the major or minor scales.

leitmotif – recurring theme in a musical or literary composition.

mezzo-soprano – middle category of female voice. Closer to the soprano than the contralto.

musical – as a noun, the term refers to a genre of popular dramatic light entertainment including strong song and dance numbers and linked to the nineteenth-century traditions of light opera, revue, and burlesque.

non-diegetic music – music that is part of an overlaid soundtrack to a film but which cannot be heard by characters onscreen.

opera – dramatic work of one or more acts set to music for singers and instrumentalists.

piano – music played softly.

polyphonic – music (usually vocal) in two or more relatively independent parts (see also 'contrapuntal').

quodlibet – light-hearted medley of well-known tunes or fragments of the same. The phrase was also used occasionally in the eighteenth century to refer to *extempore* family performances of such medleys (see Egarr 2006).

ragtime – music with a syncopated melodic line. Originated in black American communities from 1880s onwards and traditionally played on the piano.

rap – uses rhythmic vocal delivery over a musical background, with a heavy dependence on rhyme for its effects.

ritornello – in music, a short instrumental refrain or interlude in a vocal or instrumental work.

rock music – popular music from the 1950s onwards, often performed by groups and electronically amplified.

scherzo – in music, the name for a movement in orchestral music, though it was first applied to vocal music in the seventeenth century.

score – in film, the music commissioned or selected to accompany the images; this may be either diegetic or non-diegetic in form, and may also seek to blur the boundary between those states.

semi-opera – drama or entertainment with a substantial amount of vocal music in addition to instrumental movements and/or dance. Common in England in the late seventeenth and early eighteenth centuries.

soprano – highest singing voice.

soundtrack – the sound accompaniment to a film, including music (often referred to more specifically as the 'score'), but also dialogue and other sounds and acoustic effects.

swing – form of jazz prevalent in the USA in the 1930s and 1940s.

symphonic poem – also called a tone poem; an extended orchestral piece, usually in one movement, which is symphonic in scale but not a 'pure' symphony in that it usually deals with descriptive subjects taken from literary or artistic sources.

tenor – singing voice between baritone and alto and counter-tenor in range.

threnody – in music, a song of lamentation on a person's death.

timbre – character or quality of a musical sound or voice, as distinct from pitch and intensity.

Bibliography

NB: Quotations from Shakespeare throughout are taken from *The Oxford Shakespeare: The Complete Works*, gen. eds. Stanley Wells and Gary Taylor, 2nd edn. (Oxford: Oxford University Press, 2005).

Abbate, Carolyn (1991), *Unsung Voices: Opera and Musical Narrative in the Nineteenth Century* (Princeton: Princeton University Press).
——and Roger Parker (1989) (eds), *Analyzing Opera: Verdi and Wagner* (Berkeley: University of California Press).
Adams, Martin (1995), *Henry Purcell: The Origins and Development of his Musical Style* (Cambridge: Cambridge University Press).
Adamson, Sylvia, Lynnette Hunter, Lynne Magnusson, Ann Thompson, and Katie Wales (2001) (eds), *Reading Shakespeare's Dramatic Language: A Guide* (London: Arden/Thomson Learning).
Adlington, Robert (2000), *The Music of Harrison Birtwistle* (Cambridge: Cambridge University Press).
——(2005), 'Music Theatre since the 1960s', in M. Cooke 2005a: 225–43.
Adorno, Theodor W. (1991), 'On the Fetish Character in Music and the Regression of Listening', in *The Culture Industry: Selected Essays on Mass Culture*, ed. J. M. Bernstein (London: Routledge), pp. 26–52.
Andreas Sr, James (1999), 'Signifyin' on *The Tempest* in Gloria Naylor's *Mama Day*', in Desmet and Sawyer 1999: 103–18.
Ashcroft, Bill, Gareth Griffiths, and Helen Tiffin (1989), *The Empire Strikes Back: Theory and Practice in Post-colonial Literatures* (London: Routledge).
Barber, C. L. (1959), *Shakespeare's Festive Comedy: A Study of Dramatic Form and its Relation to Social Custom* (Princeton: Princeton University Press).
Barthes, Roland (1977), *Image, Music, Text*, trans. Stephen Heath (London: Fontana).
Basnett, Susan (2004), 'Engendering Anew: Shakespeare, Gender and Translation', in Hoenselaars 2004: 53–67.
Bate, Jonathan (1986), *Shakespeare and the English Romantic Imagination* (Oxford: Clarendon Press).
——(1989), *Shakespearean Constitutions: Politics, Theatre, Criticism, 1730–1830* (Oxford: Clarendon Press).

——(1992) (ed.), *The Romantics on Shakespeare* (Harmondsworth: Penguin).

——(1997), *The Genius of Shakespeare* (London: Picador).

Bennett, Susan (1996), *Performing Nostalgia: Shifting Shakespeare and the Contemporary Past* (London: Routledge).

Berry, Philippa (1999), *Shakespeare's Feminine Endings: Disfiguring Death in the Tragedies* (London: Routledge).

Bloom, Peter (1992) (ed.), *Berlioz Studies* (Cambridge: Cambridge University Press).

Boose, Lynda E., and Richard Burt (1997) (eds), *Shakespeare the Movie: Popularizing the Plays on Film, TV, and Video* (London: Routledge).

——(2003) (eds), *Shakespeare the Movie II: Popularizing the Plays on Film, TV, Video, and DVD* (London: Routledge).

Bordwell, David, and Kristen Thompson (2004), *Film Art: An Introduction*, 7th edn (London and New York: McGraw-Hill).

Born, Georgina, and David Hesmondhalgh (2000) (eds), *Western Music and its Others: Difference, Representation, and Appropriation* (Berkeley: University of California Press).

Bradley, A. C. (1991 [1904]), *Shakespearean Tragedy: Lectures on 'Hamlet', 'Othello', 'King Lear', 'Macbeth'*, introduced by John Bayley (Harmondsworth: Penguin).

Bradshaw, Graham (1983), 'A Shakespearean Perspective: Verdi and Boito as Translators', in Hepokoski 1983: 152–71.

Brett, Philip (1993), 'Britten's *Dream*', in *Musicology and Difference*, ed. Ruth A. Solie (Berkeley: University of California Press), pp. 259–80.

——(1994), 'Eros and Orientalism in Britten's Operas', in *Queering the Pitch: The New Gay and Lesbian Musicology*, ed. Philip Brett, Elizabeth Wood, and Gary C. Thomas (New York and London: Routledge & Kegan Paul), pp. 235–56.

Bridcut, John (2006), *Britten's Children* (London: Faber).

Brissenden, Alan (1981), *Shakespeare and the Dance* (Basingstoke: Macmillan).

Bristol, Michael (1996), *Big-Time Shakespeare* (London and New York: Routledge).

Brooks, Peter (1995), *The Melodramatic Imagination: Balzac, Henry James, Melodrama, and the Mode of Excess*, 2nd edn (New Haven and London: Yale University Press).

Buhler, Stephen M. (2002), 'Reviving Juliet, Repackaging Romeo: Transformations of Character in Pop and Post-Pop Music', in Burt 2002: 243–64.

——(2004), 'Form and Character in Duke Ellington and Billy Strayhorn's *Such Sweet Thunder*', unpublished conference paper in session on 'Ellington, Shakespeare, and Jazz Adaptation', Shakespeare Association of America, New Orleans.

Burnett, Mark Thornton (2000), 'Impressions of Fantasy: Adrian Noble's *A Midsummer Night's Dream*', in Burnett and Wray 2000, pp. 89–101.

——(2003), 'Contemporary Film Versions of the Tragedies', in Dutton and Howard 2003c: 262–83.

——and Ramona Wray (2000) (eds), *Shakespeare, Film, Fin-de-Siècle* (Basingstoke: Macmillan).

Burt, Richard (2002) (ed.), *Shakespeare After Mass Media* (New York: Palgrave).

Busch, Hans (1998) (ed. and trans.), *Verdi's 'Otello' and 'Simon Boccanegra' in Letters and Documents*, 2 vols (Oxford: Clarendon Press).

Carpenter, Humphrey (2003), *Benjamin Britten: A Biography* (London: Faber).

Carter, Alexander (1998) (ed.), *The Routledge Dance Studies Reader* (London: Routledge).

Carter, Angela (1985), 'Overture and Incidental Music for *A Midsummer Night's Dream*', in *Black Venus* (London: Vintage), pp. 65–76.

——(1992), *Wise Children* (London: Vintage).

Carter, Ronald (2004), *Language and Creativity: The Art of Common Talk* (London and New York: Routledge).

Chalmers, Hero (2005), *Royalist Women Writers, 1650–1689* (Oxford: Oxford University Press).

Chedgzoy, Kate (1995), *Shakespeare's Queer Children: Sexual Politics and Contemporary Culture* (Manchester: Manchester University Press).

Clark, Sandra (2001), 'Shakespeare and Other Adaptations', in Owen 2001: pp. 274–90.

Clément, Catherine (1989), *Opera or the Undoing of Women*, trans. Betsy Wing (London: Virago).

Cohan, Steven (2002) (ed.), *Hollywood Musicals: The Film Reader* (London and New York: Routledge).

Connor, Stephen (1996), *The English Novel in History, 1950–1995* (London: Routledge).

Cooke, Katherine (1972), *A. C. Bradley and his Influence in Twentieth-Century Shakespeare Criticism* (Oxford: Clarendon Press).

Cooke, Mervyn (1998a), 'The East in the West: Evocations of the Gamelan in Western Music', in *The Exotic in Western Music*, ed. Jonathan Bellman (Boston: Northeastern University Press), pp. 258–80.

——(1998b), *Jazz* (London: Thames & Hudson).

——(1999a) (ed.), *The Cambridge Companion to Benjamin Britten* (Cambridge: Cambridge University Press).

——(1999b), 'Britten and Shakespeare: *A Midsummer Night's Dream*', in Cooke 1999a: 129–46.

——(1999c), 'Distant Horizons: From Pagodaland to the Church Parables', in Cooke 1999a: 167–87.

——(2002), 'Jazz among the Classics and the Case of Duke Ellington', in Cooke and Horn 2002: 153–73.

——(2005a) (ed.), *The Cambridge Companion to Twentieth-Century Opera* (Cambridge: Cambridge University Press).

——(2005b), 'Opera and Film', in Cooke 2005a: 267–90.

——and David Horn (2002) (eds), *The Cambridge Companion to Jazz* (Cambridge: Cambridge University Press).

Cudworth, Charles (1966), 'Song and Part-song Settings of Shakespeare's Lyrics, 1660–1960', in Hartnoll 1966: 51–87.

Davies, Anthony, and Peter Holland (1994) (eds), *Shakespeare and the Moving Image: The Plays on Film and Television* (Cambridge: Cambridge University Press).

Dawson, Anthony B. (1995), *Shakespeare in Performance: 'Hamlet'* (Manchester: Manchester University Press).

Desmet, Christy, and Robert Sawyer (1999) (eds), *Shakespeare and Appropriation* (London: Routledge).

Desmond, Jane (1997) (ed.), *Meaning in Motion: New Cultural Studies of Dance* (Durham, NC, and London: Duke University Press).

Dobson, Michael (1992), *The Making of the English National Poet: Shakespeare, Adaptation, and Authorship, 1660–1769* (Oxford: Clarendon Press).

——and Stanley Wells (2001) (eds), *The Oxford Companion to Shakespeare* (Oxford: Oxford University Press).

Döring, Tobias (2005), '*A Branch of the Blue Nile*: Derek Walcott and the Tropic of Shakespeare', in Massai 2005: 15–22.

Dusinberre, Juliet (2006) (ed.), *William Shakespeare's 'As You Like it'* (London: Arden/Thomson Learning).

Dutton, Richard, and Jean E. Howard (2003a) (eds), *A Companion to Shakespeare's Works: The Comedies* (Oxford: Blackwell).

——(2003b) (eds), *A Companion to Shakespeare's Works: The Histories* (Oxford: Blackwell).

——(2003c) (eds), *A Companion to Shakespeare's Works: The Tragedies* (Oxford: Blackwell).

——(2003d) (eds), *A Companion to Shakespeare's Works: The Poems, Problem Comedies, Late Plays* (Oxford: Blackwell).

Edmondson, Paul, and Stanley Wells (2004), *Shakespeare's Sonnets* (Oxford: Oxford University Press).

Egarr, Richard (2006), 'Bach and *Cantabile* Heaven: On a New *Goldberg*', sleevenotes to Harmonia CD recording of *Goldberg Variations*, HMU 907426.

Eisler, Hans, and Theodor W. Adorno (1947), *Composing for Films* (Oxford and New York: Oxford University Press).

Erenberg, Lewis A. (1998), *Swingin' the Dream: Big Band Jazz and the Rebirth of American Culture* (Chicago: University of Chicago Press).

Everett, William A., and Paul R. Laird (2002) (eds), *The Cambridge Companion to the Musical* (Cambridge: Cambridge University Press).

Fischlin, Daniel, and Mark Fortier (2000) (eds), *Adaptations of Shakespeare: A Critical Anthology of Plays from the Seventeenth Century to the Present* (London: Routledge).

Fiske, Roger (1966), 'Shakespeare in the Concert Hall', in Hartnoll 1966: 177–241.

Folkerth, Wes (2002), *The Sound of Shakespeare* (London: Routledge).

Forster, Susan Leigh (1996), *Choreography and Narrative: Ballet's Staging of Story and Desire* (Bloomington: Indiana University Press).

Friedman, Michael D. (2004), ' "I won't dance, don't ask me": Branagh's *Love's Labour's Lost* and the American Film Musical', *Literature/Film Quarterly*, 32: 134–43.

Frith, Simon (2001), 'Pop Music', in Frith, Straw, and Street 2001: 93–108.

——Will Straw and John Street (2001) (eds), *The Cambridge Companion to Pop and Rock* (Cambridge: Cambridge University Press).

Garebian, Keith (1995), *The Making of 'West Side Story'* (Toronto: University of Toronto Press).

Gates Jr., Henry Louis (1988), *The Signifying Monkey: A Theory of African-American Literature* (New York and Oxford: Oxford University Press).

Genette, Gérard (1997 [1982]), *Palimpsests: Literature in the Second Degree*, trans. Channa Newman and Claude Dobinsky (Lincoln: University of Nebraska Press).

Giles, Peter (1994), *The History and Technique of the Countertenor* (Aldershot: Scolar Press).

Gilman, Todd S. (2001), 'London Theatre Music, 1660–1719', in Owen 2001: 243–73.

Godsalve, William H. L. (1995), *Britten's 'A Midsummer Night's Dream': Making an Opera from Shakespeare's Comedy* (London and Toronto: Associated Universities Press).

Gooch, Bryan N. S., and David Thatcher (1991), *A Shakespeare Music Catalogue*, associate editor Odean Long, with material by Charles Haywood, 5 vols (Oxford: Clarendon Press).

Gorbman, Claudia (1987), *Unheard Melodies: Narrative Film Music* (Bloomington: Indiana University Press; London: BFI Publishing).

Graziano, John (2002), 'Images of African-Americans: African-American Musical Theatre, *Show Boat* and *Porgy and Bess*', in Everett and Laird 2002: 63–76.

Grimley, Daniel M. (2002), '*Falstaff* (Tragedy): Narrative and Retrospection in Elgar's Symphonic Study', unpublished conference paper.

——(2004) (ed.), *The Cambridge Companion to Sibelius* (Cambridge: Cambridge University Press).

——and Julian Rushton (2004) (eds), *The Cambridge Companion to Elgar* (Cambridge: Cambridge University Press).

Grossberg, Lawrence (1997), *Dancing in Spite of Myself: Essays on Popular Culture* (Durham, NC: Duke University Press).

Grzegorzewska, Malgorzata (1998), 'Wooing in Festival Terms: Sonneteering Lovers, Rock, and Blues', in *Shakespeare and the Twentieth Century*, ed. Jonathan Bate, Jill L. Levenson and Dieter Mehl (London: University of Delaware Press), pp. 148–56.

Halio, Jay L. (1994), *Shakespeare in Performance: 'A Midsummer Night's Dream'* (Manchester: Manchester University Press).

Harris, Diana, and MacDonald Jackson (1997), 'Stormy Weather: Derek Jarman's *The Tempest*', *Literature/Film Quarterly*, 25: 90–8.

Hartman, Geoffrey H. (1980), *Criticism in the Wilderness: The Study of Literature Today* (New Haven and London: Yale University Press).

Hartnoll, Phyllis (1966) (ed.), *Shakespeare in Music* (London: Macmillan; New York: St Martin's Press).

Harvey, Caroline (2005), 'Words and Action', in M. Cooke 2005a: 47–59.

Hawkes, Terence (1986), *That Shakespeherian Rag: Essays on a Critical Process* (London and New York: Methuen).

Head, Dominic (2002), *The Cambridge Introduction to Modern Fiction, 1950–2000* (Cambridge: Cambridge University Press).

Helgerson, Richard (1999), 'The Buck Basket, the Witch, and the Queen of Fairies: The Women's World of Shakespeare's Windsor', in *Renaissance Culture and the Everyday*, ed. Patricia Fumerton and Simon Hunt (Philadelphia: University of Pennsylvania Press), pp. 162–82.

Henderson, Diana E. (2006) (ed.), *A Concise Companion to Shakespeare on Screen* (Oxford: Blackwell).

Hepokoski, James A. (1983), *Giuseppe Verdi: Falstaff*, Cambridge Opera Handbooks (Cambridge: Cambridge University Press).

——(1987), *Giuseppe Verdi: Otello*, Cambridge Opera Handbooks (Cambridge: Cambridge University Press).

Hodgdon, Barbara (1983), 'The Two *King Lears*: Uncovering the Film Text', *Literature/Film Quarterly*, 11: 143–51.

——(1997), 'Race-ing *Othello*, Re-Engendering White-Out', in Boose and Burt 1997: 23–44.

——(2003), 'Race-ing *Othello*, Re-Engendering White-Out', in Boose and Burt 2003: 89–104.

Hoenselaars, Ton (2004) (ed.), *Shakespeare and the Language of Translation* (London: Arden/Thomson Learning).

Holden, Anthony (2003), 'Alas, Poor Hamlet!', review of production of Ambroise Thomas's *Hamlet* at the Royal Opera House, London, *The Observer*, Review section, 18 May, p. 18.

——(2004), 'A Truly Prosperous Prospero', review of Thomas Adès's *The Tempest* at the Royal Opera House, London, *The Observer*, Review section, 15 Feb., p. 12.

Holland, Peter (1997), *English Shakespeares: Shakespeare on the English Stage in the 1990s* (Cambridge: Cambridge University Press).

Horn, David (2002), 'The Identity of Jazz', in Cooke and Horn 2002: 9–32.

Howard, Jean E., and Phyllis Rackin (1997), *Engendering a Nation: A Feminist Reading of Shakespeare's English Histories* (London: Routledge).

Howard, Katherine, and Thomas Cartelli (2006), *New Wave Shakespeare on Screen* (Cambridge: Polity).

Howard, Skiles (1998), *The Politics of Courtly Dancing in Early Modern England* (Amherst: University of Massachusetts Press).

Howard, Tony (2000), 'Shakespeare's Cinematic Offshoots', in R. Jackson 2000: 295–313.

Howe, Elizabeth (1992), *The First English Actresses: Women and Drama, 1660–1700* (Cambridge: Cambridge University Press).

Hulme, Peter, and William H. Sherman (2000) (eds), *'The Tempest' and its Travels* (London: Reaktion Books).

Ingram, R. W. (1958), 'Operatic Tendencies in Stuart Drama', *Musical Quarterly*, 44: 489–504.

Jackson, Russell (2000) (ed.), *The Cambridge Companion to Shakespeare and Film* (Cambridge: Cambridge University Press).

Jackson, Travis A. (2002), 'Jazz as Musical Practice', in Cooke and Horn 2002: 91–133.

Jardine, Lisa (1983), *Still Harping on Daughters: Women and Drama in the Age of Shakespeare* (Hemel Hempstead: Harvester Wheatsheaf).

Jennings, Luke (2006a), 'No Saxons Please, We're British', review of production of John Dryden and Henry Purcell, *King Arthur*, choreographed by Mark Morris, at the London Coliseum, *The Observer*, Review section, 2 July, p. 15.

——(2006b), 'Tutu Risqué for Our Lillibet', review of production of Frederick Ashton's *La Valse and Homage to the Queen*, *The Observer*, Review section, 11 June.

Jones, Nicholas (2004), 'Bottom's Wife: Gender and Voice in Hoffman's *Dream*', *Literature/Film Quarterly*, 32: 126–33.

Jowett, John (2003), 'Varieties of Collaboration in Shakespeare's Problem Plays and Late Plays', in Dutton and Howard 2003d: 106–28.

——(2004) (ed.), *William Shakespeare and Thomas Middleton's 'The Life of Timon of Athens'* (Oxford: Oxford University Press).

Kalinak, Kathryn (1992), *Settling the Score: Music and the Classic Hollywood Film* (Madison: University of Wisconsin Press).

Kemp, Ian (1992), '*Romeo and Juliet* and *Roméo et Juliette*', in Bloom (1992), pp. 37–79.

Kennedy, Dennis (1993), *Looking at Shakespeare: A Visual History of Twentieth-Century Performance* (Cambridge: Cambridge University Press).

Kennedy, Martin (1996) (ed.), *The Concise Oxford Dictionary of Music* (Oxford: Oxford University Press).

Kerman, Joseph (1989), *Opera as Drama*, 2nd edn (London: Faber).

—— and Thomas S. Grey (1989), 'Verdi's Groundswells: Surveying an Operatic Convention', in Abbate and Parker 1989: 153–79.

Kerrigan, John (1986) (ed.), *William Shakespeare's 'The Sonnets' and 'Love's Pilgrimage'* (Harmondsworth: Penguin).

Kidnie, Margaret Jane (2005), 'Dancing with Art: Robert Lepage's *Elsinore*', in Massai 2005: 133–40.

Kirchner, Bill (2000) (ed.), *The Oxford Companion to Jazz* (Oxford: Oxford University Press).

Kliman, Bernice W. (1995), *Shakespeare in Performance: 'Macbeth'* (Manchester: Manchester University Press).

Knight, Arthur (2001), ' "It Ain't Necessarily So That It Ain't Necessarily So": African American Recordings of *Porgy and Bess* as Film and Cultural Criticism', in *Soundtrack Available: Essays on Film and Popular Music*, ed. Pamela Robertson Wojcik and Arthur Knight (Durham, NC: Duke University Press), pp. 319–46.

Knight, G. Wilson (1960 [1930]), 'The *Othello* Music', in *The Wheel of Fire: Interpretations of Shakespearian Tragedy* (London: Methuen), pp. 97–119.

Kott, Jan (1965), *Shakespeare: Our Contemporary*, trans. Boleshaw Taborski (London: Methuen).

Krims, Adam (2000), *Rap Music and the Poetics of Identity* (Cambridge: Cambridge University Press).

Laird, Paul R. (2002), 'Choreographers, Directors, and the Fully Integrated Musical', in Everett and Laird 2002: 197–211.

Lanier, Douglas (2002), *Shakespeare and Modern Popular Culture* (Oxford: Oxford University Press).

—— (2004), 'Minstrelsy/Jazz/Rap: African-American Music and Shakespearean Legitimation', unpublished conference paper for the session on 'Ellington, Shakespeare, and Jazz Adaptation', Shakespeare Association of America, New Orleans.

Latham, Alison (2002) (ed.), *The Oxford Companion to Music* (Oxford: Oxford University Press).

Leggatt, Alexander (1991), *Shakespeare in Performance: 'King Lear'* (Manchester: Manchester University Press).

Levenson, Jill (1987), *Shakespeare in Performance: 'Romeo and Juliet'* (Manchester: Manchester University Press).

—— (2000) (ed.), *William Shakespeare's 'Romeo and Juliet'* (Oxford: Oxford University Press).

Lindley, David (2006), *Shakespeare and Music* (London: Arden/Thomson Learning).

Lodge, David (1972) (ed.), *Twentieth-Century Criticism: A Reader* (London and New York: Longman).

Loehlin, James (1996), *Shakespeare in Performance: 'Henry V'* (Manchester: Manchester University Press).

——(1997), ' "Top of the World, Ma": *Richard III* and Cinematic Convention', in Boose and Burt 1997: 67–79.

——(2000), ' "These Violent Delights Have Violent Ends": Baz Luhrmann's Millennial Shakespeare', in Burnett and Wray 2000: 121–36.

Loraux, Nicole (1987), *Tragic Ways of Killing a Woman*, trans. Anthony Forster (Cambridge, Mass: Harvard University Press).

McBurney, Gerard (2006), 'Sound and Vision', *The Guardian*, Review section, 24 June, pp. 12–13.

McClary, Susan (1998), *Rap, Minimalism, and the Structure of Time in Late Twentieth-Century Culture* (Lincoln: University of Nebraska Press).

McClung, Bruce D., and Paul R. Laird (2002), 'Musical Sophistication on Broadway: Kurt Weill and Leonard Bernstein', in Everett and Laird 2002: 167–78.

Mark, Christopher (2005), 'Opera in England: Taking the Plunge', in M. Cooke 2005a: 209–21.

Marsden, Jean I. (1991) (ed.), *The Appropriation of Shakespeare: Post-Renaissance Reconstructions of the Works and Myth* (London: Prentice-Hall).

——(2002), 'Improving Shakespeare from the Restoration to Garrick', in Wells and Stanton 2002: 21–36.

Marshall, Kelli (2005), ' "It doth forget to do the thing it should": Kenneth Branagh's *Love's Labour's Lost* and (Mis)Interpreting the Musical Genre', *Literature/Film Quarterly*, 33: 83–91.

Martin, Timothy (1991), *Joyce and Wagner: A Study of Influence* (Cambridge: Cambridge University Press).

Marvell, Andrew (2005), *The Complete Poems*, ed. Elizabeth Story Donno and Jonathan Bate (Harmondsworth: Penguin).

Massai, Sonia (2005) (ed.), *World-Wide Shakespeares: Local Appropriations in Film and Performance* (London: Routledge).

Melchiori, Giorgio (2000) (ed.), *William Shakespeare's 'The Merry Wives of Windsor'* (London: Arden/Thomson Learning).

Metzer, David (2003), *Quotation and Cultural Meaning in Twentieth-Century Music* (Cambridge: Cambridge University Press).

Moody, Jane (2002), 'Romantic Shakespeare', in Wells and Stanton 2002: 37–57.

Mundy, John (1999), *Popular Music on Screen: From Hollywood Musical to Music Videos* (Manchester: Manchester University Press).

Ojumu, Akin (2004), 'Reach for the Skies', *The Observer*, Review section, 18 April, p. 7.

Orkin, Martin (2005), *Local Shakespeares: Proximations and Power* (London: Routledge).

Owen, Susan J. (2001) (ed.), *A Companion to Restoration Drama* (Oxford: Blackwell).

Oxford English Dictionary Online. http://dictionary.oed.com

Parr, Gus (1997), 'S for Smoking', *Sight and Sound*, 7: 30–3.

Pavis, Patrice (1996) (ed.), *The Intercultural Performance Reader* (London: Routledge).

Potter, Lois (2002), *Shakespeare in Performance: 'Othello'* (Manchester: Manchester University Press).

Potter, Russell (1995), *Spectacular Vernaculars: Hip-Hop and the Politics of Postmodernism* (Albany: State University of New York Press).

Preston, Katherine K. (2002), 'American Musical Theatre before the Twentieth Century', in Everett and Laird 2002: 3–28.

Price, Curtis (1984), *Henry Purcell and the London Stage* (Cambridge: Cambridge University Press).

Quinn, Eithne (2005), *Nuthin' but a 'G' Thang: The Culture and Commerce of Gangsta Rap* (New York: Columbia University Press).

Rackin, Phyllis (2005), *Shakespeare and Women* (Oxford: Oxford University Press).

Rayner, Jay (2000), 'What a Song and Dance!', *The Observer*, Review section, 26 March.

Riley, John (2005), *Dmitri Shostakovich: A Life in Film* (London: I. B. Tauris).

Rothwell, Kenneth S. (1999), *A History of Shakespeare on Screen: A Century of Film and Television* (Cambridge: Cambridge University Press).

Rushton, Julian (1994), *Berlioz: 'Roméo et Juliette'* (Cambridge: Cambridge University Press).

Rutter, Carol (2001), *Enter the Body: Women and Representation on Shakespeare's Stage* (London: Routledge).

Sanders, Julie (2000), 'The End of History and the Last Man: Kenneth Branagh's Millennial *Hamlet*', in Burnett and Wray 2000: 147–64.

——(2001), *Novel Shakespeares: Twentieth-Century Women Writers and Appropriation* (Manchester: Manchester University Press).

——(2006), *Adaptation and Appropriation* (London: Routledge).

Schloss, Joseph Glenn (2004), *Making Beats: The Art of Sample-Based Hip-Hop* (Middleton, Conn.: Wesleyan University Press).

Schmidgall, Gary (1977), *Literature as Opera* (New York and Oxford: Oxford University Press).

——(1985), 'Verdi's *King Lear* Project', *Nineteenth-Century Music*, 9: 83–101.

——(1990), *Shakespeare and Opera* (New York and Oxford: Oxford University Press).

Schoch, Richard W. (2002), 'Pictorial Shakespeare', in Wells and Stanton 2002: 58–75.

Shepherd, Simon (2005), *Theatre, Body, and Pleasure* (London: Routledge).

Shewring, Margaret (1996), *Shakespeare in Performance: 'Richard II'* (Manchester: Manchester University Press).

Showalter, Elaine (1991), 'Representing Ophelia: Women, Madness, and the Responsibilities of Feminist Criticism', in *Shakespeare and the Question of*

Theory, ed. Patricia Parker and Geoffrey Hartman (London: Routledge), pp. 77–94.

Smith, Bruce R. (1999), *The Acoustic World of Early Modern England: Attending to the O-Factor* (Chicago: University of Chicago Press).

Smith, D. Nichol (1902), *Eighteenth-century Essays on Shakespeare* (Glasgow: James Maclehose).

Smith, James L. (1973), *Melodrama* (London: Methuen).

Smith, Jeff (1998), *The Sounds of Commerce: Marketing Popular Film Music* (New York: Columbia University Press).

Spain, Delbert (1988), *Shakespeare Sounded Soundly: The Verse Structure and the Language* (Santa Barbara, Calif.: Capra Press, Garland–Clarke Editions).

Straw, Will (1991), 'Systems of Articulation, Logics of Change: Communities and Scenes in Popular Music', *Cultural Studies*, 5: 368–88.

——(1993), 'The Booth, the Floor, and the Wall: Dance Music and the Fear of Falling', *Public*, 8: 169–82.

——(2001), 'Dance Music', in Frith, Straw, and Street 2001: 158–75.

Taylor, Gary, and Michael Warren (1983) (eds), *The Division of the Kingdoms: Shakespeare's Two Versions of 'King Lear'* (Oxford: Clarendon Press).

Taylor, Maggie (2000), 'Memory, Magic, and the Musical in Derek Jarman's *The Tempest* and *Edward II*', in *Musicals: Hollywood and Beyond* (Exeter: Intellect Books), pp. 157–62.

Teague, Frances (2002), 'Shakespeare, Beard of Avon', in Burt 2002, pp. 221–41.

——(2004), '*Play On* and *Swingin' the Dream*; or Viola and Bottom Take a Train', unpublished conference paper for the session on 'Ellington, Shakespeare and Jazz Adaptation', Shakespeare Association of America, New Orleans.

Thomas, Helen (2003), *The Body, Dance, and Cultural Theory* (Basingstoke: Palgrave Macmillan).

Thompson, Ann (1995), '"Miranda, where's your sister?": Reading Shakespeare's *The Tempest*', in *Shakespeare and Gender: A History*, ed. Deborah Barker and Ivo Kamps (London: Verso), pp. 168–97.

——and Neil Taylor (2006) (eds), *William Shakespeare's 'Hamlet'* (London: Arden/Thomson Learning).

Trapido, Barbara (1994), *Juggling* (Harmondsworth: Penguin).

Violanti, Heather (2005), 'Are the Songs of Berlin Harsh after the Words of Shakespeare?: A Look at *Love's Labour's Lost*', unpublished paper contribution to 'Shakespeare and Film Music' seminar at the British Shakespeare Association Conference, University of Newcastle.

Walker, Elsie (2002), '"Now is a time to storm": Julie Taymor's *Titus*', *Literature/Film Quarterly*, 30: 194–207.

Wall, Wendy (2003), '*The Merry Wives of Windsor*: Unhusbanding Desires in Windsor', in Dutton and Howard 2003a: 376–92.

Warfield, Scott (2002), 'From *Hair* to *Rent*: Is "Rock" a Four-Letter Word on Broadway?', in Everett and Laird 2002: 231–45.

Weis, René (1998) (ed.), *William Shakespeare's '2 Henry IV'* (Oxford: Oxford University Press).

Weller, Philip, (2005), 'Symbolist Opera: Trials, Triumphs, Tributaries', in M. Cooke 2005a: 60–84.

Wells, Stanley (2002), *Shakespeare: For All Time* (Basingstoke: Macmillan).

——and Gary Taylor (2005) (gen. eds), *The Oxford Shakespeare: The Complete Works*, associate eds John Jowett and William Montgomery, 2nd edn (Oxford: Oxford University Press).

——and Sarah Stanton (2002) (eds), *The Cambridge Companion to Shakespeare on Stage* (Cambridge: Cambridge University Press).

Willett, John (1992) (ed. and trans.), *Brecht on Theatre: The Development of an Aesthetic* (London and New York: Hill and Wang).

Williams, Gary J. (1997), *Our Moonlight Revels: Dream in the Theatre* (Iowa City: University of Iowa Press).

Wiseman, Susan (1998), *Drama and Politics in the English Civil War* (Cambridge: Cambridge University Press).

Woolf, Virginia (1992 [1941]), *Between the Acts*, ed. Gillian Beer (Harmondsworth: Penguin).

Wray, Ramona (2002), 'Nostalgia for Navarre: The Melancholic Metacinema of Kenneth Branagh's *Love's Labour's Lost*', *Literature/Film Quarterly*, 30: 171–8.

Discography

[Please note that in the case of contemporary albums and CDs I have provided the names of the artists, the title and date of the album/CD's first release, and the record company. Since these recordings are constantly being re-released under new catalogue numbers, I have not provided catalogue numbers in these instances.]

Ardley, Neil, Ian Carr, Mike Gibbs, and Stan Tracey (2005 [1975]), *Will Power: A Shakespeare Birthday Celebration in Music*, Vocalian, 2CDSML 8412.

Berlioz, Hector (2001 [1959]), *Romeo and Juliet*, on *'Requiem', 'The Death of Cleopatra', and 'Romeo and Juliet'*, performed by the New York Philharmonic, conducted by Leonard Bernstein, Sony Classical, SM2K89565.

——(2003 [1978]), *Béatrice et Bénédict*, performed by the John Alldis Choir and the London Symphony Orchestra, conducted by Sir Colin Davis, Philips, 475 221–2.

Bernstein, Leonard, et al. (1992 [1960]), *West Side Story: Film Soundtrack*, Sony SK 48211.

——(1998 [1957]), *West Side Story: Original Broadway Cast Recording*, Columbia/Sony, SMK 60724.

Bridge, Frank (2004), 'There is a willow grows aslant a brook', on *Bridge; Delius – Works for Strings*, performed by the Britten Sinfonia, conducted by Nicholas Cleobury, RCA Red Seal, B0000 99630.

Britten, Benjamin (2005), 'Nocturne', on *Britten: Song Cycles*, performed by Ian Bostridge and the Berliner Philharmoniker, conducted by Sir Simon Rattle, EMI Classics, 7243 5 58049 2 1.

——and Peter Pears (1990 [1960]), *A Midsummer Night's Dream*, performed by the Choirs of Downside and Emanuel Schools and the London Symphony Orchestra, conducted by Benjamin Britten, London Decca Records, 425 663–2.

Carthy, Martin, and Dave Swarbrick (1992), 'Perfumes of Arabia', on *Skin and Bone*, Topic Records, TSCD492.

Costello, Elvis, and the Brodsky Quartet (1993), *The Juliet Letters*, Warner Brothers/WEA.

Dire Straits (1980), *Making Movies*, Warner Brothers.

Donovan (1968), 'Under the greenwood tree', on *A Gift from a Flower to a Garden*, BGO Records.

Dvořák, Antonín (2006), *Othello: Overture Op. 93*, on *Shakespeare: Berlioz, Elgar, Dvořák*, performed by the Münchner Rundfunkorchester, conducted by John Fiore, Orfeo Records, C 999 061 Z.

Elgar, Edward (1994), *Falstaff*, on *'Enigma Variations' and 'Falstaff'*, performed by City of Birmingham Symphony Orchestra, conducted by Sir Simon Rattle, British Composers series, EMI Classics, 7243 5 55001 2 0.

——(2006), *Falstaff on Shakespeare: Berlioz, Elgar, Dvořák*, performed by the Münchner Rundfunkorchester, conducted by John Fiore, Orfeo Records, C999 061 Z.

Ellington, Duke, and his orchestra (1999 [1957]), *Such Sweet Thunder*, Columbia/Legacy, CK 65568.

Faithful, Marianne (1965), 'Full fathom five', on *Come My Way*, Lilith Records.

Finzi, Gerald (2001), *Finzi: A Centenary Collection*, performed by the English String Orchestra, conducted by William Boughton, Nimbus Records NI 5665.

——(2004), *Let Us Garlands Bring*, on *I Said to Love*, performed by Roderick Williams and Iain Burnside, Naxos, The English Song Series 12, 8.557644.

German, Edward (2005), *Hamlet – Symphonic Poem, The Tempter, Romeo and Juliet, The Willow Song and Symphony No. 1 in E Minor*, performed by the BBC Concert Orchestra, conducted by John Wilson, Dutton Laboratories, CDLX 7156.

Hackett, Steve (1997), *A Midsummer Night's Dream*, Angel Records and EMI, 7243 5 56348 2 5.

Hamill, Peter (1985), 'After the show', on *Skin*, Fie Records.

——(1999), 'A way out' and 'Ophelia', on *Live*, Fie Records.

——(2002), 'The play's the thing', on *In a Foreign Town*, Fie Records.

Henze, Hans Werner (2003), *Royal Winter Music: Sonatas on Shakespearean Characters*, performed by David Tanenbaum, Stradivarius Records, STR 33670.

Holst, Gustav (1995), *At the Boar's Head (Op. 42)*, performed by the Liverpool Philharmonic Choir and the Royal Liverpool Philharmonic Orchestra, conducted by David Atherton, on *'At the Boar's Head' and 'The Wandering Scholar'*, British Composers series, EMI Classics, 7243 5 65127 2.

The Indigo Girls (1992), *Rites of Passage*, Epic Records.

——(1994), *Swamp Ophelia*, Epic Records.

Jewel (1998), *Spirit*, WEA Records.

Kamen, Michael, et al. (2002), *When Love Speaks*, EMI and RADA, 7243 5 57321 2 5.

Kneehigh Theatre (2006), *Cymbeline: The Songs*, in association with the Royal Shakespeare Company Complete Works Festival, CD.

Korngold, Erich Wolfgang von (2002), *Much Ado About Nothing: Suite for Violin and Piano, Op. 11* on *Violin Sonata*, performed by Joseph Lin and Benjamin Loeb, Naxos, 8.557067.

Laine, Cleo, and Johnny Dankworth (1964), *Shakespeare and All That Jazz*, Universal Records.

——(2002), *The Collection*, Spectrum Records, 5447 70-2.

Lee, Peggy (1998 [1958]), 'Fever', on *The Best of Miss Peggy Lee*, Capitol Records.

Liszt, Franz (2003), *Hamlet*, on *Complete Symphonic Poems* (5 vol. box set), performed by the Budapest Symphony Orchestra, conducted by Árpád Joó, Brilliant Records, 99938 1–5.

Locke, Matthew, et al. (1998), *The Enchanted Island: Music for a Restoration 'Tempest'*, performed by the Musicians of the Globe, conducted by Philip Pickett, Philips, 456 505-2.

Luhrmann, Baz, Nellee Hooper, Craig Armstrong et al. (1996), *William Shakespeare's 'Romeo + Juliet': Music from the Motion Picture*, 2 vols, EMI 7243 8 55643 0 7 and 7243 8 59871 2 0.

Mendelssohn, Felix (1992), *A Midsummer Night's Dream*, performed by the Rotterdam Philharmonic Orchestra and members of the Peter Hall Company, EMI Classics, D 235304.

Merchant, Natalie (1998), 'Ophelia', on *Ophelia*, Elektra Records.

Nicolai, Otto (2002), *Die Lustigen Weiber von Windsor*, performed by the Choir of the Städtischen Oper, Berlin, and the Berliner Rundfunk Sinfonie Orchester, conducted by Arthur Rother, Aura Records [1943], LRC 1118.

The Parley of Instruments (2004), *Orpheus with his Lute: Music for Shakespeare from Purcell to Arne*, conducted by Peter Holman, Hyperion Records, CDA 67450.

Prokofiev, Sergei (1987), *Romeo and Juliet*, performed by the Boston Symphony Orchestra, conducted by Seiji Osawa, Deutsche Grammophon, 423 268-2.

Purcell, Henry (2001 [1971]), *The Fairy Queen*, on *'The Fairy Queen' and 'Dido and Aeneas'*, performed by the English Chamber Orchestra, conducted by Benjamin Britten, Decca, 468 561-2.

Quilter, Roger (2003), *A Quilter Companion*, Various Artists, British Composers series, EMI 7243 5 85149 2 6.

Reed, Lou (1972), *Transformer*, RCA Records.

——(1989), *New York*, Sire/London/Rhino.

Rush (1987), *All the World's a Stage*, Mercury Records.

——(1997), 'Limelight', on *Rush Retrospective, 1981–7*, Mercury Records.

Salieri, Antonio, and Carlo Prospers Defranceschi (1998), *Falstaff or the Three Tricks*, performed by the Madrigalists of Milan and the Orchestra Guido

Cantelli of Milan, conducted by Alberto Veronesi, Chandos Records 1998, CHAN 9613(2).

Schubert, Franz (1998), *Lieder*, performed by Ian Bostridge and Julius Drake, EMI Classics, 7243 5 56347 2 6.

Seeger, Pete (1966), 'Full fathom five', on *Dangerous Songs!?*, Columbia Records.

Sibelius, Jean (1990 [1956]), *The Tempest*, performed by the Royal Philharmonic Orchestra, conducted by Sir Thomas Beecham, EMI, D 152474.

Silverman, Stanley (1994), *Duke Ellington's Incidental Music for Shakespeare's 'Timon of Athens'*, Varese Records, B000024C43.

Smetana, Bedrich (1995), *Richard III* (Op. 11), on Bedrich Smetana, *Symphonic Poems*, performed by the Czech Philarmonic Orchestra, conducted by Václev Neumann, Supraphon Records, B0002528T.

Springsteen, Bruce (1973), *The Wild, the Innocent, and the E-Street Shuffle*, Columbia Records.

—— (1980), *The River*, Columbia Records.

Stenhammar, Wilhelm (2002), *Music for the Theatre*, performed by Helsingborg Symphony Orchestra, conducted by Arvo Volmer, Sterling Records, 1045.

Strauss, Richard (2005), *Macbeth*, on *Don Juan; Macbeth; Lieder*, performed by the Hallé Orchestra, conducted by Mark Elder, Hallé Records, B0007Q8M.

Tavener, John (2006), 'Song for Athene', on *Ikon*, performed by The Sixteen, conducted by Harry Christophers, Universal Music, 4763160.

Tchaikovsky, Pyotr (1992), *Romeo and Juliet*, on *Symphony No. 6 'Pathétique' and 'Romeo and Juliet'*, performed by the Orchestra symphonique de Montréal, conducted by Charles Dutoit, London Decca Records, D 125092.

Tippett, Sir Michael (2003 [1965]), *Songs for Ariel*, on *String Quartet No. 2, 'The Heart's Assurance', 'Boyhood's End', and 'Songs for Ariel'*, performed by Sir Peter Pears and Benjamin Britten, British Composers Series, EMI Classics, 7243 5 85150 2.

Various Artists (1988), *Shakespeare's Kingdom*, Hyperion Records, CDA 66136.

Various Artists (1994), *Songs to Shakespeare*, performed by Anthony Rolfe Johnson and Graham Johnson, Hyperion, B000002ZP7.

Various Artists (2001), *Shakespeare in Music*, Signum Records, B0000STPF5.

Various Artists (2004), *Shakespeare in Song*, performed by the Phoenix Bach Choir, conducted by Charles Bruffy, Chandos Records, CHSA 5031.

Various Artists (2005), *'Shall I compare thee?': Choral Songs on Shakespeare Texts*, performed by Chicago *a capella*, Cedilles Records, CDR 90000 085.

Vaughan Williams, Ralph (2001), *Sir John in Love*, performed by the Sinfonia Chorus and Northern Sinfonia, conducted by Richard Hickox, Chandos Records, CHAN 9928(2).

Verdi, Giuseppe, and Arrigo Boito (1994), *Otello*, performed by the Choir and Orchestra of the Opéra Bastille, conducted by Myung-Whun Chang, Deutsche Grammophon, 439 805–2.

——(2001), *Falstaff*, performed by the Rundfunkchor Berlin and the Berliner Philharmoniker, conducted by Claudio Abbado, Deutsche Grammophon, 471 194–2.

——and Francesco Maria Piave (1976), *Macbeth*, performed by the Choir and Orchestra of Teatro alla Scala, Milan, conducted by Claudio Abbado, Deutsche Grammophon, 449 732–2.

Waits, Tom (1978), *Blue Valentine*, Warner Brothers.

Walker, Sarah, and Graham Johnson (1988), *Shakespeare's Kingdom*, Hyperion CDA66136.

Westbrook, Mike and Kate Westbrook (1992), *Measure for Measure*, on Mike Westbrook, *The Orchestra of Smith's Academy*, ENJA Records, ENJ-9358-2.

Wilcox, Toyah (2003), *Ophelia's Shadow*, Vertical Series.

Filmography

Almereyda, Michael (2000) (dir.), *Hamlet.*
Bharadwaj, Vishal (2003) (dir.), *Maqbool.*
——(2006) (dir.), *Omkara.*
Blake Nelson, Tim (2000) (dir.), *O.*
Boorman, John (1972) (dir.), *Deliverance.*
Branagh, Kenneth (1989) (dir.), *Henry V.*
——(1993) (dir.), *Much Ado About Nothing.*
——(1996) (dir.), *Hamlet.*
——(1999) (dir.), *Love's Labour's Lost.*
Brook, Peter (1971) (dir.), *King Lear.*
Butler, David (1941) (dir.), *Playmates.*
Cukor, George (1936) (dir.), *Romeo and Juliet.*
——(1964) (dir.), *My Fair Lady.*
Fickman, Andy (2006) (dir.), *She's the Man.*
Greenaway, Peter (1991) (dir.), *Prospero's Books.*
Hall, Peter (1962) (dir.), *A Midsummer Night's Dream.*
Heckerling, Amy (1995) (dir.), *Clueless.*
Hoffman, Michael (1998) (dir.), *A Midsummer Night's Dream.*
Iscove, Robert (1999) (dir.), *She's All That.*
Jarman, Derek (1980) (dir.), *The Tempest.*
——(1991) (dir.), *Edward II.*
Jonze, Spike (1999) (dir.), *Being John Malkovich.*
——(2002) (dir.), *Adaptation.*
Junger, Gil (1999) (dir.), *10 Things I Hate About You.*
Kosintsev, Grigori (1964) (dir.), *Hamlet* [*Gamlet*].
——(1970) (dir.), *King Lear* [*Koro' Lir*].
Kurosawa, Akira (1957) (dir.), *Throne of Blood.*
——(1960) (dir.), *The Bad Sleep Well.*
——(1985) (dir.), *Ran.*
Lean, David (1962) (dir.), *Lawrence of Arabia.*
——(1965) (dir.), *Doctor Zhivago.*
Levring, Kristian (2000), *The King is Alive.*
Loncraine, Richard (1995) (dir.), *Richard III.*

Lucas, George (1973) (dir.), *American Graffiti*.

Luhrmann, Baz (1992) (dir.), *Strictly Ballroom*.

——(1996) (dir.), *William Shakespeare's 'Romeo + Juliet'*.

——(2001) (dir.), *Moulin Rouge*.

McGoohan, Patrick (1973) (dir.), *Catch My Soul*.

McTiernan, John (1993) (dir.), *Last Action Hero*.

Madden, John (1998) (dir.), *Shakespeare in Love*.

Marshall, Penny (1994) (dir.), *Renaissance Man*.

Noble, Adrian (1996) (dir.), *A Midsummer Night's Dream*.

Nunn, Trevor (1996) (dir.), *Twelfth Night*.

O'Haver, Tommy (2001) (dir.), *Get Over It*.

Olivier, Laurence (1944) (dir.), *Henry V*.

——(1948) (dir.), *Hamlet*.

Parker, Oliver (1995) (dir.), *Othello*.

Polanski, Roman (1971) (dir.), *Macbeth*.

Radford, Michael (2004) (dir.), *The Merchant of Venice*.

Reinhardt, Max, and William Dieterle (1935) (dirs), *A Midsummer Night's Dream*.

Ralph, Michael, and Basil Dearden (1962) (dirs), *All Night Long*.

Seiden, Joseph (1939) (dir.), *Paradise in Harlem*.

Sidney, George (1953) (dir.), *Kiss Me Kate*.

Stoppard, Tom (1991) (dir.), *Rosencrantz and Guildenstern Are Dead*.

Stroyeva, Vera (1954) (dir.), *Boris Godunov*.

Sutherland, Edward A. (1940) (dir.), *The Boys from Syracuse*.

Taymor, Julie (2000) (dir.), *Titus*.

Thalberg, Irving, and George Cukor (1936) (dirs), *Romeo and Juliet*.

Van Sant, Gus (1991) (dir.), *My Own Private Idaho*.

Weir, Peter (1989) (dir.), *Dead Poets' Society*.

Welles, Orson (1965) (dir.), *Chimes at Midnight*.

Wilcox, Fred McLeod (1956) (dir.), *The Forbidden Planet*.

Wise, Robert, and Jerome Robbins (1961) (dirs), *West Side Story*.

Zeffirelli, Franco (1967) (dir.), *The Taming of the Shrew*.

——(1968) (dir.), *Romeo and Juliet*.

——(1986) (dir.), *Otello*.

——(1990) (dir.), *Hamlet*.

Index

For the most part texts (theatre productions, films, and operas, for example) are indexed under the names of their authors or creators. To avoid any possible confusion with texts or productions with the same title, their generic status is indicated in parentheses. Musicals are indexed under their titles (with cross-r eferences where necessary) as there are often multiple authors, producers, directors, and creators.